CHRIST IN THE HOME

CHRIST IN THE HOME

BY RAOUL PLUS, S.J.

A translation from the French

GARDNER BROTHERS
Publishers
www.gardnerbrothers.com
2005

Nihil Obstat:
    JOHN M. A. FEARNS, S.T.D.,
        Censor Librorum

Imprimatur:
    ✠ FRANCIS CARDINAL SPELLMAN,
        Archbishop of New York

New York, June 19, 1951
    The Nihil Obstat and Imprimatur are official declarations that a book or pamphlet is free of doctrinal or moral error. No implication is contained therein that those who have granted the Nihil Obstat and Imprimatur agree with the contents, opinions or statements expressed.

COPYRIGHT, 1951, IN UNITED STATES AND GREAT BRITAIN
BY FREDERICK PUSTET CO., INC.

REPRINTED, 2005
BY GARDNER BROTHERS
www.gardnerbrothers.com

Printed in U. S. A.

Biblical Quotations have been checked with the Confraternity Edition of the New Testament and the Douay Version of the Old Testament.

*TO
JESUS, MARY, AND JOSEPH
THE HOLY FAMILY
THAT THEY MAY OBTAIN
FOR THE WORLD
THE GRACE OF MANY FAMILIES
WHO KEEP
CHRIST IN THE HOME*

TABLE OF CONTENTS

	PAGE
Preface	xv

Introductory Readings

The Saint of Modern Times	3
Sanctity of the Laity	5
Fantasy or Sacred Duty	7
My Personal Vocation	8
What Kind of Soul Am I?	10

Marriage

Before Embarking (1)	15
Before Embarking (2)	17
Requisites for a Happy Marriage	18
A Proposal	20
The End of Love?	22
One Only Being	24
Love	26
The Palace of Chance	28
Infinity Promised	30
The Nuptial Liturgy	32
The Wedding Day	34
Total Union	36
The Four Bonds of Conjugal Union	38

Life Together Is Difficult	40
Loving Each Other *In God*	41
Supernatural Love	43
United Striving for Sanctity	45
Ideals for Marriage	47
One Heart, One Soul	49
Marriage and the Bible (1)	50
Man Born of Slime	52
Some Feminine Traits	54
Marriage and the Bible (2)	55
Conjugal Duty	57
Motherhood	58
Is Birth-Control Permissible?	60
Why Have a Large Family?	62
The Bell of Life	64
The Impossibility of Having Children?	66
The Only Child	67
Christ and Marriage	69
Marriage and Baptism	71
Respect in Love	72
Marriage and the Mystical Body	74
Mutual Devotedness	76
Woman's Superiority	77
The Boss in the House	79
Marriage and the Eucharist (1)	81
Marriage and the Eucharist (2)	83
Strange Profanation	84

	PAGE
Marriage and the Eucharist (3)	86
Marriage and Sacrifice	88
A Mystic Moral Bond	90
A Father's Answer to His Daughter	92
Transported Together	94
Single Though Two	96
Marriage and the Priesthood (1)	98
Marriage and the Priesthood (2)	100
Masculine Treason	102
Marriage and the Counsels (1)	104
Marriage and the Counsels (2)	105
Marriage and Vows	107
The Social Ideal	109

The Home

Great Adventurers	113
The Psalm of Young Mothers	114
Up to Date	116
Paternal Solicitude	118
The Family	120
Heredity	122
Parental Responsibility	124
The Family Spirit	126
"The Whole Sea"	128
Homelife	130
The Family Table	132
A Christian Setting	134

	PAGE
Judicious Economy	136
The Providential Role of Insecurity	138
The Snuffbox	140
Estranged Parents	142
The Womanly Ideal	144
Her Husband's Helper	146
Good Sense	148
Women and Education	151
Endurance	153
Unbearable Husbands	154
Unbearable Wives	156
The Counsels of Madame Elizabeth	158
Woman, The Strength of Man	160
Is Genius Celibate?	161
The Power of a Smile	163
A Devastating Disposition	165
Man's Virtues versus Woman's Virtues	167
Man's Fidelity	168
A Wife with Character	170
Praiseworthy Vanity	172
A Director's Counsels	174
Friendly Argument	175
Feminine Faults	177
The Psychology of a Mother	179
Courageous Mothers	181
Courageous Fathers	183
A Mother's Zeal	185

	PAGE
Domestic Help	187
Love Out of Bounds	189
The Folly of Love Out of Bounds	191
The Prayer of the Married	192
Prayer Together	194
Prayer for Each Other	196
Marriage and a Life of Prayer	198
Choice Graces	200

Training

The First Years	205
Love for Children	207
From Three to Five	209
The Art of Giving Children Faults	211
The Untimely Laugh	213
Love versus Maternal Instinct	215
Training in Obedience	217
Children Who Command	219
Training in Docility	221
Intelligence and Firmness in a Mother	223
Picture Study	225
Impartiality	227
Difficulties of Christian Education	229
Supernatural Mothers	231
Education to the Supernatural (1)	233
Education to the Supernatural (2)	235
Education to the Supernatural (3)	237

TABLE OF CONTENTS

	PAGE
Jesus and the Child	239
The Father Who Doesn't Pray	241
Table Prayers	243
Children and Christmas	245
Eucharistic Education (1)	247
Eucharistic Education (2)	249
Eucharistic Education (3)	250
Eucharistic Education (4)	252
Eucharistic Education (5)	254
Training to Purity (1)	256
Training to Purity (2)	258
Training to Purity (3)	260
Training to Purity (4)	262
Reading	264
Training of the Emotions	267
The Child and Laziness	269
Lazy Children	271
Training in Sincerity (1)	273
Training in Sincerity (2)	275
Training in Sincerity (3)	277
Honesty and Tact	279
Is Self-Accusation Obligatory?	281
Training to Confidence	282
All My Faith	285
Formation of Character (1)	287
Formation of Character (2)	289
Formation of Character (3)	291

	PAGE
Education in Reverse	293
Important *Nevers*	295
Training the Adolescent	297
Girls versus Boys (1)	299
Girls versus Boys (2)	301
A Father's Letter	304
Misunderstood Children	306
A Defaulting Father	308
A Mother to Her Son	310
Tick Tock	312
Training in Generosity	314
Mothers and Vocations	316
Priests in the Family	318
The Mother of a Saint	320
Parents of Saints	323
Training in Charity	325
Training in Social Responsibility (1)	327
Training in Social Responsibility (2)	329
Training in Social Responsibility (3)	331
Training in Social Responsibility (4)	333
The Family and the School	335
The Secularism of Christians	337
Family Affections	339
The Hierarchy of Duties	341

PREFACE

A HOME ruled by the spirit of Christ is a happy home. It is also a school of virtue directed to spiritual transformation in Christ.

But Christ does not force His entry into a home. He enters only by invitation. He remains only when evidently welcome.

It is the wise bride and groom who let Him know by their spiritual preparation for marriage that they want Him to accompany them from the altar of their vows into the home they are about to establish. It is the wise husband and wife who let Him know they want Him always present by striving *to put on His mind* and to establish their family according to His principles.

In such a home, husband and wife and children will enjoy gladness of heart, happiness in the fulfilment of duty, and intense union of souls.

The strength and honor of the family come above all from within, from union with Christ which gives power to manifest in daily living the beautiful family virtues of patience, energy, generosity, forbearance, cheerfulness, and mutual reverence with their consequent effect of peace and contentment.

This book is an invitation to the married or those about to marry, to spend the interior effort required to unite them solidly in Christ and to make them worthy transmitters of the Christ-life to their family. It is an invitation to fulfil the high purpose of their marriage which is to help each other to sanctity and to rear saints for heaven; to possess Christ themselves as completely as possible and to give Christ to their children.

Now sanctity is the result of personal cooperation with grace. It is no passive attainment. Equally true is it that spiritual truths and principles merely *known* but not *realized* are of little force in stimulating spiritual energy and effort. Consequently this book of spiritual readings makes no attempt to present fully developed meditations. It is not to be a substitute for personal reflection and prayer. Its various topics are presented as points of departure into deeper realms of thought and prayer; by the personal following through of the ideas offered, conviction and realization will be achieved and lives transformed. A stronger bond of communication will be established between the soul and God resulting in *real* prayer and not *prayers said*. The affections made will be the outpouring of the individual's response to God and not someone else's pre-planned expression of what that response ought to be.

The essential thing is to talk over the subjects with God. It is important then to enter into His Presence before each reading by a reverent act of recollection; to beg His light to see the truth and His strength to act on conviction and realization. It is important *to see;* it is more important *to will.*

The points offered for prayerful consideration are not meant to carry the reader into the clouds of elevated speculation and theory but rather to direct the soul to study prayerfully the daily, common, routine elements of his life in order to lift them out of possible monotony and deadening repetition into the challenging and absorbing adventure of making them divine.

This book in no way presumes to replace what should be for all Christians the two essential meditation books—the *Gospels* and the *Missal.* In fact, it presupposes that its readers are Christians accustomed to live in the spirit of Our Lord's life according to the rhythm of the liturgy. It endeavors to provide variety and to bring into practical application some of the lessons hidden in the *Gospels* or the *Missal*.

Of vital importance is it, no matter what the meditation book, to draw from the little that one reads a maximum of nourishment for the soul. That is not impossible. All one need do is to beg God for His grace and to co-operate with the grace that He gives.

Such a manifestation of good will is a sincere invitation to Christ and a convincing proof that He is welcome in your life.

CHRIST WILL ENTER YOUR HOME
HE WILL REMAIN TO DWELL WITH YOU

INTRODUCTORY READINGS

The Saint of Modern Times

FORMERLY when people dreamed of sanctity or even of the interior life, they aspired to one thing only—to get away from the world, to go off to the desert, or at least to the priesthood or the religious state. To become a saint in the world, to acquire a true and profound union with God in the world, to exercise oneself in the practice of complete abnegation, and to pursue perfection in the world seemed scarcely possible.

People are beginning to realize better that there is such a thing as sanctity in the world.

We honor those who follow a priestly vocation or a consecrated life in religion. They have chosen the better part which will not be taken from them.

But are we to conclude therefore that the laity, because they live in the world, because they have entered the married state, must be content with a cheaper view of perfection? Must assume that the practice of the highest virtues is not for them? That they may not aspire to divine union and the secret joys of a valiant fidelity inspired by love?

Fortunately there are many who realize the falsity of such a conclusion. Saint Francis de Sales challenged the laity to strive for high sanctity.

"The world of today longs to contemplate the saint of modern times who will take his place beside the ancient and venerable figures of our history," observes Rademacher, the author of *Religion and Life*. "It demands the saintly man of the world who unites harmoniously in his personality all the aspects of a noble humanism established on correct values, entirely impregnated with a living faith, a strong love of God, and a supple, joyous participation in the life of the Church.... There ought to be even now on this earth a type of saintly employee, saintly merchant, saintly industrialist, saintly peasant, saintly wife, saintly woman of Christian culture and refinement. The saint's role in the world today is to be the pioneer of the new family, of the new State, of the new Society, of the new humanity, of the Kingdom of God which is always new."

No profession is of itself an obstacle to holiness. No state of life is an obstacle; and marriage, if rightly understood, not only demands holiness but leads those who fulfill all its requirements to true sanctity.

In trying to picture what the saint of the next centuries should be, Foerster, a Protestant author, did not hesitate to write: "Just as in former times the saint was characterized by his courage to confess his faith and die a martyr, since he held faith to be his highest ideal for which he must be willing to suffer; just as the saint of the Middle Ages and even of our own day, has been characterized by virginity, since then and now, and especially in our times, it requires a struggle to conquer many temptations to preserve personal purity; so perhaps the saint of the centuries to come will be the perfect wife or husband, since the vital ideal for which we should willingly suffer today is the sacredness of marriage."

There is much truth in these words. It may be though that the age of martyrs is not so far distant as the author would have us believe. And consecrated virginity, thank God, continues to hold a strong appeal for many souls. But is Foerster not pathetically correct in stating that saints in married life, in conjugal fidelity, are a crying need of our age to counteract the attacks on the family and notably the attacks on the indissolubility of marriage?

What thirst consumes me as I begin this book of spiritual readings? Is it the thirst for sanctity? How far am I willing to go?

Let me gauge the measure of my desire, of my sincerity.

Sanctity of the Laity

THE author of the so-called *Precepts of Contemporary Philosophy* may have been trying to be witty when some years before the war broke out in 1939 he wrote the following comment on sanctity:

"*Sanctity:* An idolistic word no longer having any more than historical interest. Civil and military society has preserved its heroes; religious society has lost its saints or, if any more of them remain, we no longer hear them mentioned.... The age of great Christian fervor has indeed passed away.... Without wanting to appear sacrilegious, I believe that the Catholic faith would have difficulty finding martyrs thoroughly convinced of their faith and ready to sacrifice themselves for it even to death."

True, heroic virtue is rare and where it does exist, it makes so little noise! How much real sanctity there is! Sanctity which may never be officially canonized but real just the same: the sanctity of a doctor who spends himself for the love of God and for the suffering members of Christ without counting the cost; the sanctity of a servant who lives her life of obedience and continual renunciation humbly and in a supernatural spirit—multiple types of sanctity, hidden and unknown but effective and a delight to the Heart of God. We should of course like to see sanctity more widespread, but we must not deny what already exists.

Furthermore, opportunities for martyrdom are not of general occurrence, and sanctity adorned by the martyr's palm is not the only kind of sanctity. As René Bazin so truly wrote: "Men do not seem to recognize the sacrifice of life unless it is made all at once." Martyrdom by the little fires of hidden fidelities constantly adhered to, of tormenting temptations courageously and perseveringly repulsed, of the exact and loving fulfilment of duties toward God and neighbor, of prayer faithfully practiced despite disgust, aridity and the pressure of work—is it not a martyrdom? Who can estimate the value of its countless offerings which are not publicized but which cost... and which count!

The amount of sanctity in the world today is not the essential problem; the important question is how much there ought to be, what the needs of the world demand, what the glory of God and Christianity well understood require.

Speaking one day with a group of cardinals, the Holy Father Pius X put this question to them:

"In your opinion, what is the most vital need for the salvation of society?"

"To build schools," answered one cardinal.

"No."

"To build more churches," suggested another.

"No again."

"To increase the number of priests," said a third.

"No, no," replied Pius X. "All those things are important, but what is most necessary at present is to have in every parish a group of lay people who are very virtuous, very determined, enlightened in their faith and who are true apostles."

Let us consider now just the two words "virtuous" and "determined."

The Holy Father said "virtuous"—"very virtuous" and he was speaking of lay people.

Do I belong to that number of virtuous lay people?

"What luck not to be a saint!" Doctor Vittoz of Lausanne used to say, "For then I can exert myself to become one!"

Pius X had good reason to add the word "determined" to the word "virtuous." Is my resolution to reach high sanctity resolute, determined?

Fantasy or Sacred Duty

In his interesting book, *Man the Unknown*, Alexis Carrel makes this statement:

"Each individual is set by the conditions of his development upon the road which will lead him either to the solitary mountains or to the mud of the swamps where humanity contents itself."

If not rightly understood, this statement might imply that, by a sort of pre-established harmony over which we have no control, we are inevitably directed in spite of ourselves either toward the heights or toward the lowlands.

It could be that because of inherited tendencies, family traditions, examples we may have witnessed, or the training we have received, we are more strongly drawn either to laziness or to generosity. However, everyone has the duty on his own responsibility to make himself what he ought to be. The problem of salvation and the degree of sanctity to be attained is essentially an individual problem. We save ourselves or we damn ourselves; we conquer ourselves or we let ourselves be conquered—these are all *personal* verbs.

"Everyone has the duty," that is the reality. It is not a matter of satisfying a fantasy, a more or less poetic taste for the heights. So much the better if the heights tempt me! So much the worse for me if I am the prey of a positive spirit of low ideals. I do not have to strive for the Christian ideal simply because of a certain forceful subjective attraction. No, I have an obligation to strive for it and this obligation springs from the Gospel command, a command given to all, *Be ye perfect as your heavenly Father is perfect.*

Am I perhaps too much in the habit of seeing in the Gospel only the restrictions it imposes upon me? Of viewing religion from the negative side? I must accustom myself to consider the Gospel from the positive aspect—the call to sanctity. The capital problem for the Christian who wants to be a real Christian is not the problem of sin but the problem of perfection.

Not to fall back!

Much more and much better—to rise.

In the *Journal of Salavin* by George Duhamel, Salavin laments in self-disgust, "How can one resign himself to being only what one is and how try to be other than what one is." Then he declares:

"After some indefinite time, I am going to go away."

"And where are you going?"

"Nowhere."

Evading—when it should be a matter of ascending.

For me as a Christian, the road is known. I know where to go. And the instructions are clear. Someone expressed them in three points:

1. To commit this year the least number of sins possible.
2. To acquire this year the most virtues possible.
3. To do to others the most good possible.

Here is a program that will not only avoid the abyss but lead to the heights.

My Personal Vocation

NOTHING is more interesting and at the same time more stirring than to study my particular role in the eternal destinies of the world... what God from all eternity has planned for me... what kind of saint He wants me to be... by what combination and sequence of circumstances He established me where I am... all He has given me—a Christian country, a Christian family, a Christian education, numberless graces exterior as well as interior, the Sacraments, interior inspirations, invitations to mount spiritually —and then to discover in what degree He intends to use me to lead other souls to salvation and perfection.

Religion in spirit and in truth—what is it? It consists in participating in the very sanctity of God Himself in my own personal life, and in cooperating with God to bring grace into the lives of others and to help keep them to grow in the divine life.

There is no question then of eternity forcing its way into my existence without my opening the door to it; it permeates me from within in keeping with the freedom I give it.

Nor must I be aiming only at my own sanctification. I have the responsibility of souls, not only the souls of *my own* but of multitudes who are in some way connected with my soul. The salvation of the world depends in part on the saint that I become.

One author puts this thought very well. "Each being in the universe must act with the consciousness of having been chosen for a task that he alone can accomplish. As soon as he discovers what this task is and he begins to dedicate himself to it, he can be sure that God is with him and that He watches over him. Let him be full of confidence and joy! He is associated with the work of creation." And we might add "with the work of redemption." This ought to be a continual marvel to him that weak and sinful though he knows himself to be he is nonetheless called, unquestionably called, to an action of unique value, to the exaltation of the divine in himself and the propagation and the extension of the divine in humanity!

I ought to try to realize ever more deeply the tremendous significance of my personal vocation; to consider the degree and the kind of sanctity to which I am called; to measure the extent of the field where my zeal for souls is to labor—the family, the parish, the city....

Everything in my life should be referred to God. As Saint Augustine said, *Totum exigit te qui fecit te, He from whom you received all things demands all*. I must therefore make the gifts He bestowed on me serve for His glory alone. I should not deny these gifts, nor store them away; on the contrary, I should exploit them, but for Him. To quote Saint Augustine again, "Let everything useful that I learned as a child be consecrated to Your service, O my God. Let it be for Your service that I speak, that I read, that I write, that I count!" He did not renounce the use of his mind, the exercise of his intelligence, the application of his profane sciences but he subordinated all to spreading the glory of God and extending his apostolate for souls.

I can be inspired to a like rule of life. I can use human gifts as well as divine gifts to attain the highest peak of my vocation. I am not what my neighbor is and my neighbor is not what I am. I have a role to fill and no one else but me can fill it.

I must know my capital and prudently determine my investments.

What Kind of Soul Am I?

SOMEONE has said, "All beings receive the same light but all accept it unequally. Some are like white surfaces and they shed the light all about them; these souls have the most innocence. Others are like black surfaces and they enfold the light in their own darkness; these souls are like closed coffers. Then again some divide the light keeping part for themselves and reflecting the rest as do surfaces of variegated colors and, like these same colored surfaces, change the intensity of light and shadows according to the time of day; these are the most sensitive souls. There are others who like transparent surfaces let all the light pass through them retaining nothing of it; these souls are nearest to God. Some might be compared to mirrors in which all nature and the people who look at them never cease to see themselves and to reflect themselves; these souls are nearest us and their presence alone suffices to judge us. Some make us thing of prisms in which the white light is spread out into the rainbow colors of the spectrum...."

In which class do I belong?

I need not indulge in morbid or vain introspection but try merely to get a clear view of God's intentions concerning me. I know the Parable of the Talents. I must not envy the riches of another but determine exactly the capital that God asks me to exploit for His greater glory, for my own sanctification, for the good of all souls with whom my sanctification is bound up, from those nearest to me even to the most distant at the other end of the world. *Tu quis es?* "*Who are you?*" the judges asked Our Lord, *Et quid dicis de teipso,* "*and what do you say of yourself?*"

Who am I? The mystery of each personality! It is a mystery which even the most perfect and most intimate union with another personality cannot completely pierce, as for example in marriage. There is a limitless diversity in personalities, since God made all souls originally without ever copying any previous model. How delightful this variety is: rose, anemone, violet; an extraordinary medley, gradations without limit of cut or of color....

Who am I? What are my resources? What are my good

points? What are my faults? What is the color of my desires, the force of my will, the intensity of my religious need, my thirst for an integrated life, my Christian fervor, the value of my fidelity?

Who am I? That is a different question from what I say I am or what I give to understand that I am. No, I am not a hypocrite; I do not seek to deceive for the sake of deceiving. But I am like everybody else and, without wanting to, without directly saying it, I fix up the pages of *my country's history*—I try to let myself be seen only under the most glorious aspects. People believe me to be better than I am. In any case they have a different opinion of me from what I really am.

Who am I? And what difference is there between what I am actually and what I let others discover of my person and my intimate self?

Saint Augustine prayed, "Lord, let me know myself, let me know Thee." He desired nothing else. I want to make that my prayer too.

MARRIAGE

Before Embarking (1)

WHOEVER desires to marry ought to prepare himself for that great step:

—First of all, by preserving chastity.
—Then, by praying much for his future home and family.

By preserving chastity: Whoever cannot see the need for this will not be likely to understand the need for anything. But one must be able to see the need for more than this, to desire more.

The practice of purity in its entirety involves not only the avoidance of serious wrongdoing harmful to the integrity of the body but also whatever sullies imagination, thought or desire. Consequently questionable companions, flirtations, and imprudent reading are out of the question. Custody of the eyes is essential. Death enters in through the windows of the body. Eve and David both sinned through their eyes.

For certain temperaments, such vigilance demands great generosity. No one can deny it.

"The good is more difficult than the evil," wrote Paul Claudel in response to Jacques Rivière who had explained that to remain pure was difficult. "But there is a return. The good opens up before us incomparable horizons because it alone is in keeping with our reality, our nature, our life and our vocation. This is particularly true where love is concerned. How ridiculous the romantic fever of a purely fleshly love seems to me!"

Sensing the old classic objection in his correspondent, Claudel took the offensive:

As for the emotional cramping Christianity imposes upon you, I can scarcely understand what you mean. When you speak of sins, I suppose you refer to sins of the flesh, because I cannot imagine that you have any tendency to drunkenness, avarice, acts of violence or similar things.

The first answer to your difficulty is that when we become Christians, it is not for our pleasure or personal comfort, and further, if God does us the honor of asking sacrifice of us, there is nothing to do but consent with joy.

The second answer is that these sacrifices amount to very little or practically nothing. We are still living in the old romantic idea that the supreme happiness, the greatest interest, the only delight of existence consists in our relations with women and in the sensual satisfactions we get from them. But we forget one fact, the fact that the soul, the spirit, are realities just as strong, just as demanding as the flesh—even more so; we forget that if we accord to the flesh everything it demands, we shall do so with the consequent loss of other joys, other regions of delight which will be eternally closed for us. We shall be draining a glass of bad wine in a hovel or in a drawing-room and be unmindful of that virginal sea which stretches out before others under the rising sun.

How splendidly Shakespeare has expressed the same thoughts:

> What win I, if I gain the thing I seek?
> A dream, a breath, a froth of fleeting joy.
> Who buys a minute's mirth to wail a week?
> Or sees eternity to get a toy?
> For one sweet grape who will the wine destroy?
>   Or, what fond beggar, but to touch the crown,
>   Would with the sceptre straight be strucken down?
>   (Rape of Lucrece, Stanza 31)

This is also what Saint Augustine has written in his own epigrammatic style: *momentaneum quod delectat, aeternum quod cruciat*. One instant of pleasure, an eternity of suffering....

Let me examine my own soul. Have I come to marriage entirely chaste? Chaste in body? Chaste in thought? Chaste in heart?

If my answer is *Yes*, then I must thank God. It is a choice grace.

If my answer is *No*, then what can I do to make reparation, to obtain from God the grace of entire fidelity to my duty, from now on?

Before Embarking (2)

IN addition to the preservation of chastity, the person aspiring to marriage has a second great duty—to pray much.

An old proverb wisely states, "Before embarking on the sea, pray once. Before leaving for war, pray twice. Before marrying, pray three times."

And this necessity of praying more before marriage than before a voyage or a battle is evident for several reasons. Consider the risk of associating oneself closely with a creature who has many limitations; with a creature about whom one knows very little particularly in the matter of shortcomings, since during the period of courtship and betrothal one unconsciously does everything not to reveal himself; with a creature whom one loves with all one's heart but who possesses not only lovable traits, but also faults which can cause suffering; with a creature who can bestow the greatest joy, but who can also unfortunately inflict the deepest pain.

Furthermore, in order to bear joys as well as possible trials, do we not need much help from God? And to obtain this help, must we not pray much?

Another reason for the necessity of such prayer when

one desires to establish a home is that from a union once sanctioned by the Church and consummated there is no possible withdrawal. It is a choice which is definitely established. For two changeable human beings to dare to bind themselves to each other forever in a relationship so intimate as the realities of marriage, is not God's sustaining help a prime requisite? And to obtain this help is it not necessary to pray much?

Has my life before marriage been one of sanctification and of prayer in preparation for my marriage? Or have I confided solely in the human merits existing on both sides and neglected to place under God's protection the union I was about to contract?

If I have been neglectful, I must make up for it now. There is still time.

If, on the contrary, I prayed much before my marriage, I may not leave off earnest prayer now that I am married. The greater the place God holds in my life, the greater can be my assurance that my home shall be supernaturally happy and, without a doubt, humanly happy as well.

To you, O Mary, my good Mother, I confide my marriage and my home. It seems that marriage is the means of sanctification destined for me by God as it is for the chosen soul whom you have given me.

Together we shall do our best to glorify God—this is our firm resolution. Bless us, help us, strengthen us. Sailors call you *Stella Maris*. Be for us, too, the Star of the Sea and keep us safe throughout our crossing; we put under your care our vessel and its crew. You shall be the Queen on board ship.

Requisites for a Happy Marriage

For a happy marriage, it is necessary, of course, that the engaged couple find each other congenial and enjoy each other's company.

They must agree to share loyally the joys and the sorrows of wedded union and fulfill its obligations.

Each one must be bent on procuring for the other as much happiness as possible and oblige himself beforehand to a mode of life which will disturb his partner as little as possible.

The husband must love his profession, and his wife should share this love or at least neglect nothing in order to respect and facilitate it.

They should be able to make their decisions together, not certainly without sometimes having recourse to the counsels of competent authorities, but with a beautiful and joyful independence of any member of the family who may be too prone at times to attempt to domineer over the young couple. There should, of course, be no presumption, no narrow aloofness, but a serene and supple liberty of spirit; serene and supple humility.

In order to be able to practice the sanctity of their state in all the details of their life, they must understand their duty of leaning upon God. It will not be sufficient to link together their two wills; they must be determined to pray to obtain help from on High.

They must likewise have a certain concern, a legitimate concern, for physical charm, without, however, losing sight of the fact that beauty of soul is superior to beauty of body; so that if some day the physical attraction should diminish, they will not be less eager to remain together, but each will strive to find in the other the quality upon which profound union is established.

Both of them must love children. They must develop in themselves to the best of their ability the virtues necessary for parenthood, the courage to accept as many children as God wants them to have and the wisdom to rear them well —difficult virtues requiring strong souls.

Each must be possessed of a rich power of cordiality for the members of the other's family. Both must resolve to take their *in-laws* and their household as they find them, and adopt as a principle for their contacts with them, *It was not to share hates but to share love that I entered into your family*. Consequently, they must refuse to be drawn into family quarrels, seeking rather in all their actions to promote charity, union, and peace.

Even before their marriage, the young couple should decide to keep their expenses at a minimum, according to their situation, not with avarice or niggardliness, but with the desire to live in the gospel spirit of detachment from the goods of earth. Such judicious economy, which should of course be devoid of even the appearance of stinginess, will enable them to set aside something useful and necessary for their children. It will also enable them to relieve the misery around them.

It is to be assumed that both individuals contemplating marriage have the requisite health, since marriage has been created not only for mutual support but also to transmit life.

It is further to be assumed that each of the two has kept nothing of his past life hidden from the other, and that in view of this entire loyalty which is so desirable a trait in married couples, each has kept himself pure and refrained from dangerous experiences.

A Proposal

Louis Pasteur came from a family of modest means. When he was twenty-six years old, his astonishing discovery in regard to crystals drew upon him the attention of scientists.

In 1849, he was named assistant professor in the University of Strasbourg. The rector of the university, Mr. Laurent, had three daughters. Fifteen days after Pasteur's first visit, he asked for Marie in marriage. The young scientist felt that this young woman understood life as he did and wanted the same kind of life he sought—a life of simplicity, of work, and of goodness. He sent this letter to Mr. Laurent:

> Sir, a request of great significance for me and for your family will be addressed to you in a few days and I believe it my duty to give you the following information which can help to determine your acceptance or your refusal.
>
> My father is a tanner at Arbois, a little city in the Jura region. My sisters keep house for my father since we had the sorrow of losing our mother last May. My family is in comfortable circumstances, but not wealthy. I do not evaluate what we own at more than ten thousand dollars. As for me, I decided long ago to leave my whole share to my sisters. I, then, have no fortune. All I possess is good health, a kind heart, and my position in the university.
>
> Two years ago I was graduated from *l'Ecole Normale* with the degree of agrégé in the physical sciences. Eighteen months ago I received my doctorate, and I have presented some of my works to the Academy of Science where they were very well received, especially my last one. I have the pleasure of forwarding to you with this letter a very favorable report about this particular work of mine.
>
> That describes my present status. As for the future, all I can say is that unless I should undergo a complete change in my tastes, I shall devote myself to chemical research. It is my ambition to return to Paris when I have acquired a reputation through my work. Monsieur Biot has spoken to me several times to persuade me seriously to consider the Institute. In ten or fifteen years I shall perhaps be able to consider it seriously if I work assiduously. This dream is but wasted trouble; it is not that at all which makes me love science as science.

Could a more modest, more completely sincere letter ever be sent by a young man in love?

And when he addressed himself to Marie he assured her with touching clumsiness that he was sure he could hardly be attractive for a young girl, but just let her have a little patience and she would learn his great love for her and he believed she would love him too, for "my memories tell me that when I have been very well known by persons, they have loved me."

But great as was his love for Marie, his heart was divided: Louis Pasteur loved science, he loved his crystals. He began to scruple about it, and finally wrote to his fiancée, asking her "not to be jealous if science took precedence over her in his life."

She was not jealous. Madame Pasteur married not only the man but also his passion for science. Her love had that rare quality of knowing how to efface itself, and to manifest itself precisely by not manifesting itself at all at times. She was a worthy companion of this great man, of this great scientist, of this great heart.

The End of Love?

A CERTAIN essayist makes this appalling statement: "What a sad age this is in which one makes his First Holy Communion to be through with religion, receives his bachelor's degree to be through with studying, and marries to be through with love."

Let us omit the first two statements from this consideration and take up the third.

Is it true that for some, marriage is the end of love?

That statement can be taken in different ways.

Some think that before marriage one can play at love. Then when the senses have been dulled, one shall try to find a companion for himself. "Youth must pass," people say condescendingly on observing the looseness of young men.

There are even certain pseudo-moralists who advise young girls not to marry before "deliberately having their fling as well as the boys"—advice which unfortunately some of them do not fail to follow.

This is an odious concept of love and marriage or of preparation for it. I certainly want none of it.

Again there are those who think that love is all well and good before marriage. As for marriage itself, it is first and foremost an investment. The problem is not so much to marry someone for whom one experiences a strong attraction, but rather to realize a good business deal. It is not the person one seeks, but the name, the status, the fortune. There is nothing of love in this. No, indeed, it is all a matter of interest: a concept equally as odious as the first, equally repellent.

What the author of the statement probably meant is that before marriage, the young man and woman are all fire and flame, and perhaps for a short time after marriage. Soon, or at least comparatively soon after marriage, they no longer speak of love. They have become two under the yoke—two bearing the necessary restraints of their united existences. Gone is the enchantment of betrothal days or of the early days of married life. There is nothing left but the grayish prose of humdrum existence with an individual of whom one has made a god or a goddess—a person who is after all only a poor creature.

—A man, "a poor man who eats, drinks, wears shirts and drawers, and who loses his buttons," as someone jokingly described him. "A man who will never be able to find anything in a dresser or clothes closet; who will never appreciate the cooking or the menu; who at night throws his clothes in a heap on a chair and the next morning complains that the creases in his trousers are not pressed in well enough; a man who formerly seemed like a knight, a magician, a prince charming, and whose bold gestures so commanding yet so delicate thrilled the heart and stirred one's whole being, causing one's imagination to crown him with the aureola of perfection," and who now...

—A woman, a poor creature indeed, perpetually thirsting for caresses even at the most inappropriate times; a woman who has foolish notions, headaches, fits of humor; who manifests a flare for spending which can never resist the appeal of any show window, particularly if there is an interesting clearance sale on; a woman who wants a wardrobe capable of ruining the most industrious man, the wealthiest husband—a poor sort of woman, indeed!

Is it not because of all these things, at least partially because of them, that Our Lord wanted to make marriage a rite giving divine graces—a sacrament?

Perhaps we have exaggerated the poetry of conjugal life; let us not now exaggerate the prose of life together.

As a preparation for this prose, which is always possible and often very real even in the most successful marriages, I shall aim to sanctify myself in the practice of charity and patience.

One Only Being

"LOVE seeks to escape through a single being from the mediocrity of all others." This is the definition one author gives of love.

It is not a matter of reviewing all human beings with whom one comes into contact as if they were on parade, so that with methodical, rational, and cold discernment one might pick out the chosen man or woman. It is not a selection; the object of one's desire attracts at once; it is just *he* or *she;* all the rest do not exist. As one writer put it, "Love is *monotheistic.*" There is no need at all of overthrowing idols; one pedestal alone stands, bearing the holy representation that the eyes feast upon and toward which the heart turns with an irresistible impulse.

Oh, the incomprehensible power of the heart in love promptly to divinize the poor reality it has chosen! Nothing else exists for it any longer! In the play *Asmodée*, by Mauriac, the heroine Emmanuelle, who had thought of religious life until she met Harry with whom she fell deeply in love at first sight, goes so far as to declare:

> You know when I used to hear a person say of someone, "He is everything for me," I did not know what that meant. I know now. Our pastor tells me that husbands and wives love each other in God. I can't understand that. It seems to me that if Harry were some day to be everything for me, then there would no longer be any room in my heart or in my life for anyone, not even for God.

Aside from this particular example of Emmanuelle, there is some truth in those words; they emphasize a well-known fact.

How many young girls during their engagement period, how many young wives in the months following upon their marriage, neglect the spiritual, overwhelmed as they are with human happiness! Previous to that time, all their love, all the need they felt for giving themselves was directed to divine realities. Their capacity for tenderness was showered upon Jesus and Mary; it was fed in Holy Communion.

Now another object engages all their concern. They must be vigilant that their piety does not diminish. Their needs have increased; it is not the time to decrease their cultivation of holiness. Doubtless, and above all in the case of a married woman, some spiritual exercises will not be possible; for example, daily Holy Mass and Holy Communion in certain cases will have to be sacrificed through fidelity to duty in their new state. But piety itself must not diminish as it so often does in a period of human happiness.

It is essential in the midst of marital joys, and above all in the joys preceding marriage or following immediately upon it, to strive to preserve a sense of balance and of true values. Love of God does not operate exactly as the attraction of creatures. In the one case, it is a question of an invisible reality; in the other, of a sensible reality. This last, even though closer and more accessible, never eclipses the first. Esteem as divine what is divine, and do not knowingly *divinize* or, more correctly speaking, transfigure to excess a creature, no matter how rich its gifts.

Remain if possible always *in truth*. Realize that God alone is God, and that every created being has its limitations. Strive to make your limitations and your mediocrity as little felt as possible and generously pardon the limitations and mediocrity of your companion for life.

The earth shall never be anything but the earth; it is untimely to try to make it heaven.

Love

WHY does a woman desire a man? Why does a man desire a woman? What is the explanation of that mysterious attraction which draws the two sexes toward each other?

Will anyone ever be able to explain it? Will anyone be able to exhaust the subject?

One fact is certain: Even aside from the physiological aspect of the problem, the effeminate man does not attract a woman; she makes fun of him, finds him ridiculous. So too the masculine woman weakens her power of attraction for a man, and ends by losing it entirely.

The age-old spell which each sex casts upon the other is closely allied to the fidelity with which each exactly fulfills its role. If woman copies man and man copies woman, there can be comradeship but love does not develop. In reality, they are nothing more than two caricatures, the woman being degraded to the rank of a man and a second-rate man at that, and the man to the rank of a manikin in woman's disguise. The more feminine a woman's soul and bearing, the more pleasing she is to a man; the more masculine a man's soul and bearing, the more pleasing he is to a woman.

We do not mean to say that between two poor specimens of either sex there will never be any casual or even lasting sexual appeal and experience. But we can hardly, if ever, call it love. If men and women are no more than two varieties of the same sex, a sort of neuter sex, the force which creates love disappears. Normally, as we say in electrical theory, opposite charges must exist before any sparks will shoot forth. Bring into contact two identical charges and there will be no effect; electricity of opposite polarities must be used; then and then only will there be reaction.

In the realm of love, the general rule is the same. In fact, man and woman are two different worlds. And that is as it should be, so that the *eternal secret* which each of them encloses may become the object of the other's desire and stimulate thirst for a captivating exploration.

That is love's strange power. It brings two secrets face to face, two closed worlds, two mysteries. And just because it involves a mystery, it gives rise to limitless fantasies of the imagination, to embellishments in advance of the reality. So that

One finally loves all toward which one rows.

Whether that toward which one rows is an enchanted island or one merely believes it is, what ecstasy!

Comes the meeting, the consecration of the union by marriage; each brings to the other what the other does not possess. In the one, delicate modesty and appealing reserve; in the other, conquering bravery. A couple has been born. Love has accomplished its prodigy.

Yet, how true it is, that having said all this, we have said nothing. The reality of love is unfathomable.

Could it be perhaps because it is the most beautiful masterpiece of God?

The Palace of Chance

A MODERN writer describes marriage as "having an appointment with happiness in the palace of chance."

Two persons are complete strangers to each other. One day they meet. They think they appreciate each other, understand each other. They encounter no serious obstacles; their social position is just about the same; their financial status similar; their health seems sufficient; their parents offer no objections; they become engaged. They exchange loving commonplaces wherein nothing of the depths of their souls is revealed. The days pass; the time comes—it is their wedding day.

They are married. In the beginning of their acquaintance, they did not know each other at all. They do not know each other much better now, or at least, they do not know each other intimately. They are bound together; possible mishaps matter little to them; they are going to make happiness for themselves together. It is a risk they decided to run.

That this procedure is the method followed by many can scarcely be denied.

Let us hope that we personally proceed with more prudence.

Upon the essential phases of life together, the engaged couple should hold loyal and sincere discussion. And in these discussions and exchange of ideas, each one should reveal himself as he really is, and let us hope that this revelation is one of true richness of soul.

To make a lover of a young man or young woman is not such a difficult achievement. But to discover in a young man before marriage the possibility, or better still, the assurance of a good husband who will become a father of the highest type, and in a young woman, the certain promise of the most desirable type of wife who has in her the makings of a real mother and a worthy educator—that is a masterpiece of achievement!

"To love each other before marriage! Gracious, that is simple," exclaims a character in a play, "they do not know each other! The test will be to love each other when they really do get acquainted." And he is not wrong.

In keeping with his thought is the witty answer given by a young married man to an old friend who came to visit him.

"I am an old friend of the family," explained the visitor. "I knew your wife before you married her."

"And I, unfortunately, did not know her until after I married her!"

But even when a man and woman do know each other deeply and truly before marriage, how many occasions they will still have for mutual forbearance. It is necessary for them to have daily association with each other in order to understand each other; for the woman, to understand what the masculine temperament is; for the man to understand what the feminine temperament is. That may seem like a trifling thing; yet it goes a long way toward a happy marriage. To understand each other not only as being on his part a man and on her part a woman, but as being just such a man or just such a woman, that is to say, persons who in addition to the general characteristics of their species possess particular virtues and particular faults as a result of their individual temperaments—that requires rare penetration!

A home is not drawn by lot, blindly. A palace of chance! No, indeed. If we want to turn it into a palace of happiness as far as that is possible here below, we must above all things refuse to have anything to do with chance. We must know what we are doing and where we are going.

Infinity Promised

"One of the duties of husband and wife is to pardon each other mutually for not giving infinity after practically promising it."

How much each of them expects from the other, from this union hoped for, guessed, discovered, known and loved!

"Is it true, then, that the mystery of infinity is written upon this little forehead, which is all mine," sighs the man with the Hindu poet Tagore. "You are half woman and half dream."

And what a seraphim, what a dream prince and legendary hero she believes to be marrying, she whose imagination is livelier and more powerful in evoking imagery?

Ah, the sweetness of loving, the sweetness of being two to know
The ineffable depths of the heart and its burning love's glow,
... To know all that a soul holds of power to feel,
To understand the eyes' great force magnetic, fair,
To sob softly—my forehead pressed against your hair
Because I feel so small before Love which passes.

But even in the very moment of the embrace, how difficult—impossible even—to arrive at perfect unity; physical union can be achieved, but how delicate an attainment is union of souls! As an English novelist expresses it:

> The anguish of those who love is caused by their powerlessness to surmount the barrier of their individuality. Even in love we cannot escape from the eternal solitude of ourselves. We embrace without being able to be fused into one... We yearn to be but one and we are always two... We are frustrated as two birds would be who sought to be united through a pane of glass.

Thus it is even when the two understand each other. In vain do they try to transfigure poor reality, seek to keep their idol more clearly before their vision, by closing their eyes, and by renewing marks of affection compensate for the infirmity of nature present in their very efforts at mutual tenderness; it still remains true that they always desire more than they possess; of what import is it that their substances intermingle if their consciences remain separated?

And what about those who only half understand each other or do not understand each other at all? Not only is their intimacy no mutual exchange, but their very cohabitation accentuates their isolation all the more. The poet, Anna de Noailles, who was unhappy in her married life, expressed this idea when she said, "I am alone with someone."

It is a suffering for two who do not love each other to be together; it is a suffering to be together if they do love each other, because they never know if they embrace all they really believe they embrace. Berdyaev, the author of *The Destiny of Man*, expresses this suffering of love when he says, "If unreciprocated love is tragic, reciprocated love is perhaps even more so."

How incorrect to think that there is no matter for renunciation in marriage!

The Nuptial Liturgy

ORDINARILY there is very little recollection manifested at a wedding ceremony. It is just as if the congregation had no idea of the sanctity of the place or the grandeur of the event.

Yet, all is holy.

The priest begins *In the Name of the Father and of the Son and of the Holy Ghost*, and prays that God may bless the two about to be married so that all may redound to the glory of His Name.

Then follows the exchange of consent accompanied by the rite of joining hands.

The Lord be with you, says the priest before blessing the ring...

And later, *Be unto them, O Lord, a tower of strength*. Can anything less than this Almighty protection suffice for the work of sanctification in their life together?

The Gradual of the Nuptial Mass invokes the blessing of fecundity upon the marriage. *Thy wife shall be as a fruitful vine on the sides of thy house. Thy children as olive plants about thy table.*

Marriage is not a union founded on chance or pure caprice; reason must control the glow of passion, and the union effected by marriage must be of such a nature that death alone can break it. The Gospel of Saint Matthew gives us Our Savior's own words on this subject. In answer to the question, *Is it lawful for a man to put away his wife for every cause*, Christ answered very definitely, *No*, and quoted the Scripture text, *They shall be two in one flesh.* Then He made it more emphatic by adding, *What therefore God hath joined together, let no man put asunder.*

At the Pater Noster of the Nuptial Mass, the priest does something he never does in any other Mass. He interrupts the Sacrifice, permits the Body and Blood of Christ to lie upon the altar, and turning, calls down a new benediction of God upon the bride and the groom. He recalls how the Most High God has watched over the sacred institution of marriage from the beginning of the world, to keep it intact in spite of the frailty of humanity. The rest of the prayer besides referring to the examples of faithful wives of the Old Testament—Rachel, Rebecca, Sarah—implores rich graces for the bride.

O God, by whom woman is joined to man, and that fellowship which
Thou didst ordain from the beginning is endowed with a blessing which alone was not taken away either by the punishment for the first sin or by the sentence of the flood; look in Thy mercy upon this Thy handmaid;
True and chaste let her wed in Christ...
Let the father of sin work none of his evil deeds within her...
Let her be true to one wedlock and preserve inviolable fidelity;
Let her fortify her weakness by strong discipline;
Let her be grave in demeanor and honored for her modesty.
Let her be well taught in heavenly love;
Let her be fruitful in offspring.

The priest continues the Mass and receives Holy Communion. The bride and groom should also receive the Body and Blood of Christ during this Nuptial Mass. The rubrics of the missal call for it expressly. The ideal then is to communicate not at an earlier Mass but during the Nuptial Mass itself, which nothing, not even the early hour of the day, can prevent from being solemn.

Before the Last Blessing, the priest speaks once more to the newly married couple as if he could not tire of blessing them before their great departure:

May the God of Abraham, the God of Isaac and the God of Jacob be with you, and may He fulfill His blessing in you: that you may see your children's children even to the third and fourth generation, and afterwards may you have life everlasting, by the grace of Our Lord Jesus Christ: who with the Father and the Holy Spirit liveth and reigneth forever.

The Wedding Day

WHAT a marvel of grandeur and of poetry is the nuptial liturgy! The Church, full of solicitude for the two daring young souls ready to launch out on the voyage of life, is eager to prepare them as seriously and as solidly as possible, to put before them essential principles, and to petition God to take this holy couple under His especial care, and conduct it to the great eternal family after their life of reciprocal love and confiding generosity.

Is it any wonder that such a noble and meaningful ceremony should bring to mind the First Mass of a newly-ordained priest?

Unfortunately, the worldly trappings that often accompany the marriage celebration detract considerably from the sacred atmosphere of the event. Particularly true is this of the banquet which is generally a part of the celebration.

The Church has nothing against wholesome joys, particularly family feasts to commemorate an outstanding occasion in life; but she certainly does not approve of the carousings for which wedding banquets are so frequently the excuse, or the tone of certain parties held in connection with weddings. Could anyone imagine an ordination to the priesthood celebrated in such a fashion?

After the Nuptial Mass, the world takes over, there are the congratulations, the general stir to get into the line of march in order to see and be seen; there is not a minute for prayer, for recollection, for thanksgiving. The world, even during the Mass as well as after it, assumes control of the couple and their family. Events following the marriage ceremony do nothing to correct these concessions to the world. Does it not seem reasonable that when the fundamental interests of the family are impeded by the worldly spirit, the family should do everything in its power to escape from it?

There are those who understand this: Sodalists, the Jocists, members of Catholic Action groups or similar organizations, even previous to the war, wanted to break away from these pagan practices. It is not a matter of seeing in the holy place only the Church vestibule or the Church lobby. No, no, the church is the house of God. Let everything there be holy and all that is done there be done holily, the founding of the family more than anything else!

Those groups who recognize the sanctity of the marriage ceremony have set the example of communicating at their Nuptial Mass; they have suppressed boisterous and giddy celebrations. In the same spirit they decided to delay their departure for their honeymoon and postpone the distractions it entails; so beneficial is it to remain in prolonged recollection during their first days together. They remember to make their union of souls predominate. Therefore, together they restrain themselves and by mutual accord embrace sacrifice.

Saint Paulinus, a renowned lawyer of Bordeaux, who renounced a worldly life when he was at the height of success, and with his wife retired into the city of Nola in Campania, wrote these significant lines:

Concordes animae casto sociantur amore;
Virgo puer Christi, virgo puella Dei.

which mean: "Let these souls who are one heart and soul be united in a chaste love; he, a virgin, a son of God; she, a virgin, a daughter of God."

Why not secure for these two splendid baptized souls, these two virgin souls, whom marriage has united forever, a departure worthy of them?

Total Union

IN *Les Vergers humains*, Louis Lefebvre has this charming verse in which the poet addresses his wife:

> I speak to God most often in my verse;
> I speak to my own destiny; I speak to my own son;
> With every living being, I converse
> But I speak not to you; you are myself; we are but one.

There are other exquisite examples of such perfect union between husband and wife realized not only in poetry but in the prose of everyday life.

See this husband and wife seated before the fireplace watching the play of the flames.

"What are you thinking about?" queries the wife.

"And you?"

"The same thing you're thinking of."

Idyllic, some will say. And why not, just as truly, an exact description?

Then there is the example of another couple so completely in accord at all times that the husband one day playfully petitioned his wife, "Contradict me sometimes, so that we can be two." These two fulfilled to the very letter the statement of the Bible, *They shall be two in one flesh.* They were *one*, not only in their flesh, but one in a communion of thought and opinion. They had become so thoroughly *one* that they forget to be *two*.

This could be an evil if it meant the weakening of one of the two personalities to the point of absorption by the other. Some women when first married are in such adoration before their husbands or the husbands are so infatuated with their wives that unity is effected, but it is a unity through suppression and narrowness. God grant, however, that such a unanimity never be replaced by the less happy state wherein each one clings tenaciously to self-assertion. What should be sought is unity through mutual enrichment in mutual understanding.

In some marriages this unity becomes so complete that not even death can break it. Such, for example, was the union between Queen Astrid and King Leopold III, or between Mireille Dupouey and her husband, a naval officer killed in 1915. During the seventeen years Mireille Dupouey lived after her husband's death, she continued to write letters to him as if he were still living, and to set a place at table between herself and her son for her dear departed who was forever present to her, forever one with her.

In contrast to these families where union is complete, how many there are in which dispute rages permanently; or, if not dispute, at least misunderstanding, constant bitterness.

It has been said and truly said that it is not easy for a man and woman, two poor human beings, finite, limited, and possessed of individual faults, to spend cloudless days together. "A woman must take much upon herself, to live with a man, whoever he may be," writes a moralist. "A man must take much upon himself to live with a woman even though she be most loving. How many perplexities between them, how many veiled enmities even in their most evident caresses! How many half-consented-to abdications on both sides!"

But live together they must. How can they achieve as perfect a harmony as possible?

Day after day they must seek it, study, meditate, resolve and act!

The Four Bonds of Conjugal Union

The four bonds of conjugal union are the bond of consciences, the bond of intellects, the bond of souls, and the bond of hearts.

The bond of consciences: This means that husband and wife must have the same norms for judging between right and wrong. Is it not only too clear that if they do not have an identical point of view in their appreciation of God's law, a fundamental disunity will be introduced into the very foundation of their unity? If one, for example, holds to the principle of free love while the other advocates the principle of unity in marriage, can there be complete communion? Or if one is determined to abide by the demands of the moral law in the difficult duty of procreation while the other has no intention of abstaining from the latest practices of birth control or from onanism, will there not be constant struggle in their home, and that in regard to their most intimate relations? If both are not in agreement on the question of their children's education, one will insist on secular education, the other on Catholic education, and again conflict will ensue.

The bond of intellect: This bond is not so essential as the first—it is in the realm not of strict requirement, but of the desirable. There is much to be gained from shared reading experiences, from a mutual exchange of artistic impressions and psychological observations.

For this, it is not necessary that the wife share her husband's work. It is enough if she is able to be interested in his profession. Nor is it necessary that they have the same tastes, the same outlook; a certain diversity in mentality, on the contrary, is desirable on condition that there are possibilities for mutual exchange of ideas which will lead to mutual enrichment.

That evidently supposes great simplicity in both husband and wife, a loving liberty in their communication of ideas, a very humble recognition of any superior quality in each other, an entire good faith which makes each one willing to yield to the ideas of the other when they are better.

The bond of souls: It is not sufficient to enjoy an exchange of ideas in profane matters only. It is very desirable that there be harmony of action in the domain of the spiritual, the supernatural ... prayer together ... meditation in common ... reception of Holy Communion together.

Father Doncoeur and several others go so far as to advise making the examination of conscience together with mutual admonition and mutual resolves. This would surely call for extreme delicacy and could not be so generally recommended as the suggestions given previously. But how beautiful it is when husband and wife are as an open book to each other!

Is it good to tell each other the graces received from God, the aspirations of the soul to become holy, to become a saint? Yes, certainly, on condition that all be done with simplicity, with mutual spontaneity, with nothing of constraint, exaggeration or artificiality. Why should one hide perpetually from one's life companion the best of oneself? Some individuals remain much too reticent and it is a hindrance to great depths of intimacy.

The bond of hearts: How many in marriage love each other selfishly, show themselves demanding, moody, eager to receive, but never generous in giving. There is so much selfishness in certain families even when they are very closely united.

The remedy is to supernaturalize the affections; to pass as quickly as possible from passionate love to virtuous love and to make conjugal love a permanent exercise of the theological virtue of charity.

Life Together Is Difficult

MARRIAGE is not an easy vocation. It requires great virtue of husbands and wives.

Personal experience reveals how true that is; those who cannot claim this personal experience can, in any case, accept the statement of psychologists who observe, "Marriage is the most difficult of all human relations, because it is the most intimate and the most constant. To live so close to another person—who in spite of everything remains another person—to be thus drawn together, to associate so intimately with another personality without a wound or without any shock to one's feelings is a difficult thing."

According to an old saying, "There are two moments in life when a man discovers that his wife is his dearest possession in the world—when he carries her across the threshold of his home, and when he accompanies her body to the cemetery."

But in the interval between these two moments, they must live together, dwell together, persevere together. "To die for the woman one loves is easier than to live with her" claim those who ought to know. And how many women could claim similarly, "To die for the man one loves is easier than to live with him."

They must bear with each other.

A French journalist while visiting Canada stopped for a time at Quebec. "You have no law permitting a divorce in the case of husbands and wives who do not understand each other?" he questioned.

"No."

"But what do those married persons do whose discontent is continual and whose characters are in no way compatible?"

"They endure each other."

How expressive an answer! How rich in meaning! How expressive of virtue which is perhaps heroic! They endure each other.

This is not an attempt to deny the delights of married life, but to show that more than a little generosity is required to bear its difficulties.

In *The New Jerusalem* by Chesterton, a young girl is sought in marriage. She opposes the proposal in view of differences in temperament between herself and the young man. The marriage would certainly be a risk; it would be imprudent. Michel, the suitor, retorted to this objection in his own style:

"Imprudent! Do you mean to tell me that there are any prudent marriages? You might just as well speak of prudent suicides... A young girl never knows her husband before marrying him. Unhappy? Of course, you will be unhappy. Who are you anyway to escape being unhappy, just as well as the mother who brought you into the world! Deceived? Of course you shall be deceived!"

Who proves too much, proves very little. We can, however, through the exaggeration find the strain of truth. "Michel" is a little too pessimistic. He makes a good counterpart to those who enter into marriage as if in a dream. "Marriage," wisely wrote Paul Claudel—and he gives the true idea—"is not pleasure; it is the sacrifice of pleasure; it is the study of two souls who throughout their future, for an end outside of themselves, shall have to be satisfied with each other always."

Loving Each Other *in God*

WE HAVE already seen that it is essential to advance as quickly as possible from a purely natural love to a supernatural love, from a passionate love to a virtuous love.

That is clear. No matter how perfect the partners in marriage may be, each has limitations; we can foresee immediately that at the point where the limitations of the one contact the limitations of the other, sparks will easily fly; misunderstandings, oppositions, and disagreements will arise.

No matter how much effort one puts forth to manifest only virtues, one does not have only virtues. And when one lives in constant contact with another, his faults appear quickly; "No man is great to his valet," says the proverb. Sometimes it is the very virtue of an individual which seems to annoy another. One would have liked more discretion; one is, as it were, eclipsed. Two find their self-love irritated, in conflict.

Or perhaps virtues no longer appear as virtues by reason of being so constantly manifested. Others become accustomed to seeing them and look upon them as merely natural traits. "There is nothing more than that missing for him or her to be different." It is like the sun or the light; people no longer notice them. Bread by reason of its being daily bread loses its character of "good bread."

Daily intercourse which was a joy in the beginning no longer seems such a special delight; it becomes monotonous. Husband and wife remain together by habit, common interests, honor, even a certain attachment of will, but do they continue to be bound together by love in the deepest sense of the word?

If things go on in this way, they will soon cease to be much concerned about each other; they may preserve a mutual dry esteem which habit will render still drier. Where formerly there existed a mutual ardor, nothing more remains than proper form; where formerly there was never anything more than a delicate remonstrance, there now exists depressing wrangling or a still more depressing coldness.

Married persons must come to the help of weak human nature and try to understand what supernatural love is in order to infuse it into their lives as soon as possible.

Is not the doctrine of the Church on marriage too often forgotten? How many ever reread the epistle of the Nuptial Mass? Meditate on it? In any case, how many husbands and wives read it together? Meditate on it together? That would forearm them against the invasion of worrisome misunderstandings. Why not have recourse to the well-springs of wisdom?

There are not only the epistles. There is the whole gospel. The example of Joseph and Mary at Nazareth is enlightening. What obedience and cordial simplicity in Mary! What deference and exquisite charity in Saint Joseph! And between the two what openness of heart, what elevated dealings! Jesus was the bond between Mary, the Mother, and Joseph, the foster-father.

In Christian marriage, Jesus is still the unbreakable bond—prayer together, Holy Mass and Holy Communion together.

Not only should there be prayer with each other, beside each other, but prayer for each other.

Supernatural Love

SOME persons imagine that the endeavor to transform their natural love into supernatural love will make them awkward, make them lose their spontaneity, their naturalness.

Indeed, nothing is farther from the truth, if supernatural love is rightly understood.

What does it really require?

First of all, does it not require us to fulfill the perfections of natural love? Supernatural love, far from suppressing natural love, makes it more tender, more attentive, more generous; it intensifies the sentiments of affection, esteem, admiration, gratitude, respect, and devotion which constitute the essence of true love.

Supernatural love takes away one thing only from natural and spontaneous love—selfishness, the arch-enemy of love. It demands that everything, from the greatest obligation to the simplest, be done as perfectly as possible. Then by elevating simple human love to the level of true charity, it ennobles the greatest powers of that love. It suppresses nothing. It enriches everything. Better still, it provides in advance against the danger of a diminution in human love. It pardons weaknesses, deficiencies, faults. Not that it is blind to them, but it does not become agitated by them. It bears with them, handles them tactfully, helps to overcome them. It is capable of bestowing love where all is not lovable. Penetrating beyond the exterior, it can peer into the soul and see the image of God behind a silhouette which has become less pleasing.

That is the whole secret. Supernatural love in us seeks to love in the manner and according to the desire of God; it requires us therefore to love God in those we love and then to love the good qualities He has given them and bear with the absence of those He has not given or with the characteristics He has permitted them to acquire.

Loving without any advertence to self, supernatural love is patient and constant in spite of the faults of those it loves. The Little Sister of the Poor loves her old folk despite their coughing, their unpleasant mannerisms, their varying moods. The Missionaries who care for the lepers love them in spite of their loathsome sores.

Unselfish as it is, supernatural love inspires the one who is animated by it to seek the temporal and above all the spiritual good of the one he loves before his own. Delicately it calls the attention of the loved one to his faults, not to reproach him, but to help him correct them. It does not give in to irritability or moodiness; it is quick humbly to beg pardon and to make reparation, should it ever fail. And when there has been a little outburst, how comforting it is, in the intimate converse of the evening, to acknowledge one's failings, to express sorrow, and to promise to do better in the future with the other's help!

But all this presupposes prayer and a true desire for union with God.

United Striving for Sanctity

A BEAUTIFUL work which husband and wife can pursue together is the mutual effort to correct their faults. Maurice Retour, an industrialist and one of the youngest captains of World War I of which he was a victim, suggested this to the woman he loved even during their engagement. He wrote to her, "I must confess something to you ... I became aware of your imperfections and I thought how pained I should have been if I had not been able to see clearly into your soul ... You see how frank I want to be with you. We are just engaged and yet instead of paying you compliments, I do not fear to speak to you of your imperfections which my love for you cannot hide ... Tell me you will pardon me."

Another time he wrote, "In general, engaged persons strive to shine in each other's eyes. We, on the contrary, began by showing each other all our faults ... You have acknowledged all your faults to me; I confessed to you all my weakness ... Thank you for your great confidence in me. But never forget that if I permit myself to give you advice which seems good to me, I can always be mistaken and you ought to discuss it with me. Otherwise I shall never dare to give you my opinions."

In a later letter he said to her, "I have already abused the liberty you gave me. I have told you frankly all I thought about you, nor was I afraid to recognize before you what you call your great faults. It was, I must confess, most difficult for me to tell you because I love you so much that I dread causing you the least pain." He added, "The interior life is what we need to correct our failings and we shall work from now on, if you wish, to grow in it."

This mutual effort of husband and wife to correct themselves of their faults may be much, but it is not enough. Something more beautiful remains—to strive positively for sanctity through mutual instruction, loving encouragement and a united and confiding zeal for each other's perfection.

"Why should we not live a saintly life?" asked Maurice Retour of his bride-to-be. And they decided upon some very definite principles for themselves.

"Let us put no faith in fortune, in pleasures, even in our self-love which always increases and makes us run the risk of becoming blind.... The one who receives the most grace will make the other profit by it. What do we care what the world says! It will say what it pleases, but it never will be able to say that we are not true Catholics... Our life will be holy and simple."

"As far as jewels are concerned," commented Maurice, "I understand you perfectly. If you had loved them, I should never have opposed your tastes, but I tell you frankly, I should have suffered. We shall not fail by excesses on this score. We can do so much good with money that it would be wrong, in spite of my desire to spoil you, to spend it only on you. We shall save all we can to enable us to give more to charity. We shall always go straight to our goal and make no concessions to worldliness."

There is however, nothing admirable in a gloomy life. "Our interior life must be so intense that it remains alive in all our exterior actions, our pleasures, our work, our joys and our sorrows. I do not mean an interior life which makes us withdraw into ourselves and become bores for other people. On the contrary, we ought to spread our gaiety generously about us and spend all the activity of our youth to attract those who meet us. But, in order to be saints, we must be able to conserve in the midst of the most captivating pleasures and the most intense activity an interior calm which enables us to remain self-possessed always..."

A saint who is sad is sadly in need of sanctity!

A truly inspiring program!

Ideals for Marriage

ON ONE occasion when Maurice Retour was talking with some comrades about his ideals of marriage, he saw some of them smile sceptically. He who had written, "Love has always been sacred to me. In its name I desired to remain faithful to my fiancée even before knowing her," was to discover that all his companions did not share his noble sentiments, his desire for a chaste marriage.

That did not cause him to lower his standards. He simply tried to lead his companions to a more Christian understanding of married life and if he could not do that, he at least showed his displeasure and withdrew from the discussion.

Writing to his future wife, he said, "I have heard some comments about our future, each one more offensive than the other. But I pity these unfortunate individuals who have never known how to love truly, who have never experienced real intimacy with their wife, and who have sought nothing more than appearance or the satisfaction of their caprice. They can say what they wish, they can tell me that I am young or even a little simple but I shall never change my idea. They can never destroy my confidence—first of all, my confidence in you because of God who has certainly protected me in order to find you... secondly, my confidence in myself, because I know that I am different from certain individuals about me and I am not ashamed to say so even if it does sound like pride on my part."

If that is pride, it is permissible pride! Rather is it an expression of perfect mastery! It is the magnificent dignity of the Christian who knows, of course, that he is weak but who refuses to justify in advance his failings and cowardices, and who counts not upon himself but upon God for strength to persevere.

"Pay no attention to those who tell you I shall change," he wrote. "Do not listen to those who say that men who marry young will become unfaithful later. No, I do not want anyone to believe such a monstrous thing of me."

Who was to give him the strength to resist temptations which were always possible?

"The sacrament of our marriage will impart to us the graces necessary to keep our good resolutions. How few understand this sacrament! How few prepare themselves for it and expect to receive from it the graces it can give to those who seek them worthily."

Noble and irresistible pleading! It recalls the words of Lacordaire, "When a person has not taken the trouble to overcome his passions and when the revelation of chaste joys has not come to him, he consoles himself with vices, declaring them necessary, and clothes in the mantle of pseudo-science the testimony of a corrupted heart."

Surely marriage is a sacrament, but it is not a miracle. He who has prepared for it only by youthful escapades will possibly fail to remain steadfast. But can not he who has prepared himself by the chastity of celibacy for the chastity of marriage be trusted to preserve with the help of God, a chaste marriage?

One Heart, One Soul

How happy are married persons who can say as Maurice Retour to his wife, "We love each other for our ideas. We see only God and we have become united in order to serve Him better." Such is Christian love.

"We shall ask Christ, who sanctified marriage, to give us all the graces necessary for us. We pray with force but also with joy because we have great confidence in the future since both of us expect our happiness from God alone."

And after Holy Communion which they both received on their wedding day they begged God "to make their mutual love always effect their personal sanctification, to bless their home by sending them many children, to keep in His grace themselves, their little ones and all who would ever live under their roof."

Sometimes we hear it said that there are no examples of married persons living effectively the holy law of marriage as God prescribed it and Christ ratified it.

There are many. More than one might think. And, thanks be to God, there have been some in all ages.

In the time of the early Church, Tertullian, believing his death to be approaching, wrote two books entitled *Ad Uxorem, To My Wife*. In the last chapter of the second book he gives an unforgettable picture of marriage. One cannot meditate on it too often.

He extols the happiness of marriage "which the Church approves, the Holy Sacrifice confirms, the Blessing seals, the Angels witness, and God ratifies. What an alliance is that of two faithful souls united in a single hope, under a single discipline, under a similar dependence. Both are servants of the same Master. There is no distinction of mind or of body. Both are in truth one flesh; where there is but one body, there is but one mind. They kneel in prayer together, they teach each other, support each other. They are together in church, together at the Banquet of God, together in trials, in joy. They are incapable of hiding anything from each other, of deserting each other, of annoying each other. In complete liberty, they visit the sick and help the poor. Without anxiety about each other they give alms freely, assist at Holy Mass and without any embarrassment manifest their fervor daily. They do not know what it means to make a furtive sign of the Cross, to mumble trembling greetings, to invoke silent blessings. They sing hymns and psalms vying with each other to give God the most praise. Christ rejoices to see and hear them and gives them His peace. Wherever they are, Christ is with them.

"That is marriage as the Apostle speaks of it to us ... The faithful cannot be otherwise in their marriage."

Oh, that we might fulfill this ideal in our marriage!

We must pray for it and really want it.

Marriage and the Bible

I. THE Law of Union.

How marvelous is the description of the creation of man and woman which the book of Genesis gives us.

God has created the universe. He has hurled worlds into space. Among all these worlds is the earth and on it are all the splendors of the mineral world, the plant world, and the animal world. Each time God sent forth some new creature from His creative Hands, He paused and said, "It is good!" *God saw that it was good.*

Yes, all of that creation is but a framework, a pedestal.

Whom does He intend to place within that framework, upon that pedestal?

Man.

Look at Adam. He has intelligence, free will, and a heart.

A heart—the power to love. But to whom will man direct that power of love which God has placed in him?

God placed all of creation "beneath his feet." But what does it mean for man to have everything beneath his feet if he has no one to clasp to his heart? God understood man. That is why the Most High is not satisfied upon the completion of His masterpiece. He does not say as He did after each preceding creation, *It is good*, but He says, *It is not good for man to be alone*.

Therefore, the Most High, the divine Sculptor, chisel in hand approaches His masterpiece to attack the marble anew; he lays open its side and from the avenues to the heart removes a part; this part of Adam, He forms into woman. A magnificent indication of how close must be the union between husband and wife! A union of wonderful strength, engendered by love and for love! Saint Thomas explains that "God took the substance with which He formed woman close to the heart of man. He did not take it from the head for she is not made to dominate. Neither did he take it from man's feet, for she is not made for servitude. He took it near the heart because she is made to love and to be loved."

Such is the marvel of the union of love in marriage according to God. Love will make of two beings a single *one*.

Adam acclaimed it upon awaking: *This now is bone of my bones and flesh of my flesh; she shall be called woman, because she was taken out of man*. That is why the sacred text adds: *Wherefore a man shall leave father and mother and shall cleave to his wife: and they shall be two in one flesh*.

This virginal page does not yet speak of the mother but only of the spouse. God gives Man a companion—not several but one—and this society is called conjugal society. This society will be composed of two persons, a couple, only two. So true is this that until this first woman became a mother she had no name of her own. There was only one name for both.

How wonderful is the inviolable *oneness* of the human couple according to the desire of God!

Man Born of Slime

WHAT was God's first aim in instituting marriage? Was it the mutual union of the couple? Was it procreation?

We can learn much of God's designs without departing from the story of Genesis. God desiring to multiply humankind by means of generation (the first aim) created a mutual attraction between the sexes which would lead them on to love (the second aim). That is how the matter stands from a logical point of view. Considered from the psychological point of view, the first aim is the union of the two; the child comes only as an issue and consecration of the union.

This is no time to develop a thesis. Much more valuable is it to draw inspiration for useful reflection upon the plan of God.

Adam was formed from the slime of the earth, Eve from the body of Adam. Might not this great difference in origin explain, in part at least, the essential difference between the masculine temperament and the feminine temperament? Man is coarser grained, more vehement in passion, more readily excited to physical desires. That is understandable because of his role in generation; he is constituted for conquest and, with rare exceptions, more readily advances beyond the suggestions or demands of delicacy and restraining modesty than a woman does. In many ways he evidences that he is more *earthy* than his wife. This is not a condemnation but simply a statement of a providential reality. Woman, according to Bishop Dupanloup, is more soulful than man. That, too, can be understood in the light of her role in marriage. Might it not also be explained by the fact that, born as she was from a living human being, the beginnings of her material being were nobler than Adam?

In any case, one thing is certain—God wanted Adam and Eve to be different from each other. It is a mistake for man to become effeminate, for woman to play the man. They are not made to resemble each other but to complement each other.

Let man keep the department of masculine forcefulness and let woman keep the department of necessary refinements.

Woman has probably failed at times in fidelity to her essential feminine vocation. Her game of imitating man whether attempted through perversity or thoughtlessness goes contrary to the plan of the Most High. God does well what He does. If He created Eve after Adam, it was not that He might have upon the earth only Adam and *Adam*.

Man too does not want to see just himself again in woman. Just because he has enough of being himself only, he desires something else. If woman presents nothing but an extension of masculinity, he has nothing but that to go on. He becomes completely *himself* only when a woman who is truly a woman comes to join him according to the plan willed by Providence.

Let women take on men's work, if need be, during difficult times which call men to arms; they but do their duty and we extol them for it. Aside from such an emergency, let them keep to their own field, the exercise of womanly functions, and leave to men the functions of man.

Some Feminine Traits

THE Bible clearly reveals the role designed for woman by Providence. Formed from a living person rather than from slime, her lead in the home is to be spiritual; drawn from close proximity to man's heart she is to rule by loving devotedness. Created as man's complement, she is not to become his rival but his helpmate.

It is worthy of note also that the first woman was imposed on Adam. The first man did not have a choice among several women. Eve formed by God from Adam's own being was given to Adam by God.

Ever after, aside from the periods in history when woman was nothing more than a slave or when she was given in marriage without her consent, she would be chosen by man in order to enter into marriage. As a consequence, woman has a double characteristic—an innate genius for adornment and, in regard to other women, a jealousy that can be inflamed by a mere nothing.

She has a genius for adornment. She must please. And that is right. No one need reproach her for striving to do so. "The pheasants are preening their feathers," Saint Francis de Sales humorously commented in answer to Saint Jane Frances de Chantal's letter expressing worry over her daughters' newly evidenced concern about their dress. It is excess that is blameworthy.

Charles Diehl, in the first volume of *Figures Byzantines* tells us that political reasons did not always direct the marriages contracted by the emperor of Byzantium. When the Empress Irene wanted to marry off her son Constantine, she sent messengers everywhere to find the most beautiful girl in the empire; she herself set the requirements as to age, height, and personal appearance of the candidates.

A fig for nobility! The *basilissa* needed only to be beautil. That alone qualified her to be considered sovereign; the marriage would follow. It was not therefore as wife of the emperor that she received power but rather as a sort of choice by God indicated by her beauty...

How many women at that time must have hoped to become empress.

And how many women since the Byzantine era as well as before have counted on their "beauty" to come into power and acquire a husband. Provided that she stays within her bounds when capitalizing on her real or supposed beauty, woman does not depart from her role.

She does however depart from it when concern for her looks becomes her sole interest or when she gives herself up to jealousy of actual or possible rivals.

Her aim should be to keep within the plan of Providence and never go beyond it.

Marriage and the Bible (2)

II. The Law of Procreation.

God did not create love and marriage only for the mutual pleasure of husband and wife. The purpose of their union goes beyond union. From the married couple's intimate union a third person will issue, and if the marriage is fruitful a series of *thirds*, a progeny which will be the glory of the parents.

Increase and Multiply. God could have multiplied the living without using his creatures as instruments. Adam and Eve were directly created. God needed no one. So true is this, that in the creation of the soul the Most High uses no intermediary. He reserves to Himself the power to infuse the soul into the child whose body the parents cooperate in producing.

As far as the body is concerned God permits and even desires that there should be an intermediary cause, and that constitutes a great marvel. God imparts to His creatures a share in His creative power. The parents are united in the physical expression of their conjugal love and from this bodily union, provided nothing bars the way, life will be born. For the soul there is to be no human agent. For the body a human agent shall exist. It is through the instrumentality of the parents that the body of the child will be born. But God reserves to Himself the power to put the soul into that body by a direct act of creation.

That is the basis for the sovereign beauty of fatherhood and motherhood... At the birth of her first born son, Eve, transported with joy, exclaimed, "*I have gotten a man through God.*"

There is a double law in marriage—the law of chastity and the law of fecundity. The law of chastity permits the husband and wife to regulate according to their desire the frequency of intercourse. Should they by mutual consent decide to live for a time as brother and sister, say during Lent or Advent, or at some other times in their life together, for any just and noble reasons, they may do so provided they run no risk of sin.

The principal application of the law of chastity for the married is this: If they decide either by explicit or implicit agreement to perform the marriage act, they may do nothing to prevent conception.

Let them petition God for the desired grace to practice the restraints and continence they recognize as helpful or if it is not advisable for them to abstain from physical union, the grace to do nothing counter to duty.

Conjugal Duty

THE demands of married life emanate above all from the Natural Law; in other words, right reason left to itself would reveal them to conscience. Even if Christ had never come, if Revelation had never been given, these requirements would be what they are. The Church, keeping to the doctrine of Christ merely upholds them with her supreme authority; she does not institute them. She reaffirms the law, explains its application, clarifies the ideal every time someone attempts to obscure it.

To that end we have various encyclicals of the popes as *Maximum illud* by Leo XIII and *Casti Connubii* by Pius XI and also pastoral letters issued periodically by bishops as the need arises.

One of the most complete of such letters on conjugal duty is the one written by Cardinal Mercier. Reminding the people of his diocese of the true doctrine on marriage, he explains the Christian concept of the conjugal life:

The original and primary reason for the union of man and woman is the foundation of a family, the beginning of children whom they will have the honor and the obligation to rear in the Faith and in Christian principles.

It appears, therefore, that the first effect of marriage is a duty which the married may not avoid ...

How far from truth are those who present marriage as a union whose sole purpose is physical love.

The attraction to conjugal intercourse is legitimate, beyond a doubt. But such satisfaction of the sexual appetite is justifiable only in the function for which it was destined and which it was meant to ensure.

How grave then is the sin of those who circumvent the divine law in this matter. A mortal sin is committed every time that the conception of a child is prevented by a deliberate positive act.

Deliberately, before, during or after intercourse to take precautions destined to prevent conception constitutes a formal and seriously unlawful act.

The insidious propaganda on birth control that is being spread about through pamphlets, lectures, and advertisements is nothing but an effort to make an attack on life a lawful act. Cardinal Mercier condemns doctors, pharmacists, or mid-wives who betray their social mission.

It is forbidden to attack life, even in the generative act itself, that is to say, at the very point of origin. And those who dare to kill the living one being formed in the womb of its mother, are punished by the Church with censure reserved to the bishop. That means that the priest who absolves them must obtain from the bishop special authorization to do so, although he need not mention their names.

How the thought of all the souls sacrificed through marriage frauds ought to incite me to pray for holiness of family life and general observance of conjugal duty. War is not the scourge which kills the most people. It is lust.

Motherhood

THE writer who said, "Man conquers and woman gives herself," was correct. Such indeed is the difference between man and woman in their attitude to life. His is an active heroism; hers a passive heroism. For the grown man, life is but a series of conquests; he goes from one victory to the other, carried along by the zest of it until he fails. Woman makes a gift of herself to life; she spends herself to the point of exhaustion for her husband, for her children, for those who suffer, for the unfortunate. But this gift of hers in its fullest significance is childbirth, a supreme act of passive heroism. Giving birth to a child is not a purely physical achievement. A mind, a soul come to life and uniting with the foetus form, without the mother's awareness, a man—a miracle indeed.

What is the most wonderful is the blossoming and growth of maternal love in the woman from the very moment of her child's conception, through its birth, and throughout its whole life, but particularly during its baby days.

In a certain sense, every woman from her earliest years has the makings of a mother in her. As a little girl she plays with her doll, and the game holds her interest only because her imagination transforms the rag doll or china doll she clasps in her already expert arms into a living child. So true is this, that even virginal souls who consecrate themselves to the service of the neighbor may be called *mother*; that they really are for their poor, their orphans, their sick ...

But it is quite evident that at the time of actual maternity, of physical maternity, a special creation is effected in the woman. At the same time that milk mounts to her breast, maternal love takes possession of her soul, a love of a very special quality which does not precede but which follows childbirth. Before the child appears, there can be expectation, yearning, vague tenderness like the dawn preceding day; it is not yet maternal love in the strongest and strictest sense of the word.

The child is born. The woman, even though she had been extremely lazy, manifests an astonishing energy for all that concerns her baby. Though she had been previously most shiftless now she becomes ingenious, attentive, watchful and almost anxious. No one need tell her that her tiny babe can do nothing for itself and that it is exposed to danger of death at almost every instant. She anticipates its needs; its desires and a frown appears at the least cloud that passes over the cradle. No trouble daunts her. As a young girl and young woman she grumbled over sacrifice and became irritable; now she is eager in sacrifice—hours of watching;

getting up at night; if not able to nurse the child, she makes minute preparation of formulas, and even later, pays careful attention to the kinds of food the baby may have. It all seems to come to her naturally; it seems to be second-nature. But even if she has acquired her knowledge through training and study in special courses which she may have taken with no particular relish, now she carries it out with special zest and warmth of feeling.

If her baby is well formed, beautiful, healthy and lively, she rejoices. But if, unfortunately, it is deformed, weak, listless, her love increases. It is as if she wishes to shower him with love to make up to the little one for all he lacks; as if by clasping it more tenderly to herself she can supplement its life.

Should her child later become a prodigal, she will have for him an astonishing partiality; if she believes him to be a hero, it is her prejudice in his favor! Marvelous contradiction in which maternal love reveals itself!

How eagerly she desires the father's love for the child. Then again she is afraid that the father will not be sufficiently firm and will give in to him too easily. Now the warmest caresses, now the height of disinterestedness born of maternal love!

Is Birth Control Permissible?

To LIMIT procreation by the practice of contraceptive devices without foregoing sexual union is forbidden. No one has the right to suppress life. To do away with a living adult is homicide; to do away with the living child in the course of its development within the womb of its mother is the crime of abortion; to destroy the seed of life, in the very generative act itself so as to prevent possible conception is Onanism, so called after Onan in the Old Testament who indulged in this practice.

No one has the right to place any act which by its nature is productive of life, and on his own authority, frustrate the effects of that act which is the generation of a life. Nature must be allowed to take its course. However, if for some reason decreed by Providence, conception does not take place, that is God's act. The individual has not on his own decision killed or sought to kill human life.

It has already been said that to limit procreation by abstaining from intercourse is within the right of the husband and wife.

There is however another method of birth control which has been much discussed and about which it is essential to have clear ideas. May the married couple profit by the wife's cycles of infertility, as suggested by the Rhythm theory, limiting their sexual union to such periods as seem less likely to result in conception? The answer to that question ought to be qualified.

To adopt this practice temporarily in order to space births somewhat without having to deprive themselves of each other is certainly different from making the practice habitual in order definitely to avoid having any children or to avoid it at least for a long time.

Certainly graver reasons are needed to justify the second instance than to justify the first. Are the reasons for it purely selfish? Then the married partners are at fault. They do not by their conduct violate the law of chastity in marriage, that is true, but they do violate the law of charity, or to put it more graphically, the law of fruitfulness.

The plan of God for married persons in this matter of fecundity is not that they have the largest number of children possible. Rather it is that they should have the largest number that they are capable of rearing well considering the position in which Providence has placed them or in other words taking into account the health, the economic status of the family, and other such considerations. It is a problem of honesty.

It is up to each individual to face himself squarely on this problem, if it is his, and examine himself sincerely on the complete honesty of his manner of acting. Then such a one will be ready to meditate often upon the reasons that argue for *peopling the cradles*.

Why Have a Large Family

WE HAVE seen that the practice of Rhythm, above all if it is only temporary, is legitimate and reasonable. But, even in that case, particularly when it concerns those just starting out on their marital life, it is advisable to call attention to some vital considerations to be taken into account:

—The harm it can do by separating the idea of sexual pleasure from the idea of fatherhood and motherhood.

—The harm it can do by overemphasizing the carnal side of life together at the expense of the tender and spiritual aspect.

—The harm it can do by causing inordinate abandonment to the senses during the infertile periods.

Rather than seeking out the means—even legitimate means —of limiting the offspring, what is really important for the married couple is to discover the reasons for having many children.

There are reasons of charity:

1. Toward children who depend upon the parents to be called or not called to life—to eternity.

2. Toward Christian society to which they should seek to give as many baptized souls as possible and, if God per-

mits, priests and religious for a world that needs them so much.

3. Toward their country for whom they may rear citizens who will bring her life and prosperity.

How beautiful are such reasons!

Consider these young chosen ones in perspective. It depends on me—on us—with just a little generosity on our part, to dare to bring them forth from nothingness, to call them into being, to life.

That will mean greater glory for God; it will mean for them an eternity of happiness. It is up to me—to us—to open for them the book of life, *the Book of Life;* for a life in its fuller sense is not merely a period of time, it is part of a life which will never end. In bringing forth children, parents are fashioning citizens of eternity.

It is not enough to consider the Church triumphant and how to help the greatest possible number to enter into it; we can and we ought to consider the Church militant. Are the number of baptized souls bent on living their baptism sufficient in number? Where can they better increase, develop and aid in the Christian renewal, that is, the baptismal renewal of the world than in Christian families? Are there enough priests?... War has mowed down a great number of them. Even before the war there were not enough for the work to be done. Now, the need is tragic. Bishops can only ordain... The priesthood depends mainly on marital holiness. If parents do their duty, if they are generous, there will be priests; otherwise, the Church will weaken.

As for our country, its beauty is proportionate to its men, to its men of valor. The recent wars showed the tragedy of a lack of manpower. These are of course temporal reasons, but spiritual interests are closely linked with them.

Reflect on all this... Let life live!

The Bell of Life

In 1935 there was a project on foot to install a bell of life and a dial of death in the heart of the city of Berlin. The plan may have fallen through. A large bell was to boom out every five minutes; in the interval a smaller bell was to ring nine times announcing to the neighborhood that nine children were being born in Germany during that time. Then an hour glass was to indicate to the passersby that in the space of five minutes, seven Germans had gone to their graves.

Whether realized or not, the project was worthwhile. To announce the increase of life is helpful; to call to mind the work of death more helpful still, but not the least important is to point out the triumph of life over death.

Today's meditation is to dwell on this last thought. It is not so important now to contemplate the end of life and the responsibility to be faced at that dread moment as to welcome the new cradles of life and to determine whether I am increasing for my country as I should the chiming of the life-bell.

In November 1939, a leader of a heavy artillery division at the Maginot line wrote in a letter: "I have eighteen men in my sector. They are between thirty and thirty-five years old; all except a few are married; all of them together have only eight children!"

If, as good Political Economy points out the average number of children per family for a country which does not want to die out is three—two to replace the father and mother and a third destined to fill the void caused by infant mortality—then those eighteen men should have had at least fifty-four children among them. They had eight. The deficit then: Forty-six.

There is of course no moral law that requires the married

to have three children. The example given here is simply a social or national aspect of the problem. It has already been pointed out that the moral law is determined not by the country to which one belongs—although there might be a duty to give it a thought—but by the law of chastity in marriage on the one hand and the law of fecundity on the other.

It might be well here to come back to these points. The law of fecundity expects the parents to have as many children as they are capable of rearing in a human and Christian manner. As for birth control, the law of chastity sets the rule: nothing may be done artificially to frustrate conception.

But to return to the social viewpoint—my country's future, society's need: Of what good is it to cry out *Long live my country!* if my only contribution is to her death?

More cradles than tombs! That should be our motto. How great is the disaster when the contrary is true! Does not such an argument which possibly has no force with weaklings or those too wrapped up in themselves bear weight with me? It is not the most decisive argument to encourage large families, but it is not a negligible argument.

Patriotic duty does not belong to morality in war time only. It exists and binds conscience in peace as well. In another way perhaps but just as imperatively.

Do I love my country? Do I love her enough to be willing to give her children? Certainly not primarily for the time of war, but for peace-time equally. The more valiant hearts and arms there are, the more prosperous is the country. The true wealth of a people is their wealth in men.

The Impossibility of Having Children?

We have seen clearly that it is a "serious matter" to prevent conception by any voluntary positive act and if full knowledge and complete consent of the will are present it constitutes a mortal sin. If the marital act is performed, then God may not in any way—by the opposition of the parents—be hindered from creating a soul.

—But we cannot, considering our burdens, increase the number of our children!

—That may be, responds the Moral Law; such a case is far from being imaginary. But you do not enter upon marriage only for enjoyment. In the plan of Divine Providence, pleasure is the accomplishment or the result of duty fulfilled. To separate the pleasure from the duty, to seek the first while evading the second is to go counter to the divine plan. Sexual pleasure presupposes the normal exercise of the generative function, the acceptance of the resultant burdens for which it is, as Cardinal Mercier expresses it, "the providential payment."

—But when you consider the intimacy of life together, how can we refrain for any length of time at all without giving ourselves to each other?

—There is every reason to believe that, without prayer and recourse to the sacraments, you are right. But what is your supernatural program? What are you doing to rise above the senses, to moderate the flesh?

—Can't we choose those times when fertility is least probable?

—Yes, if you have a sufficient reason, as you seem to have. And the necessity of having to practice prudent and courageous continence several days each month will in itself force you to a certain and meritorious generosity.

—Even that is not possible for us; for then we would have to renounce marital intimacies.

—Of course. But nowhere has it been said that marriage is a state where one can allow himself every liberty suggested by his caprice without exercising any judgment.

That is said nowhere; at least, not in any sane and honest books on morality. Married persons are too quick to think that, because they have not chosen "the state of perfection" in absolute virginity, the great virtues are not for them.

Even in granting themselves what they may legitimately permit themselves, the husband and wife have a large field for detachment. They ought to be willing to profit by the opportunity and not reject it on the plea of moral or physiological impossibility when it is really because of their lack of stamina, of Christian spirit, and the will to self-control.

How will such married persons aenemic in their spiritual life and accustomed to denying themselves nothing, even when the cost is not too great, deny themselves when a serious law binds them?

One must learn to will in order to know how to will. And if one falls he must not excuse but accuse himself.

You are the Judge of my past, O my God. I offer You all its efforts and its weaknesses. Give me the grace to be generous in the future.

The Only Child

THERE is, as we have seen, a double duty involved in the marital bond:

—The duty of chastity: In no way to attack the law of life.

—The duty of charity or fruitfulness: To do one's best for the production of life.

It is impossible—and that is self-evident—to set a definite

figure as the gauge of duty in procreation. A very competent authority on this subject, Father P. Boisgelat, S. J., has this to say:

> Who keeps below his minimum possibilities fails in the duty of his state of life and sins through selfishness. Who strives for his possibilities and realizes them does his duty. Who exceeds the maximum of his possibilities sins by imprudence and intemperance.
>
> As for this level of possibility about which he speaks, it must be determined by each one's conscience without selfishness and without imprudence.
>
> One must on his part confide in God, abandoning to Divine Providence the possibility of unforeseen misfortunes, such as the unexpected and early death of the father, a possible lower economic status in the future, war...
>
> Duty obliges us to foresee only what is foreseeable and likely; all the rest must be confided to God.

There are couples who eagerly desire one child but not several children. They want the one either to have a tangible proof that they have made a fruitful marriage or to create a precious and living bond between them. They desire only the one because they do not want to be encumbered; they do not want to limit the regular tenor of their lives, the quality and variety of their wardrobe, and they are afraid to run the risk to their health that every new birth might bring; they dread the crying and the inconvenience caused by very little children. These reasons and others just as selfish are worth nothing. Serious reasons are necessary to dispense from serious duty.

The idea of limiting the family in order to give to the one (or to the very small number) resources which will eliminate the necessity of working or assure the whole benefit of the entire fortune is not in itself selfish on the part of the parents. It is extremely harmful however. We are not born to avoid work here below. Each one is obliged to contribute his maximum effort to the welfare of society. *We are not here to reign, but to wrestle.*

Parents do not manifest much esteem for the fruit of their blood if they do not deem it capable of gaining, by its own power, a place in life whenever it so desires.

Then, too, is there not always the danger that the only child will receive too soft a training, that he will be spoilt and be of an inferior character?

Should this only child die young, what anguish for the father and mother! They themselves become the very first victims of their damnable birth control.

Christ and Marriage

OUR LORD did not come to destroy but to fulfill the law. Marriage was to remain exactly what it was in the Natural Law: the exchange of two wills for the purpose of procreation. Our Savior who knew very well the difficulties of the marital state made a sacrament of this mutual exchange of wills, a rite that imparts grace. Each of the two in becoming united to the other will enrich that other one with an increase of sanctifying grace. Both should be in the state of grace before the marriage takes place since it is a sacrament of the living, which means that its purpose is to intensify the divine life already existing in the soul. By their gift of themselves to each other they also obtain for each other a gift of new growth in the divine.

Because marriage is fundamentally a contract—a double *yes* giving to each of the two complete right to the other— it has this special feature that there is no other minister than the two concerned. Sometimes people say, "That's *Father So and So;* he married us." The expression is incorrect. It is not the priest who marries the bride and groom; they marry themselves. They themselves are the *ministers* of the sacrament which they *receive* at the same time. The priest is there only in the capacity of a witness representing the Church; as the witness required for the validity of the marriage; but a witness only.

What eminent dignity therefore has the sacrament of Matrimony! What eminent dignity have the bride and groom! They are for each other transmitters of the divine.

The bonds which they contract bear upon two points: the *oneness* of the couple, the *indissolubility* of their bonds. Our Lord, who made of marriage a grace-giving rite, also stressed the double obligation of unity and indissolubility.

Oneness. They form a single unit. They shall be two in one flesh, says *Genesis*. But due to human grossness, forms of polygamy were introduced. Our Savior forbade them, and the Church has always taken care to require the observance of the law. Love itself demands it. Marriage is such an intimate reality. To live it with several individuals at the same time is condemned by natural feeling itself. Divine law merely reaffirms this basic requirement. Furthermore, family stability as well as the happiness of the children militate equally in favor of oneness.

Indissolubility: Marriage creates a *oneness* forever; a oneness that can be dissolved only by the death of either partner. The encyclical of Pius XI, *Casti-Connubii* reminds the world of this:

For each individual marriage, inasmuch as it is a conjugal union of a particular man and woman, arises only from the free consent of each of the spouses; and this free act of the will, by which each party hands over and accepts those rights proper to the state of marriage is so necessary to constitute true marriage that it cannot be supplied by any human power.

This freedom, however, regards only the point whether the

contracting parties really wish to enter upon matrimony or to marry this particular person; but the nature of matrimony is entirely independent of the free will of man, so that if one has once contracted matrimony he is thereby subject to its Divinely made laws and its essential properties.

Marriage and Baptism

CHRIST came to restore to us the divine life lost by original sin. He instituted baptism as the practical means of entering upon the supernatural. The baptized person is not only a soul and a body, but a soul in which God lives.

According to one of the Fathers of the Church baptism is a marriage between God and the soul; he goes so far as to call the soul *Spirita Sancta* the feminine form for the Holy Spirit (Spiritus Sanctus). Without this marriage of God and the soul, the individual can have no spiritual fecundity. It is impossible: The most noble human act performed by one in mortal sin has no value at all for heaven.

What then is the marriage of two beings of flesh and bone?

It is the image on an earthly plane of a union which is more beautiful although invisible—the union of God and the soul.

Baptism, marriage—two sacraments of union—and the second will always be but a symbol of the first. Union of God with the soul, union of husband and wife. Two sacraments of union; two sacraments of fecundity. Without God, the soul can do nothing fruitful for heaven; without each other, husband and wife cannot beget children. And just as Saint Paul could call all sin adultery since it is deliberate divorce from God, so every break in the marriage bond is blameworthy and true adultery.

Both baptism and marriage then are sacraments of inviolable union. A rupture of the union whether a divorce from God or a divorce from one's partner in marriage can in either case be called adultery.

What better guarantee have the wedded couple of their reciprocal fidelity than their common life in the state of grace! Each of the two refusing to be divorced from God is thus more sure of the other. United as they are by the same promise, by conjugal embraces, they are likewise united with each other by the same Holy Spirit who forms the Bond between them. Any husband or wife who denies this is already committing an offence against the integrity of the gift of self. Each of the two must live the truth of Tertullian's definition of a soul in grace. "What is a Christian?" he asked. "A Christian is a soul in a body and God in that soul." To give to one's partner in marriage only the first two elements and refuse the third is not to give all, not to give the best. Truly it is a plunder, a plunder which injures husband and wife. Is it possible not to realize this? It remains profoundly true just the same: Indeed, it is a double betrayal. For who can say that one who has been coward enough to betray God will not be just as likely to betray the partner of his life?

So true is this, that only fidelity to God can give completeness to marriage.

Respect in Love

COMPLETE fidelity in marriage is essential. It is however only a minimum. *To treat each other as living tabernacles of God*—that is what marriage between two baptized persons demands.

Know you that the sacrament of Christian initiation transforms a person into a living temple of the Most High?
You know.

Well then, behind this more or less attractive human silhouette which is the person of the marriage partner, body and soul, there is God dwelling within and living His Divine life in the depths of the soul. Consequently when poor health or advancing age cause husband or wife to grow less attractive exteriorly, that is not a reason for love to wane.

How many know that when husband and wife in the state of grace embrace each other by conjugal privilege, they clasp the Holy Trinity, who unites them even more closely than their human embrace? Far from coming between them, what supernatural intimacy and what magnificent dignity does it give to their union! How it elevates, and idealizes what in itself is good though still carnal and therefore capable of easily becoming earthy and, for some, difficult to consider as something noble.

It is rare to find Christians who truly have faith at least faith in the fundamental mystery of the life of the baptized. Father Charles de Foucauld wrote to his married sister who was the mother of a family:

God is in us, in the depths of our soul... always, always, always there, listening to us and asking us to chat a bit with Him. And that is, as much as my weakness will permit, my very life, my darling. Try, that more and more it may become yours; that will not isolate you, nor draw you away from your other occupations. It only requires a minute; then, instead of being alone, there will be two of you to fulfill your tasks. From time to time lower your eyes toward your heart, recollect yourself for a mere quarter of a minute and say: "You are there, my God. I love You." It will take you no more time than that and all that you do will be much better done having such a help. And what help it is! Little by little, you will acquire the habit and you will finally be always aware of this sweet companion within yourself, this God of our hearts... Let us pray for each other that we may both keep this dear Guest of our souls loving company.

If husband and wife were equally convinced of the living splendor their souls actually present, how the marital act, so holy to begin with, would become for them an act of divine faith, an act penetrated by the highest supernatural spirit.

I want to meditate often on my baptism, and the mystery of the divine life in me. I want to become accustomed to treat myself as a living tabernacle of my Lord, to regard the companion of my life as the thrice holy shrine of the Divinity, for I know this to be a reality.

The just live by faith. I want to live by faith.

Marriage and the Mystical Body

CHRIST came to restore the divine life lost to us by sin. But how? He did not save us only by some act external to Himself as one might lay down a sum of money to ransom a slave but by incorporating us in Himself, by making all of us with Him a single organism. *I am the Vine, you are the branches.* Christ is the Head, we the members and together we are the whole body, Christ. The aggregate of all the members, all the branches united constitutes the Church joined by an unbreakable bond to Christ, its Leader and Head.

And Christian marriage will be... and will only be... but the symbol of this union of Christ with His Church, of the Church with its Head Saint. Paul at the end of his Epistle to the Christians at Ephesus gives no other rule of love and of security in their union to the married than the counsel to copy this union in their life. He says to wives. *Let women be subject to their husbands as to the Lord: because the husband is the head of his wife as Christ is the head of the Church being Himself Savior of the body. But just as the Church is subject to Christ, so also let wives be to their husbands in all things.*

Then addressing himself to husbands, he continues: *Husbands love your wives, just as Christ also loved the Church and delivered Himself up for her.* This is the way husbands ought to love their wives and recalling the words of *Genesis. They shall be two in one flesh,* Saint Paul concludes, *This is a great mystery.... I* mean *in reference to Christ and to the Church.*

Is it possible to imagine a divorce between Christ and the Church, between the Church and Christ? By the same token, it should be impossible to conceive of a divorce between a man and woman in Christian marriage, the man being but a double, an image of Christ; the woman a double, an image of the Church.

This is but a negative aspect... not to be disunited. The union of Christ with the Church which baptism symbolizes invites the married to have for each other the most profound and entire consecration to each other. It is this entire consecration to each other which Saint Paul demands.

It is not without reason that the liturgy of the nuptial mass contains this particular epistle of Saint Paul. Unfortunately how few understand something of the significance of these texts!

How much more fitting would it be, at the time of the marriage, to profit by the marriage discourse to explain to those concerned the sublime meaning of the ceremony and the obligations which will ensue instead of handing out just so much twaddle and bestowing so many compliments!

The whole difficulty is that it would necessitate touching upon the profound Gospel spirit and, for the majority of persons, the Gospel is a dead letter. As a consequence, everyone keeps to the low level of hackneyed themes understandable to all.

I shall come back often to this Epistle of my nuptial Mass; it will help me to deepen my Christianity.

Mutual Devotedness

The emphasis upon the duty of reciprocal devotedness of husband and wife is evident in the previous quotation from Saint Paul. So that the Church may remain intact, beautiful, and immaculate, Christ is lavish in His care of her. In return the Church leaves nothing undone to bring glory to her Divine Spouse.

That is how husbands and wives should treat each other. The husband must be another Christ, a faithful copy of Christ. He ought to neglect nothing for the honor and the welfare of his wife; he should even be ready, if the need arose, to shed his blood for her. She, on her part, ought to do everything to revere her husband. It must be a mutual rivalry of love.

Just as there exists between Christ and the Church, in perfect harmony with their mutual devotedness, a bond of authority on the one side and of submission on the other, so too in the home, the husband is entrusted with the lead in their advance together and the wife joins her efforts to his in sentiments of loving submission.

The wife's duty of subordination to her husband does not arise from woman's incapacity but from the different functions each of the two are to exercise. When each fulfills well the proper function, the unity of the home is assured. The wife is not a slave; she is a companion. On essential points there is no subordination but necessary equality.

The man has no right to come to marriage sullied and yet demand that his wife be still a virgin. The man does not have permission to betray the home, and the wife the obligation to remain faithful. And when it is a question of the marriage right, the duty is conjugal, equal for each: When the husband asks the wife to give herself to him she must grant the request. But there is a reciprocal duty. When she makes the same request of him, he too must grant it.

The duty of subordination holds only where the direction of the home is concerned. It does not give the husband the right to impose any of his whims upon his wife. In fact, should he go so far as to make demands contrary to the law of God, she has the duty to resist him with all gentleness but also with the necessary firmness. Rightly understood, then, the wife's submission to her husband is not at all demeaning. Moreover, to obey is never to descend but to ascend.

Let husband and wife strive not so much to equal each other as to be worthy of each other. Let the husband put into the exercise of his authority the reserve and prudence which win confidence and let the wife strive to be an accomplished woman not masculine but feminine.

The interesting character of the home is not a man, a woman, but the couple; not an individual, but the family, the harmonious development of the family cell; not duality as such but the advance *in common* of the two.

Woman's Superiority

IN HIS book *Il Sangue di Cristo*, Igino Giordani pronounces this judgment:

Even when he is good, man always reminds one a little of a heron; he stands on one foot and assumes poses. He turns to the right, then to the left, and what concern he shows for his appearance!

The Christian woman fulfills the more obscure domestic tasks, services humble and hidden. The woman is to be like

Mary. She will become familiar with the tasks that require abnegation. Is it not perhaps easier to ascend the pulpit than to watch at the bedside of the dying? There are plenty of such examples. Saint Augustine wrote stacks of books but who made a confessor of the faith out of this professor? His mother—with her tears.

More women than men enter religion; yet they do not have the satisfaction of the priesthood. It is perhaps because of these interceding and retiring women that all does not go up in the smoke of vanity's fireworks.

Men might perhaps retort that on the score of vanity, women do not yield to them a point. If they, the men, know how to pose to advantage, and women, just to win admiration, also do their share of strutting, and with an earnestness worthy of a better cause. Would they be such slaves to fashion if they did not have—and how much more than men—the mania for excelling their rivals and gaining notice?

Certainly in self sacrifice and above all in the daily humble hidden devotedness which the tasks of the home require, woman is in the lead. That does not mean that man, in his profession, does not know how to sacrifice himself for the one he loves. Would he spend himself as he does if he did not know that a smile would reward him in the evening and a gentle voice would sing his praises? Nevertheless, in general, the opinion of Giordani can be accepted as well as the proofs he gives for it.

We need not consider religious life now. It has no point here. All we need do is look to the Christian home to find without difficulty numerous and sometimes touching examples of devotedness which nothing can exhaust. Here is a wife; she has a husband who gets beside himself with rage; he has real fits of temper, the blood rushes to his head and he is practically on the verge of a stroke. Will the woman let him to his fate and punish him for his violence by depriving him at least for a time of her attentions? Not at all!

Wasn't it Shakespeare who gave us this delightful scene: A sheriff is enraged against his wife. She leaves the room. Perhaps she has gone off to pout because she is away for a while. But no! Here she comes, her arms loaded down, and sets about preparing mustard packs for her husband's feet and cold packs for his head to avert the ill effects of his moments of fury.

It might be just an episode in a play but it is none the less symbolic.

That is woman for you!

The Boss in the House

AFTER a meditation on his duty of ruling his future home, Maurice Retour wrote the following ideas to his fiancée: "In all the families I have visited, the husbands want to appear to rule their wives while the wives quietly claim that they rule their husbands. I eagerly desire to have influence on your soul to help you ascend; but I desire just as eagerly to have you exercise a great influence on mine. Let us leave to others such petty behavior and thank God in all humility that He has enlightened us."

In another letter he came back to the same idea "I wish to be master before the law, I even want to be responsible to God for the morality of our home, but for all the details of our life there is no master. I have never had greater disdain for anyone than I have for a married man who presumes to dominate his wife. I have seen some husbands grow actually stubborn over some detail so that they do not have the appearance before others of giving in to their wives. I think such husbands are idiots." Then as a reason for his opinion he adds, "Two persons living together necessarily have an influence upon each other, but I promise you never to try by any subtlety to hold you under my dominion. We shall live side by side without a thought for such notions.

I want to believe that we can belong to each other in order to enjoy life but with a love that will bring us ever close to God.... God must always be foremost and He must be our goal even in our love, now and always."

All husbands are not of that calibre. In a novel by a German author, a certain baron gives his idea on how women should be treated.

"They must be made to feel their inferiority otherwise they will be spoiled.

"If you get married, do as I do. Never tell her beforehand about a trip or a horseback ride. Just lead in your horse. 'Where are you going, my dear?' she will ask the first or second time. Give no answer, but continue putting on your gloves. 'Are you going to let me alone like this?' she will add stroking your cheeks. You seize your riding whip quickly and say, 'Yes, I have to go to town. I have this and that to do. Goodby. And if I'm not back at nine o'clock for supper, don't wait for me.' She trembles, but you don't pay any attention. She runs after you, but you signal with your whip for her to go back. She runs to the window, leans out and waves her handkerchief crying 'Adrien!' But let her white banner wave and don't bother. Dig in your spurs and get going! I swear that that's the way to keep women respectful. By the third time, my wife asked no more questions and God be praised, the wailing has come to an end."

A mere comparison of these two different attitudes makes the right one stand out clearly. There are some husbands who are blackguards; others who are gentlemen.

My choice is made.

Marriage and the Eucharist (1)

A YOUNG lady before her marriage wrote to her future husband asking him to go to Holy Communion with her as often as possible; "The Eucharist is the sacrament of those who are engaged to be married because it is the Sacrament of Love." So impressed was the young man by her thought and so much good did he derive from it, that he engraved the sentence on her tombstone when she was taken from him by an early death.

Marriage and the Eucharist... how true that they are both sacraments of love.

What does love require?

Love expresses itself by these three needs: the need of the presence of the beloved, the need of union, the need of exchange of sacrifices. Each of the two sacraments satisfies this triple need.

Need of presence. In the Eucharist: *This is My Body.* God present in us in His divine nature by sanctifying grace received at baptism found the means to unite to Himself a human nature: *The Word was made flesh.* He was certain that under that new form He would find a way to make Himself present to humanity. Therefore, the Eucharist.

In marriage: Needless to mention the yearning the couple have to be together. If they talk, it will only be to tell each other how glad they are to be near each other. They may say nothing, but then in the deep silence which envelops them their souls will be knit together, they will commune and exchange the best of themselves. Silence between lovers is often more eloquent than words; the following advice of a Chinese sage to a young girl considering a proposal of marriage evidenced judgment and experience:

If he tells you, "I love you more than all the world," turn away your head and nonchalantly fuss with your hair. If he tells you, "I love you more than the golden rod in the temple," adjust the folds of your dress and reproach him laughingly as if amused at his impiety.

If he passes beneath your window on a white horse to say goodby because he prefers to die by a thrust of the sword than to despair, give him a flower and wish him a happy trip.

But if he remains beside you, numb as a slave before a king and clumsy to the point of spilling tea on your blue tablecloth, then smile at him tenderly as you would for the one whom you wish to accept for always.

Even though at the beginning of marriage, being together is unalloyed joy and there is no need to urge cohabitation upon the newlyweds, it can happen that in the long run unpleasantnesses arise; the charm of being together wanes perhaps because faults show up more readily than in the past or because the couple's concept of marriage was overly romantic, not preparing them for the possible flaws in each other or simply because a man will never be anything else but a man and a woman never anything else but a woman, that is, two limited beings who can not avoid discovering their limitations sooner or later.

No one is obliged to marry. But once married, cohabitation is a duty. Canon Law states: "The spouses must observe the community of the conjugal life." Saint Alphonsus says even more specifically, "The married are bound to cohabitation in one house to the sharing of bed and board." Separation regarding the last two points can for just reasons, be permitted in certain cases. Grave reasons are necessary to dispense husbands and wives from living under the same roof; there is always the danger of scandal to be feared and, under the stress of temptations which may arise, also the danger of transforming simple separation of bodies into real divorce.

Marriage and the Eucharist (2)

LOVE, which thrives on the mutual presence of the two who cherish each other and yearn for each other, also seeks physical expression.

It is true for marriage; it is true for the Eucharist.

That physical expression is a need of love, both experience and the most elementary psychology more than amply prove. Doesn't a mother often say to her baby whom she is smothering with kisses, "I could just eat you up," as if she vainly dreamed of being able to reincorporate it?

What is impossible to the mother is possible to Our Lord. He wanted to give Himself to us as food not so much that we might incorporate Him in ourselves as that He might incorporate us in Himself. In the case of ordinary food, it is the one who eats who assimilates. In the Eucharist, it is the Living Bread which assimilates us in Itself: *Take and eat, this is My Body; take and drink, this is My Blood. If you do not eat the Flesh of the Son of Man, you shall not have life in you. He who eats My Flesh and drinks My Blood shall have life everlasting.*

The Eucharist requires that we take it and consume it. The Host is not made for the eyes, to be seen, but to be eaten. It is not enough to look and to adore; we must receive and assimilate: *Take and eat.* The Real Presence is already a great gift and to be present at Benediction of the Most Blessed Sacrament a precious exercise which the Church praises. But that is not the whole significance of the Eucharist. The Eucharist demands communion, the common union... and what a closely bound community... of two beings who love each other, Christ and the Christian.

Because love is the ideal basis for the sacrament of matrimony, marriage in its turn dreams of physical expression.

Since it is concerned with uniting not angelic but human

natures, that is, spirits within bodies, marriage, while it involves a union of souls, also normally involves a union of bodies which should facilitate the union of souls. It is the entire being of the one which seeks to become united with the entire being of the other.

It can then readily be understood how in view of the particular intimacy sought through bodily union, delicacy claims privacy. It is a good act without question and willed by God who by His nature can permit not even the shadow of sin. The Church, in the course of her history, condemned those overly severe moralists who wanted to oblige the married to go to confession before receiving Holy Communion if they had previously had intercourse.

There is no question about the couple's right to all those marks of affection and tenderness which normally accompany the generative act. Still, between Christian husbands and wives, a wise modesty, not in the least fearful, but decently reserved, will be the rule.

The strict right by which sin is measured is one thing; quite different is the domain of perfection or even of imperfection which extends far beyond that and which is properly the course of Christian refinement.

Strange Profanation

MARRIAGE as a sacrament which should be based on love, looks to the conjugal act as an expression of love. And since this embrace is in the nature of the closest of intimacies, everyone understands that it demands unity of the couple. We have spoken of that before. But it is essential to be convinced of it on account of the objections that come up frequently in conversations and the arguments advanced by certain modern authors like Blum, or Montherlant or Lawrence. This last mentioned writer gives us a scene like the following:

Jack who is married to Monica by whom he has several children makes advances to Mary:

"Oh, Jack! You are married to Monica."
"Am I? But she doesn't belong entirely to me; she has her babies now. I shall love her again when she is free. Everything in season, even women. Now I love you after going for a long time without ever thinking of you. A man is not made for a single affair."
"O God," she cried. "You must be crazy. You still love Monica."
"I shall love Monica again later. Now I love you. I don't change, but sometimes it is the one, sometimes it is the other. Why not?"

Yes, Why not? Simply because the rule as regards marriage is not the mere caprice of man and the satisfaction of his sensual desires; because woman has a right to respect and to the pledge that has been given her; because marriage is made not for the individual but for the family, the social unit, and to carry on in such a fashion is the break down of the family.

But Jack—or rather Lawrence—hears nothing of all that.

Mary, all alone, was incomplete. All women are but parts of a complete thing when they are left to themselves... They are but fragments... All women are but fragments.

Where does such a theory originate if not in the unbounded sensuality of man? But Jack listens to nothing. What do judgments other than his own mean to him? As he said, "He hated the thought of being closed up with one woman and some youngsters in one house. No, several women, several houses, groups of youngsters; a camp not a home! Some women, not one woman. Let the world's conventions be ignored. He was not one of those men for whom one woman was enough."

Why doesn't the logic of sensuality accord woman what man so brutally claims for himself? Are there two Moral Laws?

Here is another character, Helen. She is a doctor's wife and his most devoted assistant. But she divorces him for a snob whose life is all race horses and receptions. There she is, soaked in worldliness. She gets another divorce to marry a young poet, the latest rage, and transforms herself into an intellectual... Marvelous richness of the feminine soul! Says your sophisticate, she is like a fountain of glistening water which catches its coloring, green, red, or blue according to the men she chooses in turn!

Are we dreaming? That's the kind of thing we are likely to hear in certain gatherings and cocktail parties.

What a profanation of love!

Complete oblivion of the significance of the conjugal act! It is not only two distinct physical acts, but, through the medium of the body, a most ineffable exchange between two souls.

Marriage and the Eucharist (3)

MARRIAGE as a sacrament that should be based on love in the beginning and that must foster love in those who receive it together expects the mutual presence of a respectful and devoted cohabitation. From the very nature of marriage there devolves the duty of union and of procreation.

Marriage requires still more... mutual sacrifice. And here again its similarity to the Eucharist is remarkable.

Our Lord instituted the Eucharist not only to give us His Presence, not only to provide us with the benefits of Holy Communion. Rich though these benefits be, they do not constitute the culminating benefit. What is the great wealth of the Eucharist?

On Calvary, Our Lord offered Himself all alone to His Father. But by His sacrifice He merited for us the grace to be grafted on Him. Stretched upon the bloody Arbor of Calvary Christ's Hands and Feet and Side were cruelly notched; through the benefits of these divine openings we have gained the privilege, we wild offshoots since the time of Adam, branches deprived of divine life, to be set, to be grafted to the single Vine, the only Possessor of sanctifying sap.

Made other *Christs* that day, all Christians ... *Christiani* ... received the power, each time that the *Lord Christ Jesus* would repeat His sacrificial oblation of Calvary through the hands of His priest for the glory of the Father and the salvation of the world, to offer it with Him. This repetition of that offering is the Mass. Jesus, the divine Mediator, assumes again His attitude of Mediator; held between heaven and earth by the hands of the priest, He reiterates the dispositions of the complete immolation of Calvary.

On Golgotha, He was alone to carry through the sacrifice, the bloody sacrifice. Having been made that day by Him into *Christ*, we, since we are inseparable from Him except by sin, have the mission, whenever Christ renews His oblation, to offer it and to offer ourselves to Him. Effective participation in Mass is to be united with the Divine Head and all members of the Mystical Body in the intimacy of the same oblation renewed.

Jesus brings to us the benefits of His very own sacrifice; we bring to Him the offering of our own sacrifice. It is this part of the offering that the martyr's relic in the altar stone and the drop of water into the wine at the Offertory represent; the union of two sacrifices in the unity of the same sacrifice.

Marriage will have to reach heights like that to succeed in satisfying the utmost demands of love. The husband must be ready to sacrifice all for his wife; the wife must be ready to sacrifice all for her husband. From these conjoined sacrifices, love is made; love likewise demands these conjoined sacrifices.

What shall I do to show my wife that I love her? What fine deed can I accomplish, what prowess display, what humble, noble act perform? That is the spirit of chivalry.

And the wife: What shall I do to make my husband happy? What will give him pleasure?

This is the nourishment and the condition of love, the relish for mutual sacrifice.

Marriage and Sacrifice

IT IS not only the highest Catholic doctrine which requires the spirit of sacrifice of the married couple but more immediate common experience.

To live mutually in the closest proximity, in constant forgetfulness of self so that each of the two thinks only of the other requires something more than mere human attraction.

"Do not believe those who tell you that the road of love offers only the softest moss for your feet to tread. There are some sharp pebbles on the trail blazed by Adam and Eve."

The married woman who wrote those lines in verse, said the same thing in prose, a prose strangely poetic:

"To enter into marriage with the idea that someday they will be rid of self is like putting a moth into a piece of wool. Whatever may be the embroidery, the gold threads, the rich colors, the piece of wool is destined to be eaten, chewed with holes and finally completely devoured. It would be necessary for two saints to marry to be sure that no bitter word would ever be exchanged between them; even then it is not predictable what misunderstandings might crop up. Did not Saint Paul and Saint Barnabas have to separate because they had too many altercations? Then, can these two unfortunate children of Adam and Eve destined to struggle in life with all that life brings in our days of recurring difficulties expect never to have any temptations to wound each other and never to succumb to such provocations?"

If marriage is difficult even when the husband is a saint and the wife is a saint, how can we estimate the sacrifices it will require when the couple are to put it briefly but "poor good Christians."

Here however we are discussing the case of two who are sustained by dogma, morals, and the sacraments. But suppose one of the couple is a sort of pagan, or if baptized, so far removed from his baptism that nothing recalls any longer the mark of the children of God. What a secret cause for suffering!

Such was the suffering of Elizabeth Leseur who was happy in her married life in the sense that her husband was completely loyal to her but unhappy in her home because on the fundamental point for union, there was disunion, a separated life, the wife being Christian to the degree of astonishing intimacy with God and the husband remaining perfectly satisfied with the superficial life of so-called society.

Even when souls live in closest harmony, there will always be, even in the best of homes, a hidden cause for mutual suffering, which one author calls, "the eternal tragedy of the family, due to the fact that man and woman represent two distinct worlds whose limits never overlap." For woman love is everything. For man it is but a part of life. The woman's whole life rotates about the interior of the home, unless necessity forces her to work to earn a livelihood. The husband lives whole days much more outside the home than in it; he has his business, his office, his store, his shop, his factory. Except for the early days of his married life, he is absorbed more by ambition than by love; in any case, his heart alone is not busy throughout his days, but also and frequently more often, his head.

Sometimes the wife suffers from not having her husband sufficiently to herself; the husband suffers because he appears not to be devoting himself sufficiently to his wife. Over and above other causes of tragedy, here is the eternal and hidden drama. Much virtue is needed by both to accept the suffering they unwittingly cause each other.

A Mystic Moral Bond

ASIDE from the helps of Faith, two things especially can aid the married couple to practice mutual forbearance and to accept the sacrifices inherent in life together.

The first is the fact of their mutual share in the birth of their progeny.

Saint Augustine speaks beautifully of the two little arms of a child which draw the father and mother more closely together within the circle of their embrace as if to symbolize the living bond of union the child really is between them.

Even when one's choice of a marriage partner has been perfect, when ardent tenderness is evinced on both sides, there can still develop a period of tenseness and strained relations. Who can best reconcile the two souls momentarily at odds, upset for a time, or somewhat estranged?

The child.

Someone has said it well: "Life is long, an individual

changes in the course of ten, fifteen, twenty years shared with another. If the couple that has a had a fall out, has known love in its fulness.... I mean by that the love of hearts and souls above all..., if the two have the noble and deep memories which constitute our true nourishment during our voyage on earth, if they are above all bound together by the children that their love has brought into the world, then there is a good chance that even though they are caught by the undertow of passion, they will emerge safe and sound."

In addition to having children... that bond of love between the father and mother even in the greatest stress and strain... what most contributes to a speedy reconciliation after the clashes that eventually arise or the misunderstandings which set them at odds is the thought that they must endure, they must remain together.

What is to be thought of the following practice which is becoming quite customary? In the preparation of the trousseau, only the bride's initial is engraved on the silverware or embroidered on the linen. Does it not seem to be a provision for the possibility of a future separation?

By the constant repetition of the idea that man is fickle and that "her husband is the only man a woman can never get used to," the novel, the theater, the movies, set the stamp of approval on the "doctrine" of the broken marriage bond as something normal, something to be expected.

"On the contrary," says Henriette Charasson, who is a married woman and an author quoted before, "if husbands and wives realized that they were united for life, if they knew that nothing could permit them to establish another family elsewhere, how vigilant they would be not to let their precious and singular love be weakened; how they would seek, throughout their daily ups and downs, to keep vibrant, burning, and radiant, the love which binds them not only by the bond of their flesh but by the bond of their soul."

We must thank God if He has blessed our home by giving us many precious children; thank Him also for the Christian conviction which we received formerly in our homes, convictions which will never permit us to consider the possibility of the least fissure in our own family now.

A Father's Answer to His Daughter

IN THE book *My Children and I* by Jerome K. Jerome, which is as full of humor as of common sense, a young girl tells her father that she is frightened at the possibility of love's brevity.

"Love," she says, "is only a stratagem of nature to have fun at our expense. He will tell me that I am everything to him. That will last six months, maybe a year if I am lucky, provided I don't come home with a red nose from walking in the wind; provided he doesn't catch me with my hair in curlers. It is not I whom he needs but what I represent to him of youth, novelty, mystery. And when he shall be satisfied in that? . . ."

Her father answers, "When the wonder and the poetry of desire shall be extinguished what will remain for you will be what already existed before the desire. If passion alone binds you, then God help you! If you have looked for pleasure only, Poor You! But if behind the lover, there is a man (let us add a Christian); if behind this supposed goddess, sick with love, there is an upright and courageous woman (again let us add Christian); then, life is before you, not behind you. To live is to give not to receive. Too few realize that it is the work which is the joy not the pay; the game, not the points scored; the playing, not the gain. Fools marry, calculating the advantages they can draw from marriage, and that results in absolutely nothing. But the true rewards of marriage are called work, duty, responsibility. There are names more beautiful than goddess, angel, star, and queen; they are wife and mother.

Marriage is a sacrifice.

In order to live these four last words, "Marriage is a sacrifice," it is not enough to have started off on a good footing, to be enthusiastic about fine ideals, to put all hope in mutual tenderness.

Since marriage calls for more than ordinary sacrifice, it will be necessary in order to remain faithful to the habit of sacrifice, to have more than ordinary helps.

We have already meditated on the similarity between the Eucharist and marriage; we have seen that not only is there a bond of resemblance between these two sacraments but that there is in the Eucharist, above all in participation in the Eucharistic sacrifice and in Holy Communion a singular help for the married.

Prayer together must also be a help. Someone has rightly said, "The greatest sign of conjugal love is not given by encircling arms in an embrace but by bended knees in common prayer."

In his *Confessions*, Saint Augustine describes his last evening with his mother at Ostia. It is worth quoting. When a husband and wife have reached such a degree of soul-union in God, they can face all life's tempests without trembling.

"Forgetting the past and looking toward the future, we pondered together in Your Presence, O my God, the living Truth, on what the eternal life of the elect would be like. ... We came to this conclusion: The sensible pleasures of the flesh in their intensest degree and in all the attractiveness that material things can have, offer nothing that can compare with the sweetness of the life beyond, nor do they even deserve mention. In a transport of love, we tried to lift ourselves to You there...."

I must understand more clearly than in the past how essential it is to be rooted in prayer and if possible in prayer together.

I will meditate on this again.

Transported Together

WE ARE not considering the word "transported" in its emotional and rapturous sense, not as a paroxysm of exaltation, but rather in the sense of an ascent in a vehicle toward a determined destination.

Marriage is a trip for two. A trip. They travel ahead, enjoying mutual happiness on earth even as their destination gets nearer; and farther on, over there, up yonder, they shall both have the happiness of paradise.

Do I have my destination, our common destination, sufficiently before my eyes... sanctity here below, then death; then in the next life, the reward for our mutual efforts on earth?

How quickly we slip along hardly noticing our advance; I am scarcely aware of having started on the way. How distant the end seems; it escapes my sight; I am all taken up with what is right before me; I can't see the forest for the trees.

Am I advancing? In sanctity? In union with God? In patience? In purity? In charity? In generosity?

How many questions? Am I really asking them of myself? And if I am, how must I answer them if I want to be honest?

But I am not alone. This is a trip in company with others. We are several; we are two not counting the children.

How do I conduct myself toward this company, my co-travelers?

How do I act toward the partner of my life?

A recent "before and after" cartoon gave a series of pictures indicating changes in attitude toward one's life companion: During the engagement period, the young man is holding the umbrella very solicitously over his fiancée's head with no regard for the rain pouring down on him. Shortly after marriage, he holds the umbrella between them so that each receives an equal share of the raindrops. A long time later in marriage, the husband is no longer concerned about his wife; he holds the umbrella over his head and lets his wife get soaked to saturation.

Is that a reality or only an accusation? Selfishness so quickly regains its empire. It is not always bad will; inattention, perhaps, plain and simple. Yes, but isn't even that too bad?

What happened to all the little attentions of courtship and the honeymoon days? Those countless delicate considerations? The constant thought of the other?

There is the root of much suffering especially for the wife who is keener, more affectionate, more sensitive; she thinks she is cast off. She lets it be known on occasions. Oh, not bluntly, but with that subtle art she has for allusions, implications, and expressive silences. She might upbraid: "If you were in such a situation, if you were with such and such a person, I am sure you would be so obliging, so engaging, so attentive. But it is only I. Consequently you don't have to bother, isn't that so?" And, little by little, bitterness creeps in. It was nothing at all to start with. They made something—matter for friction.

I know a priest who wanted to preserve until he was at least eighty all the freshness of his priesthood: "I shall never let myself get used to celebrating Holy Mass." I should be able to say the same thing in regard to the sacrament I have received, the sacrament of marriage: "I will preserve my love in all its freshness. I shall remain considerate, delicately attentive. I shall do everything in my power to travel forward together not only in peace but in light and mutual joy."

Single Though Two

ANNA DE NOAILLES, a French poetess, summed up her unhappy married life in the words, "I am alone with someone."

It is an expressive but sinister remark.

People marry in order to be two, but two in one, not to continue to be alone, alone although with someone.

Aloneness for two can have a double cause:

1. Waiting too long to have children through a mutual agreement at the beginning of married life.

2. Loving each other too much perhaps. Too much, selfishly of course. Man and wife united, together, yes; and in this sense, it is not the solitude of which Anna de Noailles spoke. But if their union for two deserves rather to be called selfishness for two, it is not a true union.

These are the reefs upon which many a marriage has been wrecked.

Granted that if they do nothing to prevent generation, they do not sin... at least not against the law of chastity for marriage; but besides going counter to the law of fecundity, they are running the risk of sterility.

If they wait too long to have their brood, the nest hardens, loses its softness and adaptability. They get so accustomed to being only two that the presence of a third, even though the fruit of their union, does not seem desirable. There will always be time later, later! Let us enjoy each other first.

Selfishness for two: conjugal solitude. And let us add, a risk for later on. The wife will probably suffer from not being able to be a mother; the husband gets used to seeing in her only a wife. "It is in springtime," the proverb picturesquely says, "that the father bird learns to do his duty." The wife is very imprudent if she lets her husband prolong unduly a sort of bachelorhood; let her teach him how to assume his duties without too much delay.

There can be another reason more harmful still for this being alone though two and that is born of opposition of characters.

Generally it does not appear in the first years of married life. Everything is marvelous then, sunshine and moonlight. Though there may be exceptions, they are rare.

But there comes a time when tension creeps in, more or less restrained, then hidden resentment, finally opposition if not with weapons at least by tongue lashings, sullen silences, disagreeable attitudes. There is in every man, even a married man the stuff of an old bachelor; in every woman, even a married woman, something of ... well, a person shouldn't really use that word to speak of unmarried women.

When husbands and wives notice their rising irritability, they should take hold of their hearts with both hands so to speak and refrain from words they will regret soon after. If they have the courage, let them have an understanding with each other as soon as possible. They should learn not to notice every little thing; to forget with untiring patience all the little pricks; to remember only the joys they lived through together; to make a bouquet of them, not a faded bouquet like dried out artificial flowers that are kept in a drawer, but alive and fresh, beautiful enough to be put in full view on the mantlepiece.

Everything that is typical of the single life is taboo. They are united. They are to remain united. Two in one. *In one:* It is not always easy; it is always necessary.

Marriage and the Priesthood (1)

THERE is a greater resemblance between the sacrament of matrimony and the sacrament of Holy Orders than is immediately evident. The encyclical *Casti Connubii* of Pope XI does not fail to point it out. Here are a few similarities:

1. Although the sacrament of matrimony does not like Holy Orders impart a special character to the soul, it does consecrate "ministers" appointed to communicate grace. The priest is but a witness at the marriage. It is not the priest who marries but the man and woman who marry themselves who by exchanging their mutual "yes" give to each other more divine life. A sublime dignity which we have considered before.

2. Both marriage and Holy Orders give and sustain life. Holy Orders, supernatural life; marriage, natural life. The object of marriage, however, is not only the formation of bodies, but also the education of souls; procreation is nothing if it does not duplicate itself in education. It is up to the parents to get their children baptized, to prepare them for their First Holy Communion, to help in their religious formation, to assist them to remain in grace, a ministry which paves the way for the ministry of the priest, makes it possible and doubles its value.

3. Marriage and Holy Orders are both "social sacraments"; they are not intended only and principally for the personal sanctification of the recipients but are directed more especially to the general good of the Christian community. The priest is not a priest for himself; he is ordained for the sheep entrusted to him; he is commissioned to work for the flock the bishop designates for him. Parents are not

married only for their own good; they are married for the good of the children who will be born of them.

When the number of priests decreases, what harm results for the spiritual future of society! (Isn't today's terrible proof of this a real anguish for the heart?) If marriage is not undertaken by the fit, or the fit determined to fulfill its obligations, what harm will ensue for the temporal future of society!

4. Those who receive the sacrament of matrimony are vowed just as truly as is the priest to the exercise of charity.

For the priest it is clear. A bishop is established in the state of perfection by his very function which is to spend himself—to the giving of his life if necessary—for the welfare of the faithful. Because he is perpetually in the state of complete charity, we say that he is in the state of perfection, perfection consisting in the more or less extensive and permanent exercise of charity. Priests share in this state of holiness of the bishop. They must spend themselves for their sheep, be ready day and night to bring them spiritual help, to do all in their power to instruct them in the Word of God, to prevent them from losing their souls, to lead them back to the fold if they are tempted to go astray.

The married are, in their turn, and in a broad sense, established to a degree in a state which can, if they live it as they should, bring them to high perfection.

Ought not the husband exert himself with his whole soul for the well-being of his wife and children; should he not work and spend himself for love of them?

And what about the wife and mother? The pelican appears on the chasuble of the priest to symbolize his duty to imitate Christ by giving his very heart's blood for the faithful. Could it not also be a symbol for maternal sacrifice?

Marriage and the Priesthood (2)

PRIESTS receive Holy Orders at the foot of the altar, so too do the bride and groom receive the sacrament of matrimony.

It is as if the Church appointed the same place for the reception of both sacraments because she wished to emphasize the relationship between matrimony and Holy Orders.

Now that we have seen the points of resemblance between them, we are ready to draw some profitable conclusions:

1. The two who are married are called to help each other in the life of grace. Therefore the couple will become channels in the communication of grace in proportion to each one's own wealth in the divine life. What a long preparation the priest must have for his priesthood—long years in the seminary, the reception of minor Orders before admittance to the priesthood, the retreats before each of his ordinations.

By contrast, how many enter upon marriage with no preparation. Even when they do prepare for it and give it thought, how superficial and brief their preparation is; how easily lost are the effects by a flood of social events and distractions. Strange conduct!

2. The two joined by marriage will have to propagate life, and what is more, a life which will resemble theirs. A most frequent comment made over a new baby, a comment which is quite telling is "Why, he's his father all over," or "She's a vest-pocket edition of her mother." What if this is to be true morally as well? What am I, the father, like? Or I, the mother? Do I really want this little one to resemble me? Oh, no! I want it to be better, much better than I!

But am I free, as I go along, to weaken what I expect to

transmit and what I expect to keep for myself? No. I can refrain from begetting children, but if I do have them, I must know that they will resemble me. I ought not to have to say as someone said, "My children will be like me, but you will have to forgive them for it."

Is that not a thought that should move me strongly to sanctify myself?

Since I am not only to beget children, but I must also rear them, ought I not examine myself on the degree of my virtue? Is it such that I can really contribute to the advancement of other souls, to contribute to the growth of the Mystical Body of Christ, to intensify the supernatural in the souls around me—my partner in marriage, my children?

The Curé of Ars once asked a priest who was complaining over his lack of influence on his parishioners: "Have you fasted, taken the discipline, struggled in prayer?" In other words, "Have you pushed your efforts in prayer, penance, and sanctification to the highest point?"

Perhaps I complain of my powerlessness with one of the children. Have I taken all the means to draw down God's maximum graces upon me? Souls cost dearly. To be sure there is always individual free will to contend with; it can resist God; it can resist the prayer and the parents' striving after holiness. I may not get discouraged. Have I not perhaps been measuring out my generosity a bit too carefully? I shall try to reach the heights. We cannot lift up unless we ourselves are higher.

I should see, in the light of the parallel between the sacrament of matrimony and the sacrament of Holy Orders, the extent of my responsibilities. Like priests, I have a heavy responsibility. A magnificent responsibility but a frightening responsibility! If I am only *so-so*, I shall—according to the logic of things and barring a miracle of God's grace—rear souls who are only *so-so*.

Is that what I want?

Have I up to now measured how far-reaching my mission actually is?

Masculine Treason

WOMEN have their faults; while they are generally more irritating than man's, they are less to be feared. Man more readily betrays; he is more truly all of a piece; when he falls, it is the whole way.

That should not cause a wife to be constantly on needles and pins; it is harmful for the man and she does herself great harm by so acting, for nothing will as quickly drive her husband into another woman's arms as jealousy in his lawful wife.

The knowledge of man's tendency should incite the husband to watch over himself more closely to avoid imprudence that might run into flirtation, then into a friendship, then into adultery. The spirit is willing but the flesh is weak, above all in the strong sex.

Even in cases where the quality of the person, the honor of the family name, nobility of origin would seem to give every guarantee of perseverance in good, we sometimes meet lamentable examples of a man's infidelity to his home.

In the diary of Eugénie de Caucy, the second wife of Marshal Oudinot, it is related that on Sunday of shrove-tide 1820, there was a very spectacular showing of *Le Carnival de Venise* at the Opéra.

The Duke de Berry had left the theatre before the last act to escort his wife to her carriage. Upon turning to go back to his box he was mortally wounded by the anarchist Louvel.

He asked for a priest and then made another request: "I want to see *all my children*." The people about him knew only of *Mademoiselle*, the four year old daughter, the child of his marriage with the Duchesse.

His wife, the Duchess, did not dare to understand his request. He explained, "My wife, I admit, I have several children. Through a liaison of mine in England I had two daughters."

He died shortly after, asking mercy for his murderer and regretting from the depths of his soul, a little late to be sure, his unfaithful conduct.

Many thoughts suggest themselves on hearing such a story. First of all, think of dying in such a setting! Yet, there is certainly nothing wrong with attending a play if the play is morally good; we just have to remember to be always ready wherever we are; death can strike us in society and even while we are in the proximate occasion of sin.

Another more appalling thought is the wife's ignorance of her husband's life. How can a man so betray the one to whom he has pledged his faith? Furthermore, how brazen, to ask a young girl to be his wife, the cherished companion of his life after giving if not his heart at least his body to another woman! Truly, man is not charming! Not that woman is incapable of betrayal and of giving herself unlawfully, but we should like to think that it happens more rarely.

Finally a third observation comes to mind—the picture of this man lying in his blood, confessing his past and by this act of humility, which is to his credit, trying to redeem the failings of the past.

Thanks to God's grace, I have not similar failings on my conscience. But are there not many thoughts, many desires, certain types of reading, much imprudence even in act, and unwarranted liberties of which I have been guilty? If those about me knew what I really am, how would they judge me?

Marriage and the Counsels (1)

Is it possible to arrive at perfection without following the evangelical counsels?

Put in this way, the question can have two answers depending on whether the effective practice of the counsels is to be understood or simply the spirit of the counsels.

1. Perfection consists in the exercise of charity as the duty of one's state implies it. *Be ye perfect as your heavenly Father is perfect* was said to all not just to priests and religious.

And again to all, *Thou shalt love the Lord, thy God, with thy whole heart, and with thy whole soul and with thy whole mind and with all thy strength.*

The perfection of charity is commanded to all and not only counselled.

That the evangelical counsels are a help to the exercise of the virtue of charity for those who have elected to live by them is certain; they are not the only means.

The Gospel makes it perfectly clear: There is the observance of the Commandments—a necessity for all; there is the observance of the counsels—for those who desire it; those only would be obliged to adopt this second means who have evidence that without them they could not attain their salvation—a rare case indeed.

2. But it appears to be a very difficult thing to arrive at the perfection of charity without adopting the spirit of the counsels.

In fact there are three great obstacles to the perfect service of God: excessive attachment to the goods of earth; the tendency to seek purely selfish satisfactions where the affections of the heart are concerned; finally the habit of obeying not so much God's will for our life as personal caprice and the false demands of the world.

From this it is evident that the pursuit of perfection presupposes the spirit of detachment; it means using things, as Saint Paul would say, *as if we did not use them at all*. That suggestion is good not only for life in the cloister but every bit as good if not more so, in view of the greater difficulty, in the simple life of observing the Commandments. The spirit of poverty in either case is essential.

The pursuit of perfection while living in the midst of the world likewise calls for the spirit of chastity, the chastity of the heart—not to the point of having to deprive themselves of everything as those do who are vowed to the virginal state but to the point of the privations necessary to meet the demands of the conjugal state. Therefore, the spirit of chastity is equally essential.

Striving for perfection in the midst of the world still allows the individual entire liberty regarding many of the details of life, the so-called good things of life as well as ideas, companionship, dress. The soldier Ernest Psichari yearned as he used to say "to be free of everything except Jesus Christ."

Strive for obedience to God alone who said *Seek ye first the kingdom of God and all the rest shall be added unto you*. I must not let "the rest" take precedence over "the Kingdom."

Obedience to God should not be marked by formal passivity but by vision and conviction. Let me measure the distance from the place I am now to the summit of Christianity.

Marriage and the Counsels (2)

This subject has too great significance for one meditation only.

Before the Fall there was a triple harmony in man:

—Harmony between God and the soul: Adam and Eve

conversed familiarly with the Most High who used to walk with them at twilight in Paradise; He often left His footprints in the sands of their garden.

—Harmony within man himself between his body and soul: The senses were active but they were submissive to reason and will; concupiscence existed but it was just concupiscence not evil concupiscence; the powers of desire were not inordinate.

—Harmony all about man, between him and nature: The animals were subject to him and were not hostile to him. Inanimate nature did not refuse its secrets to his work which was but a joyous extension of his activity and not as it has become in part at least—fatiguing labor. *You shall eat your bread in the sweat of your brow.*

Then came the Fall. Immediately this beautiful balance was destroyed. Man revolted against God. The result: Man's senses rose up against right reason and will enlightened by faith; nature and all about man turned hostile. There would be wild beasts and venomous creatures among the animals; the earth would resist his toil and the labor of generations to come, revealing its treasures only with discouraging parsimony and at the cost of fearful toil and sweat.

What should be most profitable for my meditation is the consideration of the revolt in man himself, his lower powers against his higher powers. From then on man would have to struggle against the triple and fatal inclination which was born in him:

—An inclination to take an exaggerated possession of the goods of the earth, the fruit of concupiscence of the eyes: Man will rush after all that glitters. How many crimes have been committed because of an unregulated love of money!

—An inclination to seek after excessive carnal satisfactions contrary to true discipline of the senses and the commands of God. What crimes have not the follies of lust produced!

—An inclination to pride: Man, proud of his liberty, but not sufficiently concerned about keeping it in dependence on reason and the Divine Will, runs the risk of forgetting the majesty and sovereignty of God and the prime duty of obedience to the Master of all.

How can one struggle effectively against this triple and dangerous inclination?

Do violence to self, declare spiritual writers with good common sense. First and foremost among them in suggesting this technique is Saint Ignatius of Loyola. Choose the counterpart: poverty, chastity, obedience.

Religious men and women make it the matter of a vow. Their lives serve as an inspiring example to draw forward those whose lesser courage or less demanding vocation have kept in the common way of life.

I shall hold religious life in high esteem. Although my vocation is different I shall learn to live in a wise spirit of detachment from created things, of chastity according to my state, and of obedience to the Holy Spirit.

Marriage and Vows

THE problem of personal vocation, as I have seen from my meditations, is not a problem to be solved in the abstract, in pure theory, but in the concrete, taking each particular case into consideration. The best vocation in an individual case is not the vocation which is best *in itself* but the best *in fact*, that is the one which Divine Providence prepares for each person.

I have recognized mine quite clearly. I have no worry on that score.

Without wishing to belittle in the least the merits of those who pronounce religious vows—for they are priviliged souls—can I not in a way compare my life with theirs and find a resemblance between them?

In the writings of his mother which the poet Lamartine published we find these lines:

> Today I attended the Investment of some hospital sisters. The sermon which was addressed to them was beautiful: The speaker told them that they had chosen for life a state of penance and of mortification. A crown of thorns was placed upon their heads to symbolize this ... I greatly admired their self-sacrifice; but I reflected that the state of a mother of a family can approach the perfection of theirs if she fulfills her duties.
>
> A person doesn't give enough thought to the fact that when she marries she also makes a vow of poverty since she practically puts her fortune into her husband's hands, and that he has something to say about how she spends money.
>
> She makes a vow of obedience to her husband and a vow of chastity inasmuch as she is not permitted to seek to please any other man. She also dedicates herself to the exercise of charity toward her husband and her children; she has the obligation to care for them in sickness and to give them her wise counsel.

Isn't there much truth in this comparison? Evidently in the case of marriage, husbands and wives are largely compensated for the sacrifices they have to make by the joy that comes to them from life together. In the virginal state there is no such human compensation. That is no reason to underestimate the value of the married state. Because the one state is more beautiful, it does not follow that the other is not very beautiful.

It may well be that a certain father or mother who hesitated before entering the married state because they felt called to the life of consecrated virginity fulfilled God's plans for religious vocations better by their marriage; God used them as instruments for a series of vocations that would develop among their offspring.

When Pius X was promoted to the bishopric of Mantua, he paid a visit to his mother at Riese. "Mamma, look at my beautiful episcopal ring." His eighty year old mother let her wrinkled fingers pass over the ring thoughtfully. Then she said, "It is true, Guiseppe; your ring is beautiful; but you would not have had it, if I had not had this one," and she held up her wedding ring.

The Social Ideal

YOUNG Maurice Retour found himself at the head of a textile factory upon the early death of his father.

Shortly before his marriage, he wrote to his bride-to-be.

To know that more than three hundred persons depend on you for their daily bread, to be certain that with work, intelligence, and patience you can make them earn more, what else would you need to become inspired with the desire to discover all possible improvements.

He let his fiancée know that he planned to have her share in the furtherance of his enterprise. He added:

To be a Christian, to have the happiness of knowing your wife will one day work hand in hand with you, to feel that you possess this sister-soul to help bring to success the noble and beautiful ideal you dreamed of accomplishing is almost too great a bliss; it's enough to make you beside yourself with joy.

The young industrialist, in full agreement with his wife, set himself to the duty of providing the desired improvements: a free Saturday, a cafeteria for the workers, a benefit fund. Naturally he was criticized by his fellow industrialists who did not have a like Christian sense. But he held his own and went even farther. Sometimes before some of his reforms which had as their only purpose better conditions for the workers, a number of the workers themselves either from force of habit or ill-will evidenced displeasure. He still kept to his plan, tried to win them over and was patient with them.

In spite of his firm principles, the exactness of his economic and sociological knowledge, his good judgment, his Christian spirit which guaranteed the usefulness of his efforts, he was still eager to be supported in his labors; he told his wife his difficulties and asked for her opinion and advice. He counted on her either to help him to study and to grow in his understanding of social problems or more often still to have a part in his work.

In the fight against alcoholism, in the care of the workers' children, in the visitation of the sick, in planning for big celebrations, in organizing vacation camps, what a wide field there was for the wife of an industrialist!

Maurice Retour did not believe in getting himself involved in so many activities that he would neglect his factory; interest in free schools, attendance at Saint Vincent de Paul meetings were all fine, but they should not separate him from his factory.

We ought to think first of our workers, of their children, of those who are in our direct contact in order not to scatter our efforts in all directions uselessly. Let us try to sow a bit of happiness about us... Let us give as much as we can to others ... We are responsible for the good we do not do... All our life spent in this work hand in hand, united in the same ideal, the same faith, the same great love would not be too much.

From the Front in 1915, he often wrote asking for news: "Tell me about our dear workers of whom I think so often."

What a god-send when a wife finds in her husband such a magnificent social spirit; when an industrialist finds in his wife someone who understands him and backs him up!

THE HOME

Great Adventurers

CHARLES PÉGUY called fathers of families, "these great adventurers of the modern world."

How correct he was! What courage is needed to step out before life, with a companion on one's arm, aspiring to have children and hoping that Mother Earth will be able to support and nourish their own little world!

Certainly the joy that attends the birth of a babe is sweet. Here is how a father describes it:

> When one sees a little one so weak yet so well formed one loves the Creator still more and how much more one thanks Him for giving us life! What a beautiful mystery maternity is! To see a young mother feeding her babe suffices to incite one to adore God. There is nothing more touching than to see this dear little treasure resting in the arms of its mother. It was baptized on March 28. What a majestic ceremony it was and how proud one feels to be able to say his son is a Christian!

But what anguish is suffered if the children are sick; if the mother's strength fails beneath her work. How anxious one grows when the little ones cough and gasp for breath. And even if all goes well as far as health is concerned, there is no end to buying clothes, having shoes resoled, and providing food for the ever hungry mouths.

When the children grow up, one must be concerned about their education. One must start thinking about high school and college for the boys and the girls. Which school is best? Which teachers are best qualified? Will they take the same interest in our children that we the parents do? Will they give them what they really need to face life? ...

Then come the sudden worries—auto accidents, accidents in sports, war in which the worst bodily dangers threaten!

But worse still and more serious by far are the soul dangers—the boy who keeps bad hours, who has an evil tongue and a shifty glance, who evades questions and begins to lie.

Yes, indeed, what magnificent and courageous adventurers are fathers of families!

A reporter recounted the enthusiastic acclaim the people of Paris gave the intrepid sailor Alain Gerbault who had succeeded in sailing around the world in a very frail skiff.

"For my part," said the reporter, "I gave to Alain Gerbault the recognition that was his due."

But in the crowd that had gathered about the famous sailor, the newspaper man found himself next to a family of rather humble means to judge by their appearance, although they did not lack dignity. There were five children with the father and mother, all modestly and neatly dressed. The father was explaining to his sons, "Oh, what an admirable type is this Gerbault! What a hero!"

"I shared that idea," commented the reporter, "but I thought that father was also a hero to pilot a skiff loaded down with children on the parisian ocean as he was doing ... I even wondered if it were not more admirable than to guide a boat on the high sea with only oneself to think of."

The Psalm of Young Mothers

A YOUNG mother—very true to her role of mother and at the same time very artistic—got the idea of comparing her role with that of cloistered sisters. Between her washing, her cooking and the care of her youngest, she managed to compose *The Psalm of Young Mothers* which appeared in the 1938 November issue of *Marriage Chrétien*. It is full of love, full of spontaneity. Every young mother will recognize herself in these passages we are quoting:

"O my God
Like our sisters in the cloister
We have left all for you;
We have not imprisoned the youth of our faces in a guimpe and under a veil,
And though we have cut our hair, it is not in any spirit of penance...

Deign nevertheless, O Lord, to cast a look of complaisance
On the humble little sacrifices
Which we offer You all day long,
Since the day our groaning flesh gave life to all these little Christians
We are rearing for You.

Our liberty, O God, is in the hands of these little tyrants who claim it every minute.
The house has become our cloister,
Our life has its unchanging Rule,
And each day its Office, always the same;
The Hours for dressing and for walks,
The Hours for feeding and for school,
We are bound by the thousand little demands of life.
Detached by necessity every moment from our own will,
We live in obedience.

Even our nights do not belong to us;
We too have our nocturnal Office,
When we must rise quickly for a sick child,
Or when between midnight and two o'clock,
When we are in the full sleep we need so badly
A little untimely chanter
Begins to sing his Matins.

We practically live retired from the world:
There is so much to be done in the house.
There is no possibility of going out anyway without a faithful sitter for the little ones.
We measure out the time for visits parsimoniously.

We have no sisters to relieve us on another shift.
And when the calls for service reach high pitch for us
We have to sweep, to wash the dishes, scrape the carrots for the stew, prepare a smooth purée for baby and keep on going without stopping
From the children's room to the kitchen and to and fro.
We do big washings we rub and we rinse
Aprons and shirts, underclothes and socks
And all the baby's special things.
In this life of sacrifice, come to our help, O Jesus!

Up to Date

ONE of our modern novels gives us the following situation:

Gina Valette is a woman who is "up to date" in the unpleasant sense of the term. Very rich and provided with a husband who thoroughly spoils her, she has dogs, cats, a parrot, and a monkey, but no children. Her brilliant existence palls on her. Among her friends are mothers with children who courageously use their modest resources to advantage and rear quite a family. Often when an epidemic breaks out among the children of a family, a friend of the family will take two or three of the others for the time.

To cure Gina of her depressed spirits, her friend Jamine persuades her to take young Gilles Perdrinix whose five brothers and sisters have the chickenpox. Gina is bewildered; she knows perfectly how to care for a monkey but she finds herself embarrassed before this little Perdrinix boy who judged her severely from the height of his four years.

"How ignorant she is! How much is lacking in her training!" Little Gilles sighed to think of it. "She knows how to smoke," he said to himself sadly, "but she can't give me a lift to button my shirt." He did not complain nor did he reproach her; but on seeing her so clumsy, he thought she had much to learn to become a woman like other women.

Happily there are other kinds.

A mother of a family and a brilliant author wrote in the preface of a volume on *The Mother* which she was requested to write by the editor of a series entitled *The Up to Date Woman*, "How shall I ever write this little book? There are no up-to-date mothers. There are only *Mammas*."

And with charming dash coupled with irresistible conviction she gave young wives this advice:

> Little Lady, you are embarking upon married life on the arm of a husband who is all taken up with you, who probably wants nothing more than to believe in you, to follow you and to approve of everything that touches the essence of your being. Do not listen to those frustrated women or those soured unmarried girls, or those *Jezebels* who have nothing of the matron about them but their age and have no real experience; do not let them draw you out of the right way. Be convinced, that the joy which babies bring is inexpressible and makes up for all the torment and fatigue of bearing them. Be certain that the sight of that plump, smooth little body; of those dimpled hands and feet, both like pink silk yet provided with sharp nails; of that darling little mouth with its toothless smile, so simple and so trustful that the bright look, so marvelously pure, the soft cheeks, the silky hair, the utter quiet abandonment of this little being who issued forth from us floods our soul with an intense and intimate ecstasy such as I have never known before.

If only the up-to-date woman would be a mother for the future.

After the dark hours of the war, new life must be born.

There will be lives only if there are mothers, mothers who respond to their essential and divine vocation.

Even if there were not this motive of special need, eternal reasons still have force—the law of fecundity and the law of chastity: Although it is permissible for married persons to abstain from the conjugal act or to perform it only when there is the least possibility of conception provided their reasons are not selfish; if they do perform the marital act they may do nothing to prevent the generation of a life which is in the plan of God. That is clear.

Give me, O my God, the grace through respect for You and for Your work, always to have a devotion to and a respect for life; grant that I may never sully my own existence by any criminal attempt upon new life. Grant me also the grace to be in Your Hands a not too unworthy instrument of Your creative power. Let me be "up-to-date" whenever it is a question of enrolling a new name in the Book of Life.

Paternal Solicitude

IN ORDER to fulfil his task conscientiously, a father needs singular qualities.

First among these qualities is an *unfailing courage*. In homes where life is easy—and in what family today is life easy—he can rest on the fortune amassed by his ancestors. But that melts so soon. In homes where the family lives truly on the *daily bread*, how much he must exert himself to earn that bread for the day. There's more than one meal that has to be provided for a single day. And the clothing? And the shoes? And the bills—from the doctor, the pharmacist, the grocer? Days follow upon each other, weeks overlap and months roll by; the home is augmented by one more. How shall he cope with this world of his?

With courage, the father needs a *quiet confidence* in God. Surely, if they understand their duty well, true fathers know how to space births somewhat without failing in the least against the laws of marriage; and this for some requires heroic courage. But even then when one does not tempt Divine Providence but lives in a prudent and continent moderation, it is still necessary in order to keep above the surface of life to cast anchor in the deep and wait for the desired help from God—imperturbably serene through it all.

And who will measure the *untiring patience* that he will need to bear those almost necessary difficulties of character in a most loving and attentive wife; to endure the crying and weeping of the babies at night; to bear with the noisy games of the growing children when he wants to work in quiet; to try to make the income at least balance expenses; to build up a declining business; to find new openings for his products; to develop a better and wider clientele. Patience alone will see him through!

How he will need *authority* with the children to re-enforce the mother's control who, either because she is too busy or too easy going, lets them take advantage of her now and then!

He will not have this authority without *insight* which will help him distinguish the pre-dominant character traits of each child and determine the best means to provide for the training of all so that their virtues are developed and their faults are checked; to read their souls, their inmost thoughts, the progress of their dreams for the future...

All in all, what skill, what firmness, what adaptability, what sanctity he will need! And here is just a poor father consecrated such by circumstances and who, just a young fellow himself, has never weighed his future responsibilities —or not very seriously weighed them!

Oh, how deeply I feel, Holy Virgin Mary, that you must

help me. Our Lady of great courage, give me strength! Virgin most patient, give me patience! Seat of Wisdom, give me insight into characters! Mother and Queen of Jesus, give me a gentle, but firm authority!

Holy Mary, give me holiness more than all else! I have not attained the degree God wants of me for my mission in life; I am well aware of that. Draw me, O Immaculate Virgin, draw me to the heights; you are so near to God; you dwell in the radiance of His light and His omnipotence; lead me on, higher!

The Family

THE family, a workshop of life for earth, a workshop for eternity!

1. *A Workshop of Life:* What power to have control over the creation of life! God, who could have created human beings all by Himself wished to give His creatures the gift of a power which belonged only to Him. Consequently, souls will not come into the light unless parents consent to it. They will not create souls, to be sure, but by generating bodies they furnish God the means of increasing the number of souls.

Have I meditated often enough upon this magnificent power which has been conferred on me? A power which I share equally with her who is the companion of my existence? Have I meditated on the glory of fatherhood? The glory of motherhood? Have I considered what a grave sin it is to place the act which generates life and then to prevent through perverted will the coming of life to a potential human being? Or to snuff out the life which is developing in the womb of the mother?

The author of the novel *Jeanne*, though not a Christian, clearly pleads the cause of Christian morals in the play he produced from his novel. The following scene gives in brief the theme of the whole play:

MADELEINE—Jeanne is always present... Do you know the dream I often have? I see a little hand which is trying to open a door. We are very comfortable you and I and we both push against the door with all our strength so that Jeanne cannot come in to take away a little of our ease, our luxury, our warmth... Then the little hand falls down and we begin to count gold pieces so as not to hear anything... A little whimper...

ANDRÉ—That's a nightmare!...

MADELEINE—For you yes. Remorse is a policeman...

ANDRÉ—Don't you love me anymore, Madeleine?

MADELEINE—Since we were accomplices... I loved you to folly, but this love was snatched away with my child. When I came back from that abortionist, you noticed no change in my attitude. But André it was another woman you clasped in your arms... a sort of dead...

ANDRÉ—Then, always, forever, that will be between us?

MADELEINE—Not between us, with us!

Have I ever thought of the tragic intimate dramas that conjugal cheating gives rise to in the lives of parents? Have I thought of the harm done to society in times of peace? To the country I love, weakening its defenses, threatening its safety in times of war? To the Church who would have had some saints among those children who were denied birth, in any case, some priests and religious... Have I thought of all that?

2. *A Workshop for Eternity:* The family not only contributes an increase to earthly existence but it also increases more divine life on earth, and that in two ways—from the moment of its establishment and later: The day the man and woman receive the sacrament of Matrimony, they produce, if we may so dare to speak, more divine life; each of the two

become richer in the life of the Trinity within themselves; the Eternal is intermingled to a greater degree in the existence of both. Then come the children. Each will possess within itself the germ of eternity, something of the life which will never end. Death will come to end life here below, but this life is destined to bloom again: "I believe in the resurrection of the body and life everlasting" we recite in the Creed.

To be sure, the children have free will, they can fail to attain their destiny. The devil and evil concupiscence must always be conquered. But if their origin is Christian, if the parents have done all they possibly could to do their duty and rear their offspring as they ought, it would be failing in Hope to think of the family's being eternally cut off from some of its members.

I shall pray fervently that we may all be reunited in heaven, that we eternally sing the *Sanctus* as a chorus with not one of us missing.

Heredity

THE *profession* of fatherhood and motherhood has its responsibilities even before the birth of the children. Someone has said, "Every man is an heir; every man is an ancestor." Just as we receive through our ancestral line many of our traits, so too we found a line of descendants, and we transmit to those descendants something of what we are ourselves.

If we were free to transmit only the good, how truly it would be worth transmitting! But it does not work that way. It is impossible to foresee what part of us will pass on to our successors. Whoever performs the work of imparting life runs the risk of imparting to the one born of him some of his worst with the best. Wherever there is propagation by generation the mystery of heredity has its place, a frightening place. It is not in vain that God gives this warning in the twentieth Book of Exodus: *I am the Lord thy God, mighty, jealous, visiting the iniquity of the fathers upon the children unto the third and fourth generations of them that hate Me; And showing mercy unto thousands to them that love Me and keep my Commandments.* There is a similar idea expressed in the prophecy of Ezechiel.

A certain father took part as a young man in a sinful escapade. He corrupted his blood; a germ entered into him. Should he be astonished then that at the moment in which he transmits life, that very life will be contaminated? He took precautions; he was cured. That is possible. It is not always certain. There are often unpleasant surprises. Even when the malady does not recur in the first generation, it is possible that it may reappear in the second or third or even later.

It is the same in the case of lesser evils which nevertheless leave their corrupting effects—habits of laziness, intemperance in the use of liquor, a wasting of one's forces. It all tells.

The mother also formerly lived too fast. Her life was characterized by an excessive effort to follow the capricious changes in styles, too intense a participation in strenuous sports, an abuse of strong liquors or over-indulgence in smoking, too much loss of sleep because of empty and sophisticated night-life or hours of reading thrillers or indiscriminate running to movies. Here she is now leaning over her baby's cradle. The little thing is weak and puny looking as if it were trouble just to breathe. The doctor is called. There are certainly many reasons for sicknesses and weakness in babies other than the imprudences of the mother and father. But is it not true that in many cases if the doctor were sincere he would have to say: "Madam, there are maladies here which wisdom could prevent but which science cannot circumvent." To have healthy and vigorous children, parents must deserve it.

But far be from us any unjust generalizations! It often happens that in the most deserving families where parents have always done their duty, God may send weak and sickly children either for the sanctification of the parents or for reasons known to Himself alone.

But it still remains true that in many a household an unbelievable thoughtlessness serves as the prelude for so serious an act as the procreative act. How many fathers and mothers ought to meditate on the words spoken by Our Lord with a different implication to the women of Jerusalem as He trudged along to Calvary, *Weep over Yourselves and your children.*

What a tragic mystery is human heredity! Physical impurities, and in part, tendencies which foster moral weaknesses can be transmitted to one's descendants. Some children will issue forth victorious over terrible struggles only painfully because there is weighing upon them the crushing weight of faults or frightful frivolities to which others before them have consented!

Parental Responsibility

IT is worth considering more than once the responsibility that can rest with the parents when some children do not achieve their full possibility or even turn out badly.

Let us of course give due blame to the evil concupiscence which can provoke a painful transformation in children even when the parents have done everything possible.

It remains true just the same that in a good number of cases, the father and the mother or one or the other must plead guilty.

A boy is sent to college. He gets along fine until the sophomore year. From then on he bungles everything, abandons right conduct, falls in with dangerous companions, carries on high to such an extent that he has to be expelled. And when a professor expresses astonishment, the dean will give this explanation: "It's his background; unfavorable heredity; his brothers were just the same. The mother is a saint, but the father is one of those unfortunate individuals who is ruled by his senses; he has caused much suffering to his wife. It is just the traces of the father showing up in the children."

The explanation can be taken for what it is worth. The law of heredity is not a mathematical law. There is no doubt, however, that it is operative, more operative than one thinks.

When heredity is not to blame, it can often be a matter of bad training. How good parents are, how very good, too good, too weak! It is their own formation which is faulty; it should be done over.

A mother brought her young son to the doctor for an examination. The doctor prescribed a remedy. "The medicine was not pleasant to take but it was very potent," he said. Well and good; they had the prescription filled.

Some time later they returned to the doctor.

—"Well, now, how's our patient?"

—"Not any better, doctor."

—"How's that? Didn't the medicine take effect?"

—"No, doctor, it was too hard to take; he wouldn't touch it!"

How much botch-work of that kind goes on! Parents satisfy the child's every whim. They recoil before the first tears, before the mere signs of an outburst, before less than that—a frown, a pout, or a dejected look. They are lost!

Reversing the scriptural phrase, *Cain, where is thy*

brother Abel? an author speaking of social problems, which can well be duplicated in the family and in education asked, "Abel, what have you done with Cain?" In other words: "You good people, are you not responsible through your faults or your incapacities that some good individuals have become bad?"

I have charge of a soul; I may have a plural charge—several souls. What has been my conduct until now? Do I not have to reproach myself with many faults or at least many weaknesses? And I am surprised at the results obtained! Are they not the logical outcome of my bungling?

Let me examine myself; consider the whole problem seriously; if it is necessary, let me reform.

The Family Spirit

BEFORE the war, family spirit was on the decline and on the verge of being lost. There were exterior and interior reasons.

Exterior reasons: Means of travel had become easier and encouraged people to go out as much as possible. At times, the whole household would take the train or auto for an excursion but more often than not one or other member of the family would go off for himself with the car.

Young girls began to leave home more than formerly for purposes of study, Red Cross causes, Social Service training or simply to take a position. Many who had no such need at all left home for no other reason than not to have to remain at home. Anything rather than stay home!

Various activities and organizations were always sufficient excuse or pretext for absence. Household activities held no appeal for these young women and often repelled them. The remembrance of confidences from their mother in some of their intimate sessions frightened some of them.

The world with its perpetual and superficial and useless activity drew many young men and even more young women into its crazy dance and encouraged the desertion of the home.

Interior Reasons: Some homes make no attempt to be attractive; life in them seems too austere to the children; the mother is too busy, the father is always grouchy, upset by the least noise, easily irritated and perhaps, even without knowing it, frigid and abrupt in his manner of speaking ... Sometimes there is an unfortunate lack of harmony between the parents. The atmosphere is always charged with a threatening storm. There is no relaxing, no peace, no trust ... Each one wants his liberty, to go his own way. The children caught between two fires do not know to which saint they should dedicate themselves. Therefore they too go away, or if they can't they close up within themselves ... Each one in the house stands on his dignity.

It is quite true that children have become more difficult to train. They always have been difficult but they are more of a problem today than in the past. A tendency developed to give them greater leeway which created a greater distance than was wise between fathers and sons and especially between mothers and daughters; it was an imaginary difficulty rather than a real one in many cases but only too frequently it gave rise to a cruel estrangement.

No one can prevent the difference of twenty years more or less between father and son or mother and daughter; that it should be a difference is to be expected; but that it should be a barrier, no! And while there are parents who cannot remember that they were once twenty years old, most of them can.

"I dream of a daughter who will be like me but also very different," wrote a mother; "because I should not like to produce only a duplicate but neither should I like to be only a rough draft of a more perfect pattern."

Then she continues to explain that her daughter will be able to come to her in all confidence to tell her about her first infatuation; she will understand her and will even tell her how she herself at about the age of eighteen fell madly in love with a violinist of exceptional talent and that her own mother so completely entered into sympathy with her that she helped her daughter compose the burning letter of admiration in which her newly-born ardor was poured out... Together mother and daughter waited for the fervent response... which had never come!

Poor children, who feel that their parents do not understand them! But if they do understand! It is their duty not to approve of everything, but they understand! Then they are ready to help, not always by writing a love-letter, but to encourage, to warn, to support the children in their undertakings, to sustain their enthusiasm, to lead them to their goal.

"The Whole Sea"

PEOPLE sometimes say: "What is the use of trying to rear children as good Christians; they will be lost sight of once they enter upon life in the midst of the great masses. Will any one so much as notice their presence? Will they be able to leave their mark? Will they not run the risk of being crushed by the amorphous mass and quickly covered over by some all-embracing platitudes?" Or again, "What is the use of trying to establish a home that is a Christian community, a veritable monastery of Christian virtues—and by that we don't mean an atmosphere like a morgue but an exemplary group governed by Christian devotion and love—when all about us there are only mediocre families? They are not bad but worldly, with no depth to their Christianity. We would be drowned by all the rest!"

Pascal gave the answer to these questions when he said, "The whole sea rises for one stone that is thrown into it." Though it appear but an insignificant pebble in value, it at least assures one's contribution to a common work. Has it not always been the minority groups who transformed the world?

You say, "What is the use of troubling ourselves and working to form Christians and real men when all about us the mass of humanity is becoming more and more dechristianized and less virile? Lacordaire suggests an answer similar to Pascal's, "Simple drops of water that we are, we wonder what need the ocean has of us; the ocean could tell us that it is made up of nothing else but little drops of water."

That is true of individuals; it is true of families.

If we could do nothing to effect numbers we can at least effect quality—the policy of the leaven. What matters the thickness and weight of the dough, if the leaven which works in it possesses irresistible force?

Let us throw dynamic Christian personalities into society; where can they be better prepared than in Christian families and institutions? We ought to, that's sure. In the midst of indifferent families, let us settle some distinctly Christian families who do not compromise when duty is involved, who radiate joy, manifest the beauty of virtuous living and bear witness to Christ by apostolic zeal. And then count on God to assure the result.

The result is certain. We must have faith in Him and believe in the power of radiating centers.

"Unless there are in our cities and towns, homes where Christian life flourishes, every hope for Christian civilization is doomed," wrote a university man of note shortly before the war.

To Christianize a town, a village, a neighborhood, in short any *milieu* involves more than multiplying activities which do not even get into the blood-stream of real living; it means an invention of new ways of life, as for example group formation of families who give a public example of Christian virtues by living in loving and fraternal communities, breaking with the forms of mediocre living and substituting for it in their relations with others a true form of friendship rooted in the Gospel spirit.

What was true before the war is even truer now. There is still a desperate need for a renovation of the Christian world, and of the whole world for that matter; this renovation will be achieved only through Christian families, by thorough-going Christians within these solid Christian homes, and fervent community groups of Christian families.

Home Life

SOMEONE has suggested the following "slogans" *for a Happy Home Life:*

1. *Always appear before your family in a good humor.* Nothing is so depressing for the rest of the family as a father or mother out of sorts. See that the family never has to suffer because of your attack of nerves or your irritability.

2. *Never weary in cheering your family with your smile.* It is not enough to avoid depressing the family; that is purely negative. You must brighten them up, let their spirits expand. Be especially vigilant when the little ones are around. You must give them the alms of a smile, hard though it be at times. What a pity when children have to say, "I don't like it at our house."

3. *Tell what you may tell openly:* If something must not be told, then don't tell it. If you may share it then do so. We ought to let others profit by our experience, above all, the family.

4. *Amiably show the greatest interest in the least things:* The problems of family life are generally not affairs of state. However, everything that concerns the persons we love most in the world should be worthy of interest: the baby's first tooth, the honor ribbon won at school, the entrance of one of the little ones into the Holy Childhood Association.

5. *Banish exaggerated asceticism from your life heroically:* If your home is Christian and each member of the family is learning to carry his cross, then it is essential to avoid making others suffer by a too ostentatious or inopportune austerity. Besides there is abundant opportunity for self-renunciation in devoting oneself to procuring joy for others. Marie Antoinette de Geuser used to sacrifice her great longing for recollection and her taste for a simple life by accompanying her brothers to evening affairs for which she wore dresses that she said "made her look vain."

6. *Be very attentive to treat all alike.* Nothing is so disrupting to home life as the evidence of favoritism for one or the other child. The same measure for all!

7. *Never think of yourself but always of them in a joyous spirit:* Henry the Fourth used to crawl around on all fours, with his children on his back, to enliven the family get-together. Louis Racine, the son of the famous Racine, relates of his father, "My father was never so happy as when he was free to leave the royal court and spend a few days with us. Even in the presence of strangers, he dared to be a father; he belonged to all our games. I remember our procession in the garden in which my sisters were the

clergy, I was the pastor and the author of *Athalie* came along carrying the cross, singing with us."

8. *Never begin an argument, always speak prudently.* Discussion should not be banned unless it develops into bickering or argument. A free habit of exchanging ideas on a broadening subject cannot but be profitable; the children should even be encouraged and led into it to develop in them a wise and discriminating mind and a habit of suspended judgment. Unsavory and disturbing subjects as well as those beyond their depth ought naturally be avoided.

9. *Act patiently always, answering graciously always:* That it takes the "patience of an angel" to rule vigilantly over the little world of the family is beyond question. I must apply myself to it affably.

10. *By good-will you will gain hearts and souls without exception:* Love much—that is the key to it all.

These slogans for a Happy Home Life are not marvels of prose but they do express a precious rule of wise family discipline.

The Family Table

MEALTIME should serve not only to nourish the body but also to comfort the soul.

Someone wittily said: "Repast, repose." Whoever it was made a good point.

While the children are still little the mother and father will probably breakfast alone. When they are older, if the father cannot be present because of his work, the mother at least should be present to set the example for table etiquette, to make sure that the children eat enough, properly, without greediness, and without rejecting what is not to their liking. This is the hour for the household to shake off sleepiness which still stupefies them, and to season the atmosphere with joy and genial good spirit.

At the main meals all except the babies will be present. The parents should exercise the greatest care not to come to table laden with their worries, a prey to the preoccupations of their duties or their professional activities. The only possible exception to this rule would probably be during a time of family bereavement or exceptional sorrow. But even then a just mean should be observed so that the young ones need not be unduly depressed. They ought to keep all their verve and to a certain point, their power of fancy.

Except when it is essential that the whole family share the concerns of all in common, the father and mother should not come to table looking downhearted and pass the mealtime discussing their hard lot in life. Children are quick to sense the worry of their parents, they feel that things are not going well, if there is tension or estrangement, if evil has hit the home. When they perceive things of this sort, their little hearts contract and a certain unease strangles them.

And why make someone who is not equal to it *bear the burden and heat of the day?*

After the first few moments in which the father and mother exchange a few words about decisions they must make concerning affairs which need not be kept from the children, they ought to direct the conversation here and there to the younger and the older; let them tell how they spent the morning or afternoon; show an interest in the efforts of all, in the work they did, the virtues they practised or the disappointments they met. Even if the father and mother have heavy cares, they should force themselves to escape from them long enough to be attentive listeners to the thousand details that all wish to recount. Each one must know that he can speak freely, provided that it is always politely, discreetly and charitably. Should there be some little chatterboxes, they must be taught to moderate their intemperance which would prevent others from having their say. If one of the children seems to be in bad humor, he should be stimulated by a little kindly teasing, a kind word or an opportune question.

When the children pull out all the stops, call for *pianissimo;* when they observe too long a pause speed up the tempo. Should one or the other strike a false note get him back in the key again.

The parents should not be satisfied with listening to the little stories of their children. They too should contribute to the broadening of their knowledge by giving them worthwhile information, relating an amusing or instructive story or starting a discussion on an interesting subject.

René Bazin, the novelist, speaks of those families in the North of France who still keep to the custom of beginning the meal with a short reading from the life of some saint or famous hero. Wasn't it Father Lourdel who entered the White Fathers after hearing the story of the African martyrs? All that relaxes, elevates, and lends variety. It might even be a reading from the letter of a relative or a selection from a newspaper. The main idea should be to entertain and as far as possible expand hearts.

A Christian Setting

ONE of the most touching descriptions is found in the account by Louis Veuillot of his visit to the home of one of his old friends whom he had not seen since the day of his marriage fifteen years before.

The visitor was admitted by the old servant who did not recognize him; he had to give his name. "Come," she said, "The Master is upstairs with Madam in their own room."

They went up. It was still the blue room whose picturesque decoration his old friend had admired so much in days past.

He recognized his friend despite the work of the years upon his features; his eyes were still keen, but it was evident that he had been weeping. The wife he remembered only vaguely.

"In my memory she was the fairy of youth dressed in flowing robes, crowned with flowers, with a smile on her lips, approaching reality over the green roads of Spring. A smile that nothing chased away, a mind that had never known fear, ears which had heard nothing but gentle words, hands which carried only wreaths of flowers, she personified the morning, the gloom, the promise of life. So she appeared to me on her Wedding Day—a Christian woman yet a child, a harmony of beauty, faith, love, candor. She was earnest because she believed; happy because she loved; radiant because she was pure.

"Now after fifteen years she is a wife who has aged from the cares of her home; she is a daughter in mourning for her mother, a mother in mourning for her children.

"On her pallid face the torrent of her tears have furrowed more deeply the traces of the years; in her heart, submission to the Cross; she stifles the sob of Rachel. I remembered that we used to call her *Stella matutina, Morning star*; now, I thought, we would have to call her *Mater dolorosa, Mother of sorrows*."

Then his eyes glanced at the walls of the room. They were not adorned as before. Formerly, there had been no crucifix. Now there was one. It occupied the place once held by a picture of Diana, the Goddess of the Chase. A little distance away, there was a picture of Mary at the Foot of the Cross. "We put it there to replace some poetic pictures at the time our first child died," the husband explained.

He continued, "This design above the dressing table where we used to have the painting of *The Great Festival of Watteau* is a copy of my father's tombstone in the village cemetery. It is over in that direction that I began to build and the cypress trees around the house are the first trees I planted. Here at the side is the picture of my wife's mother; she died in this room which we alone can use from now on. These other pictures are what remains to us now of all the dear souls who reared us, worked and suffered for us and provided so tenderly for our happiness. And here is a picture of our dear little Therese, our little saint, the second child God took from us. She left us last year when she was only six years old. She cried out before she died, 'God, God, where is God? I want to go to God!' She took with her the last happy days of her mother."

All that does not depress souls. Earth after all is not heaven. It is only the vestibule. That in itself is beautiful. And, as the author explains at the end of his description, "separations only increase our confidence, love and peace."

Judicious Economy

CHRISTIANITY demands detachment. Of all, interior detachment—*to use things as if we did not use them.* Of some, complete exterior detachment—the vow of poverty for religious which differs in degree of severity according to the Rules of the Order entered, from the actual and rigid deprivation of the disciples of Saint Francis of Assisi to the simple dependence relative to the possession of things or administration of money required in Congregations which are less austere.

But what should be the degree of effective poverty required or at least desired in people of the world?

We hear people speak of the "duty of improvidence" or

the "virtue of insecurity." What are we to think of these expressions and the ideal they express?

It is certain that love of gain is dangerous and that privation when accepted in the right spirit detaches.

It is equally certain that normal gain, that is to say not beyond bounds and obtained through honest means, is legitimate. Furthermore, economy, when it is not grounded in avarice or inordinate attachment to money but in the virtue of prudence, is not to be condemned.

With the good sense for which he is famous, Saint Francis de Sales says very aptly in Part One, Chapter Three of his *Introduction to a Devout Life:* "If husbands would not desire to amass any more than Capuchin monks, would not their piety be ridiculous, ill-regulated, and unbearable?"

Pope Pius XI, as well as Leo XIII, far from condemning economy expressed the wish that all should be in a position to benefit from it. Here is what is expressly stated in the Encyclical, *Quadragesimo Anno,* a replica one ought say of the famous Encyclical on *The Condition of the Working Classes* written forty years earlier:

"It is necessary to do everything possible that the share of wealth which accumulates (in certain hands) may be reduced to a more equitable measure and that a sufficient abundance of it is divided among the workers...so that they may increase *through economy* a patrimony capable of permitting them to meet the burdens of their family."

There are in these lines a condemnation of excess and the justification of the practice of economy.

Excess constitutes the hoarding of wealth, the accumulation of reserves for one's own personal use and with no thought at all for the common good—"to put in reserve and accumulate for one or several persons, under the form of gold, moneys, bank notes or even certain company titles, an excessive power of purchase instead of spreading it for the common good of the whole of humanity," is the way Pius XI expresses it.

The practice of economy is clearly indicated: "Under the direction of the Eternal Law and the universal government of Divine Providence, notes Leo XIII, man is his law and his providence." We must not ask God to reward our folly, our folly of spending wildly, putting nothing aside with the presumptuous assurance oneself, "God will help me if I fall into want."

There must be no passivity in our abandonment. We have to cooperate with God. Do one's best and then count on Providence should be our motto.

Far from us be any such thing as pagan foresight which makes us practically ignore the role of Divine Providence and count only on the money we have piled up; which makes us lose sight of the real purpose behind the practice of economy which is decidedly not to guarantee protection from want to a few but to help along toward the well being of all. Must we remind ourselves that superabundant capital may not be spent according to the whims of the owner. The surplus wealth which people possess, as our Lord has clearly pointed out, must be considered as a "trust-fund to be administered for the good of others, a stewardship, a guardianship which is to be exercised for the good of the community and in the interests of the community."

The Providential Role of Insecurity

GOD is not the enemy of security. He wants man to earn the daily bread for his old age by his labor. He wants society to guard against depressions and to guarantee to all a life protected by law. He requires certain privileged individuals to come to the aid of their brothers in need, especially, as it frequently happens, when society is powerless to help.

Does that imply then that God cannot permit insecurity for someone's good? Certainly not.

It is so easy to abuse security:

—Perhaps through *selfishness* by skimping one's life, refusing the entrance of love into one's life or setting up barriers to the possible gift of children from Divine Providence.

—Perhaps by purely pagan prudence, the attitude of the wicked rich in the Gospel, I will pull down my barns, and build larger ones.

—Perhaps by pride. What is Divine Providence anyway? I have money and the means of making it bring in more. God doesn't count.

In addition to its already precious role of crushing false hopes of security conceived by pagan-mindedness, insecurity has power proper to itself.

It *forces us to think of God*. Here I am, I have done all that I could, worked my best, saved without being niggardly but with legitimate prudence and now I am struck by a catastrophe—the death of the head of the family, or an untimely accident, war... I have nothing left, or if it is not so bad as that, Trial has at least made deep inroads on the possessions I had.

What should I do? Get discouraged? Never!

I will call up all my energy; try to salvage from the present situation whatever can help my best efforts and count on Divine Providence without in the least neglecting foresight. God helps those who help themselves.

I must believe that Our Lord surrounds those who find themselves in need through no fault of their own with a special predilection. "Do not forget," wrote a navy lieutenant to his wife at the outbreak of the war of 1914, "that uncertainty permits us to count more on God...riches hide some of God's delicate attentions from us...We have the best of the game with God."

What a beautiful expression of faith! Since human aid can so easily fail, God owes it to Himself to come to the aid of those who put their trust in Him. "We have the best of the game with God!"

Consequently, abandonment to God is in keeping with wise foresight.

A person does his best to avoid falling into a state of need. If God requires that all or much of his efforts come to naught, he ought not despair; let him submit valiantly to the yoke again; if he has a lively faith, he will thank God for having permitted "the caresses of poverty." The individual of himself could never have achieved the actual poverty of religious life; he can now at least accept the privations permitted by Providence and strive to live more literally the Gospel precept: *Make for yourself purses that do not grow old, a treasure unfailing in heaven, where neither thief draws near nor moth destroys.* Luke XII, 33.

The Snuff Box

FATHER VAUGHAN, known from the poorest to the most distinguished sections of London, as a famous preacher, the brother of several prelates one of whom was the Cardinal Archbishop of Westminster, learned much from his father who was a colonel in the British Army.

One day, at table, the little fellow took a very greedy portion of jam. His father reproved him for it and clinched his correction with the comment, "Whoever wants to become a man—a gentleman—knows how to conquer himself."

The child was hurt and becoming somewhat impudent retorted, "Oh, after all, Papa, you have your snuff box!"

Colonel Vaughan immediately put his hand into his pocket, drew out the snuff box and before the whole group threw it into the fire.

The history of the Vaughan family provides many such incidents which make profitable reading.

That's what we call fair play. If one wants to get another to do something, he must first of all do it himself. There should be justice. Not that children have a right to judge their parents, but parents should be careful not to give their children occasion to judge them badly.

We are sometimes amazed when young people who were very pious at one time and who have received a Christian education from start to finish, later on abandon the practice of their Faith. We must go back to the source. The mother was a practicing Catholic, the father suited himself about attendance at Mass; he had very quickly given up family prayer. The children rarely saw him perform an act of worship. No other explanation is needed to clarify everything.

The same holds true for the spirit of sacrifice, for prayer, and for refined manners.

Here is a child at table who has a mania for crumbling his bread into little pieces or to scatter crumbs all about his plate. The mother corrects him, for it.—"Oh but Papa does it too!"

So it goes with everything. People say they are *terrible* children. Why of course, all children are terrible. They record with unerring fidelity the examples they witness. And since examples strike incomparably harder than words, parents preach in vain, if they themselves do not practice; instead of forming, they deform. Who knows whether the little irregularities of today will not culminate in the regrettable crimes of tomorrow.

Great consideration should be given to the fact that "the

child is father to the man." Parents are therefore bound to watch themselves, their habits, their behavior, their speech.

Parents will be so free at table; they criticize the Pope, the bishops, the pastor, such and such persons among their relatives and acquaintances; their judgments are only too frequently severe or at least imprudent. Need they be astonished if later their children "who come from such Christian families," are free in passing criticisms about their highest superiors and other persons most deserving of respect. Whose fault is it?

"But they're so little; they don't understand what we're talking about!" How do you know? Although they do not understand everything or at least not right away, some impression will stay with them, and the habit of judging indiscriminately will be well planted to sprout later. What great damage is done! What out-and-out imprudence!

I will pay great attention to my children. They can be my best educators. I should give them the least possible occasion to teach me a lesson.

Estranged Parents

THERE can be such separation of soul between parents that they finally live their own lives; they no longer live together as husband and wife; they are father and mother, but not exactly husband and wife—a situation unmeasurably sad.

Sadder still is the home in which the father and mother still maintain husband and wife relations but do not understand each other at all; they are perpetually arguing or sulking or exchanging sharp words; they no longer love each other and consequently find that their life together offers nothing but constant occasions to make each other suffer.

If these unfortunate individuals have children, especially younger children, have they never wondered what possible questions might be tormenting their little heads; what bewildered anguish strangles their little souls which vainly seek to bestow their frail yet ardent love somewhere in this remote region made bleak and barren by battles.

How can they decide whose part to take? They can't. "Whom do you prefer, your mamma or your papa?" someone asked a little boy. He hesitated a moment, then said, "I prefer them both." And even if the child's heart leans more toward the one than the other, how could it decide who is more in the right or more in the wrong?

Those wretched parents who are so out of harmony with each other ought to meditate often on the touching prayer of the little child who got the idea of walking his estranged parents down to the beach one fine evening; as he walked along the way with his father and mother on either side of him, silent and glum, mulling over their own sad thoughts, he said softly—but still loud enough for his parents to hear—this little prayer of his own making:

O my dear little God. I feel so bad because Papa is angry at Mamma! Oh, if You knew how bad I feel! Please make it so he won't be angry anymore, so I won't be afraid anymore and so these terrible things, which you know about, may go far away from me because I am just a little child. Make it that I can love Papa and Mamma again with all my heart, my whole heart all full, because You see, my little God when somebody is angry I feel too bad and I am too afraid and, then, You know I am just a little child! Amen.

The Church is opposed to divorce, because it is an attack on the reality of love—and it is just that, for what is a love that is not indissoluble or the intimacies of marriage if they can be enjoyed with someone else during the lifetime of one's husband or wife; because divorce is the ruination of the family as Paul Bourget has the Jesuit Father Evrard explain in his novel *A Divorce:* A boat happened to be at a port where one of the passengers wished to go ashore; there was an epidemic on board ship; no one was allowed to leave the boat. The particular individual was inconvenienced by it but the good of the society overruled. So too, it is much better that the home be saddened than that the family be sacrificed. The Church is also opposed to divorce because it brings nothing but unhappiness to the child.

The same is true when the divorce is not a formal breaking up of the family; it is enough for the parents to be at odds, to cause the child to suffer, and generally, quite intensely.

Charity to their children obliges the parents to try everything to reestablish their union which is jeopardized.

God bless the homes in which the arms of little children guard forever the close union between the father and the mother.

The Womanly Ideal

PERHAPS no one has more beautifully extolled the womanly ideal than Charles Péguy.

What he admired first and foremost in woman was her special faculty for putting soul into the daily humdrum of the eternal repetitions of everyday life in the home. He has Our Lord say:

> My love goes out to you, O most precious one
> To you, most submissive at the feet of destiny,
> Most subject to the masters of the feast,
> Most eager and most solicitous.
>
> I love you so much, O most earnest one,
> You who are most responsive to claims of work
> Most unknown and most glorious
> Most attentive to the care of the fold.

The smallest action, the most ordinary, the most routine, though submerged in the greatest monotony of recurring days and engulfed by the unfolding centuries, can be of immense value if performed with a great love:

> .... You spend yourself utterly, O only needy one,
> In washing dishes and keeping house
> O Woman, you who set in order both labors and days.

But then, woman, is not only a worker, a housekeeper, she is a *mother*, a mother who is solicitous for her little ones, a mother who never tires of contemplating the infinite hidden away behind a curved forehead or stubborn eyes. Man does not sense it. He is not sufficiently delicate or spiritual for that. Woman alone has a glance sufficiently keen and supernatural to discover not only the corporal needs of a fragile and tiny body but also the deep and innocent soul washed by the waters of baptism and rich with countless graces which must be put to good use in the future.

Nothing is so beautiful as a child falling asleep while saying his prayers, says God (according to Péguy)
I tell you nothing in the world is so beautiful...
Yes, I tell you, I don't know anything so beautiful in all the world
As a little child falling asleep saying his prayers
Under the wings of its Guardian Angel
A little child, who laughs at the angels while beginning to fall asleep
And who gets his prayers all mixed up because he no longer has his mind on them
Who mixes up the words of the *Our Father* with the words of the *Hail Mary*
While a veil is already falling upon his eyelids
The veil of night upon his sight and upon his voice.

Truly, it is woman's honor and her duty, as a consequence of her vocation, to be very near to souls and to the supernatural world. Then too woman is more loving than man. She has a sense of pity and compassion. She always has something in common with the sympathetic traits manifested by Joan of Arc even as a little girl. One day she saw two little starving and sad-hearted children walking along a roadway. "It grieved me so much, I gave them all my bread, my noon-day lunch and my four o'clock snack. Their joy hurt me: I thought of all the other starving people who had nothing to eat, so many starving people, countless hungry people. I felt that I was going to break out weeping. I gave them my bread. A beautiful gesture! But they will be hungry again tonight; they will be hungry again tomorrow... There, they have gone into the future, into distress, into the anxiety for the future... O, my God, who will give them their daily bread?"

Joan's great compassion for souls tore even more at her heart than her anguish over the physical hunger of bodies. "If only we could see the beginning of Your reign established, o my Lord!" she prayed.

Honor to Woman for the greatness of her heart!

Her Husband's Helper

PASTEUR's wife was a precious aid to the renowned scientist who was her husband.

The help she gave him was not always scientific, intellectual, technical. In the organization of most homes, wives will not have to give their husbands only that type of help. Moral support is more essential.

It was a little home in which unity and understanding flourished but where money was scarce. The husband needed an auto for his work; he had an old jalopy and it had taken him three long months to pay for it. One day shortly after his last payment, the rear axle broke while he was turning a corner. The poor fellow returned home utterly discouraged. His wife who was courageous, confident, and who was furthermore expecting a baby, said not a word of reproach or discouragement. On the contrary she tried to console him:

"Look, we are happy; God loves us. We ought to pay Him a little ransom for all the joys He has given us. Come, let us pray and not lose hope. He can't abandon us." Their hearts raised together to God, they found themselves more closely united than ever in their human love. Together they had drawn from the same Spring of Hope, the same Font of Goodness. They were united in perfect Unity.

It is clear that a wife ought to expect to find in her husband a strong man, someone who does not go to pieces at the first set-back; who knows how to struggle with the tempests and bring their bark safely into port. She certainly does not expect him to exhibit his virility by vain attitudes or a show-off's behavior; she does not expect him to swagger or substitute boasting or protestations for ability to act, for solidity of character, and for real bravery. She naturally much prefers one who is truly a master, a master in his profession or in his work whatever it is, a master in the conduct of the home, able to make decisions and to assume responsibility. She wants no irresolute or timid chap who takes two steps back for every step forward or whose will is changeable, capricious, petty; nor does she want a man who gets submerged by details and forgets the whole, but a man endowed with an eye for detail coupled with a power for organization. She does not want a man whom prejudices blind and who is not sure of himself; no, she wants a man who can be resolute without being tyrannical, determined without being narrow and stubborn when a need arises for changing one's tactics—a man of peace, of thought, and of perseverance...

What a list of virtues! Can they ever be found in one single soul? Let us suppose a man has the whole array of these virtues or even the principal ones among them, will he not even then need moral support at some time or other?

There are moments of discouragement, dark hours either because events bring sorrow and anguish or because nature grows weak or health fails or vigor of character temporarily subsides.

How helpful it is in these situations which are not at all impossible to be able to find reenforcement in the companion of his life! They started out as two but life together has made them one; each of them must support the other in view of their common work.

To each the task is a true principle but when danger threatens, it is not too much to have to face the same threat together....

What security for the wife to know that she can find in her husband the help she dreamed of! For the husband when he can be certain of being understood by his wife in periods of material or spiritual difficulty and not only understood but supported, cheered, and comforted!

Thank You, O my God, for giving me in my life-companion the intelligent, disinterested, attentive aide You knew I would need, You said, *It is not good for man to be alone.* You gave me another self. Help me to find in this other half of me, my other self, the strength to be strong.

Good Sense

A SISTER missionary describes the following family episode which took place in Congo:

Strong stalwart Batéké who had recently married came looking for me one morning with a very dejected appearance, or perhaps, disgusted would be more correct.

"Well now, my friend, what's the matter? Aren't things going well? Is your wife sick?"

"Oh no, Sister, she's not sick" (this in a very dry tone)

"What's the matter then?"

"Ah, that one" (meaning his wife). She doesn't have any sense.

"Nothing to eat! She's always outdoors talking. Nothing is good in the hut. She needs..."

"Well bring her here," I interrupted to show myself willing to help. "I will scold her and remind her of her duties."

"Oh no, that's not enough!"

"What then," I asked slightly worried.

"That one, (still referring to his wife) ought to come here for at least a month to get a head on her shoulders!"

"All right! Bring her."

The next day my Batéké came back pulling "that one," who looked very sheepish, after him.

"How is it my daughter," I asked her reproachfully, "that you don't understand your new duties better? If you do not know how to keep house or prepare a meal for your husband, it would be better to come back with us for several days, maybe a month. Do you want to?"

"Oh yes," she sighed.

"That is fine," beamed the happy husband.

Obediently the young wife began her new apprenticeship to learn how to prepare good cassava and fish with oil dressing, the staple food of her lord and master.

Batéké came to see his recluse before the month was up.

"You can take your wife back now," I offered, "she will be wise and capable from now on."

"No, No," protested the obstinate husband. "She must stay the thirty days."

And at the end of thirty days the couple was reunited. The

last news of them was good. My Batéké is satisfied. "*That one has sense now.*"

What is possible in Congo is scarcely possible among us. A husband cannot send his wife back to school for a course in Home Economics or back home to her mother to be instructed in her duties ... As a consequence his home is run helter skelter fashion. Nothing is ready on time, the food is spoiled, the clothing is not properly cared for, the bills are not paid, the accounts are not kept straight, the children are not dressed on time—there is general hubbub. How can there be peace in such a home where a woman has no sense?

Sometimes it is the man of the house who lacks sense. He manifests no business ability at all; wastes time and money; has no feeling for organization or sense of value; invests foolishly on the word of others and is an easy mark for wily and scheming confidence men. He is hesitant; can never make up his mind or if he does make a decision, he corrects it the next moment; begins everything but finishes nothing; undertakes a profession in which he expects to move mountains and work marvels only to abandon it several months later through lassitude or because he ambitions a career more to his liking and more lucrative.

This changing humor makes him choose one school after another for his children; none of them are ever exactly what he wants. Naturally the children suffer from it, they can't profit by their classes, lose out on grades, and are in danger of becoming changeable too.

For a man above all the qualities of the heart can never replace solidity of the mind. He has to have a head on his shoulders, quick discernment, accurate knowledge, the power to decide, if not promptly in delicate matters at least always firmly, the ability to revise his decision when advisable and when the evidence demands it, because obstinacy has no value and reveals even more than indecision that a person lacks sense; but he must also have the power to hold his own against wind and tide, even when the odds seem against him, provided of course, that what he looks upon as opposition is not some difficult obligation of the moment he should be meeting rather than fighting.

Women and Education

A WOMAN educator of note in her book *L'Education selon l'Esprit*, expresses an opinion that deserves full acceptance: "What is best for a young woman is not to be entirely absorbed in material works and the care of children but to keep a little freedom of time and of mind to continue her intellectual development. The gift she makes of herself to her own will be only the more precious; the services she will render them will be of a superior quality. She herself will be ennobled by these disinterested pleasures, defended against the temptations that are born of fatigue, boredom, and a barren interior life.

There are unfortunately some young women for whom this advice would be most difficult if not impossible to follow; they are obliged to work in the time they have free from family duties to provide for the necessities of life. But there are those who have leisure. That they ought to profit by it to cultivate their minds is quite evident.

The principal reason is the one already mentioned—to be able to give something of the intellectual riches they have acquired to their children later. One needs to know so many things to enlighten their young minds, to open up their little souls just at the threshold of life; their questions should be answered by something better than an irritable "Stop bothering me!"

Another advantage of growing in culture is that it helps one struggle against a sense of futility. Not that the thousand occupations demanded in a home are futile. But there are, over and above the essential things, a thousand little nothings with which one can fritter her time. That is the immense domain of the futile in which women flit about untiringly as a bird hops from bar to bar in its cage, a pretty bird of paradise.

But there is something worse than to be busy with little nothings and that is to do nothing. There is just a void, an exaggerated place left open for day dreaming—and the normal consequence—an open door for temptation.

"Because what's to be done in a home unless one dreams?"

If one does not apply the mind to serious and uplifting reflections, the devil will be right on hand to turn it to fantastic hopes: one relives stories read, reviews step by step girlish infatuations, ruminates over the imaginary or real deficiencies in her husband... Temptations are not far away!

Even if conscience preserves such a one from sin, she is always in danger of trouble, extreme sensitiveness and boredom from the drudgery of daily tasks.

Good reading which elevates the soul and stimulates thinking, which supplements religious knowledge, puts one in contact with great souls, will inspire to virtue and produce wonderful effects in the individual.

At the present time when the apostolate must deal with so many problems, is it asking too much of the one who expects to do good to be highly competent? The religious renaissance must begin with the educated groups. Ideas will always rule the world.

What poverty it is for women, so devoted as they are to the apostolate, to lack ideas; to live only by routine! They have forgotten but one thing—to light their lamps!

Endurance

ABBÉ PERREYVE wrote to a young man of twenty who had told him of his hopes to marry:

Ah, my friend, next to the happiness of serving God in consecrated virginity, what is more beautiful than to link one's life with that of a cherished woman; to share one's whole soul, that is all his sorrows; to begin with her that brief pilgrimage on which there are so many joys and tears that there is scarcely time to do a little good? What is more worthy of an immortal soul than to give his love in youth to the soul he must love always and before God to purify the ardor of his desires by submitting them to the duties of fidelity and of paternity?

Do not laugh at love as those foolish souls do who are incapable of it. There is no nobler word among men. Love is not the pleasure, not the selfishness of enjoyment; it is not the delusion of a brutal passion. The one who loves gives himself more than anything else. The highest degree of love is sacrifice. That is why he only knows how to love who immolates his rest, his joys, his fortune even life itself for the being he ought to love on earth and in heaven.

Wherever marriage is seriously and correctly regarded the word sacrifice is part of its vocabulary. There is no doubt about it, marriage brings with it the sweetest of human joys that can be tasted on this earth; but it also involves self-abnegations that are essential.

The Countess of Adhemar wrote to Abbé Frémont:

Man and woman are united, not as they often believe with the best faith in the world, to *give* each other happiness, but, in reality, to *seek* it of each other. As their individual concepts of happiness may differ, there ensues for both of them a painful awakening.

That excellent bulletin the *Association du Mariage Chrétien* carried a fine article by an author who identified himself with the initials C.B. The ideas expressed in it have much to contribute here:

Love is not a bargain, it is not even an exchange; it is a sacrifice which should always be mutual. Each giving up and sacrificing the best of himself so that the best of the other's self may live and grow.

Clearly the great test is endurance. Oh, if only the honeymoon could last forever. But that cannot be. They must pass from blind love to clear-sighted love; time requires this transformation but "the line" is not easy to cross—it is not easy to go from the torrid to the temperate zone. They must protect themselves against being deluded about this.

"Two young people go up to the altar for the beautiful nuptial ceremony," writes Father Lacordaire, "They bring with them all the joy and all the sincerity of their youth; they swear eternal love for each other.

"But soon their joy diminishes, fidelity stumbles, the eternity of their pledges is broken to bits.

"What happened? Nothing. Hour followed hour; they are what they were except for one hour more. But one hour is much."

The author adds it is true "outside of God."

In order to triumph over time, over its duration, over monotony, over the friction resulting from character differences which become more evident with time, a supernatural spirit is absolutely necessary; it alone is able to call forth sacrifice, persevering sacrifice inspired by love.

Unbearable Husbands

To a brother of his who was very impatient, Saint Francis de Sales could not refrain from saying one day, "There is one woman in the world who must be very happy."

"Who," asked his brother.

"The woman you might have married had you married."

Madam Acarie, a mother of six children was left a widow in 1613. She later entered Carmel taking the name Marie of the Incarnation. Her husband had been an unpleasant character and helped not a little to enrich her with the virtues that led to her beatification. Once in a rare spell of good humor he admitted, "They say she will be a saint some day; I shall have helped her become one; they will speak of me at her canonization."

Guy de Rabutin-Chantal, the father-in-law of Saint Jane Frances de Chantal, who took the saint to his home after her husband's death was extremely hard to live with.

"He belonged to those well meaning and difficult old men who work efficaciously to make saints out of their women when they have in them the stuff from which saints are made," commented one of his biographers.

After the death of a celebrated philosopher, his wife obtained an audience with the king of Sweden. The latter inquired with kindly interest about the habits of the deceased. The wife, in a sudden outburst, exclaimed, "Your Majesty, he was unbearable!" A certain historian recording her remark added, "If all biographers were as sincere as that lady, they would be able to engrave her judgment on her pedestal of all the monuments raised to heroes."

Without accepting that opinion about heroes as our own —and admitting possibly that we are more willing to forgive them their foibles than others—is not the severe judgment on husbands a revelation of not too good an opinion?

And we could extend the litany. Chaliapine relates that a Russian general of his acquaintance used to give way to terrible fits of temper at home. The life of the general's wife was a veritable hell. Happily one day she discovered a clever strategy. At the moment her husband's fury started to let loose, she dashed to piano and struck up the national anthem. Must we believe the marvelous results obtained? The general stood at attention; his anger cooled off.

Every woman can't have a general for a husband nor one so susceptible to harmony either. We know that music refines manners. How marvelous it can be on that point. But the best music for the wife in cases of this kind will be the music of silence.

Saint Monica's husband used to drink heavily and when he came home with insults on his lips or speaking unbecoming or unintelligible words the poor wife had to practice a patience that we can readily imagine. She answered nothing and waited until the storm passed to remind him gently and lovingly of the law of God. She won almost unhoped for results, which testified to her sanctity: she obtained the complete cure of her husband who became a temperate and controlled man.

Is there anything obnoxious in me which brings sufferings into my home? I will correct it as soon as possible.

Unbearable Wives

YESTERDAY the men were on trial. The chapter on the ladies will be no less edifying.

"What you need," said a man to one of his bachelor friends who was disturbed by a vague nervous disorder, "what you need is a wife to share your troubles."

"But I don't have any troubles."

"That is all right. You will have them after you marry."

Such a story is not very expressive of esteem for marriage. Woman certainly has the power to console, but also the power to cause suffering.

The husband scolds, the wife gets angry. Does that make things any better? The husband, once the outburst is over forgets about it; not so the wife. She holds in reserve, unless she is very good, amazing desires for revenge. Moreover, she is argumentative.

"Look darling, look at the pretty bird that's with those two crows."

"Yes, I see, but there aren't just two crows, there are three."

"No, darling, look, there are only two."

"But I tell you there are three. It's always like that. I never have the right to be in the right."

And soon the tears drop from her lashes.

Some women will pout rather than argue.

After a dispute which was of no great moment, a certain wife, pricked in her vanity, risked this imprudent threat. "If you don't yield to me, I won't talk to you for fifteen days." The husband paid no attention and thought that after a short while life would settle down to normal again. But it didn't. Silence. Silence. She would not deign to answer his questions even those asked with the most angelic sweetness.

The husband, beside himself, came to a decision. He began to empty out all the cabinets and table drawers, take the pictures off the walls and was about to attack the drapes with a pair of scissors.

"What are you doing there?"

"I am looking for your tongue."

Bursts of laughter restored peace. The pity is that the bursts of laughter had not occurred fifteen days earlier.

Tenacity has great worth. A woman probably has too much of it. She may expect to let it compensate for a certain strength she lacks. She realizes she is wrong because she is intelligent. She does not think she ought to yield because a miserable vanity gets in between her conscience and her decision.

It still remains that it is the woman in spite of her limitations and weaknesses who most often creates the happiness of the home and the man who spoils it. The moralist was not wrong who said,

"With all their faults, their perfidy, their subterfuge, their envy and their lies, with their strong perfumes, their paint and their powder, their imperfections and their wretchedness, poor women are so much more courageous, more generous, more patient, more virtuous, more faithful than we men!"

Let each of the married partners judge himself or herself by his or her own conscience, and mindful of the happiness of the other, correct as soon as possible what might trouble the harmony of the home.

The Counsels of Madame Elizabeth

THE sister of Louis XVI, Madame Elizabeth who was a woman of fine psychological acumen and deep nobility of character gave to one of her ladies in waiting who had recently married this practical advice:

Above all seek to please your husband... he has good qualities but he can also have some that are not so pleasing. Make it a rule for yourself never to concentrate on these and above all never permit yourself to talk of them; you owe it to him as you owe it to yourself. Try to look at his heart; if you truly possess it, you will always be happy. Make his house agreeable for him; let him always find in it a woman eager to please him, busy with her duties, with her children, and you will in this way win his confidence; when you once have that, you will be able to do, with the mind heaven has given you and a bit of cleverness, anything you wish.

The outcome is interesting. Everyone knows it: "Man reigns but woman governs."

"I will do it if God wills it," said the husband of a rather dictatorial wife.

"Now you are talking nonsense," said his friend, "why you haven't even asked your wife's permission."

Woman instinctively, and above all when she loves, loves to be docile. Nothing costs her too much and at times she goes to the point of sacrifices extremely taxing for herself if her heart is captive. But at the same time she loves to dominate.

The heroine of a comedy revealed, with exaggeration of course, a trait that is often found in woman. The said heroine had not yet married but she already was engaged in making her fiancée dance to her thirty-six wills and to goad him on with a thousand pin pricks: "I prick him, I make him go, I already treat him as my husband."

Even when they are not so naughty, women by using to advantage their weakness and their charm usually succeed in making their husbands pretty much as they want them.

In his genially caustic style Emile Faguet used to say, "Women are divided into three classes: those who are inclined to obey sometimes, those who never obey, those who always command."

Let women never use their power for the egotistic satisfaction of their self-love. Let them rather have in view only God's glory and, especially in the spiritual government of their home, let them know how to make God's glory understood as it ought to be. They should be able to gain a hearing in the most vital matters when duty is at stake or when the worship due to God is involved; in other matters let them be ready to yield. They will purchase by their perpetual abnegation in these lesser things the right to be listened to in more important matters and their husbands will realize that when they do resist their wishes it is not because of vanity but because of virtue.

Woman, the Strength of Man

Is it not often true in a home that "the strength of the man is many times in the woman."

Man, who in principle at least and often in fact possesses physical resistance and moral energy, is sometimes singularly deficient; he hides under the appearance of strength an intimate need to lean on someone, to be led, encouraged, assisted.

Is it not also true that one great source of happiness in marriage is the reciprocal help the two give each other, the husband to his wife, the wife to her husband?

Joseph Proudhon from whom we would not expect such correct ideas, has given us some beautiful pages on the help that woman is called to give to her husband. He took for his theme the Bible text: *And the Lord God said: It is not good for man to be alone: let us make him a help like unto himself.*

Woman is a helper for man because by showing him the ideality of his being she becomes for him a principle of admiration, a gift of strength, of prudence, of justice, of courage, of patience, of holiness, of hope, of consolation without which he would be incapable of bearing up under the burden of life, of preserving his dignity, of fulfiling his destiny of bearing with himself.

Woman is man's helper first of all in work by her attentions, her sweet company, her vigilant charity. It is she who wipes his forehead that is moist with perspiration, who rests his tired head upon her knees, who cools the fever of his blood and pours balm into his wounds. She is his sister of charity. Ah! let her only look at him, let her season the bread she brings him with her tenderness: he will be strong as two, he will work like four.

She is his helper in the things of the mind by her reserve,

her simplicity, her prudence, by the vivacity and the charm of her intuitions.

She is his helper in justice, she is the angel of patience, of resignation, of tolerance, the guardian of his faith, the mirror of his conscience, the source of his devotedness.

Man can brook no criticism, no censure from man; even friendship is powerless to conquer his obstinacy. Still less will he suffer harm or insult. Woman alone knows how to make him come back and prepares him for repentance and for pardon.

Against love and its entanglements, woman, marvelous being that she is, is for man the only remedy.

Under whatever aspect he regards her, she is the fortress of his conscience, the splendor of his soul, the principle of his happiness, the star of his life, the flower of his being.

What praise for woman! What responsibility for her to be in her home, the fortress of conscience, almost a living translation of divine commands!

Let her strive to deserve this role by the solidity of her principles, the energy of her convictions, the convincing strength of her calm statements.

Is Genius Celibate?

CERTAIN authors have denied that woman is a help for man at least intellectually and often also morally. They claim that feminine contact and the demands of the home weaken the strong; the words of the physiologist Garnier, "genius is celibate" have been capitalized on by some.

One of the great advocates of this thesis is Tolstoi who did not hesitate fourteen months after his marriage to have one of the characters in his book *War and Peace* say:

Never marry, never, my friend. That is my advice. Do not marry, at least not before you can say to yourself that you have accomplished the whole of your destiny before discovering woman such as she is. Otherwise you will be cruelly disillusioned. Marry when you are no longer anything but an old man, good for nothing; otherwise all there is of good and noble in you will perish; all will be spent in little things. Yes, if in the future you expect anything of yourself, you will feel that all is finished for you, except the parlor where you will be on the same footing as a court valet or a fool... My wife is an admirable woman. She is one of those rare women with whom one can be tranquil about his honor, but, my God, what would I not give not to be married... You are the first person, the only person to whom I say that, because I love you.

Tolstoi himself left his home to escape from this sad sensation of a missed life.

The part that is true about all this is that for certain individuals and in certain careers the choice of a companion for life is of paramount importance.

Ozanam, who was a professor at the Sorbonne, wondered if he would ever find the woman of his dream; not only someone who would love him, but someone who would understand him; be willing to see him buried in books and apparently neglect her to keep company with ideas; someone who in the intimate converse of conjugal life would not be silent, unintelligent, or unreceptive but capable of taking an interest in her husband's studies and even help him in his work.

Jean du Plessis de Grenedan, a marine officer, used to wonder if he would ever find the woman he hoped for; a woman who would accept the career of her husband and not melt into tears at every leave-taking as if her husband heartlessly went away to make her suffer; who would not, except for serious reasons unbiased by whim, require him to give up going to sea and accept a land commission; someone who would not be depressed during his long absences.

Because of a too selfish idea of home-life, some women do weaken their husbands, hamper their vocation, their profession or their apostolate. They have that type of jealousy which considers all that is not given to them as stolen from them. They are satisfied only if they can keep the chosen one of their heart always with them and have him constantly at their feet.

A wife should stimulate and encourage but never paralyze.

The Power of a Smile

THERE is in Rome not far from the basilica of Saint Agnes, which was built over the spot at which she was martyred, another church—Our Lady of Peace. It is more or less a custom for newlyweds to attend Mass here the day following their marriage; it is as if they realized that Mary's help is none too much to help them preserve peace in their homes.

Nothing so helps to preserve the mutual attraction husband and wife have for each other as cheerfulness, the habit of taking everything in good part, of keeping one's balance in the midst of disturbing circumstances, of bearing personal anxieties without letting them become noticeable, so as not to sadden the other. Nothing so quickly kills this attraction as nagging over little things, pettiness in any form, referring to the blunders of the other, magnifying some omissions, manifesting suspicion. The ideal of cheerfulness is to display as spontaneously as possible, without the least trace of effort an amiable gaiety ever ready to smile.

Wrangling, ill-humor or simply sulkiness are the great enemies of homes. Particularly when these things have their source in the wife is there grave danger; for husbands may be tempted to seek outside the home and out of the path of duty the ray of sunshine they cannot find at home.

Little heed should be paid to imprudent comments on the part of neighbors and acquaintances, supposedly so well-meaning, who think they are rendering a service by revealing, confidentially of course, the goings-on of this one and that one. Little heed should be given to insinuations that are made sometimes without any foundation; they have a peculiar power to throw a gloom over the soul if they get a hearing. Peace is lost to the soul; someone's perfidy or inopportune truthfulness killed it.

No matter what happens keep your power to smile.

A certain wife was on the verge of despair; bits of gossip she picked up here and there and other evidence which she thought she discovered revealed to her that her husband was in love with another woman. This woman had been flitting about the unfortunate man; at first he pretended not to notice it; one day out of a sense of duty he actually put her in her place. But then, little by little, her persistence won out and he yielded ground. He was not far from actual betrayal of his home.

His wife, not knowing what to do, went to her confessor. The priest first put her through an examination of conscience: "Have you always in your home life manifested patience, no matter what happened; a joy that uplifts, a reserve which attracts, a calmness which inspires confidence?"

She had to confess that she had failed many times against these virtues. Instead of showing herself more attractive, she had allowed her wounded self-love—which could easily be understood—get the upper hand; she did not hide her suspicious attitude and began to give way to little expressions of spitefulness. Such unwise tactics, instead of retaining her husband's loyalty, helped to strengthen the attraction of her rival.

"Act differently," the confessor advised her. "Learn to smile!"

A short while after, the husband in a moment of confidence confessed the risk he had run and revealed that the smile of his wife and her confident joyous spirit had saved him from the abyss. "I did not have the right to destroy such happiness, to annihilate a hope that was so evident."

Wives would do well to follow this very judicious advice: "Love your husbands as if you were sure of their hearts and act as if you still had to win them."

A Devastating Disposition

EVEN when a person has great desires for good he can fall far short of the program for holiness he dreamed of following; he lets himself slip into faults of speech or unpleasant attitudes—yes, unfortunately he may fall more seriously or come perilously near betraying his strongest obligations.

If then he finds himself constantly confronted with harshness, reproaches, a set face, he may perhaps drift farther away from his duty instead of being sorry for his negligences and failings.

He has a much better chance of getting back to the right path if he is met not with irritability and sharpness but with a receptive gentleness that announces and promises pardon without having to express it, yet is withal earnest and firm.

Does God deal otherwise with us? He tried throughout the Old Testament to adopt a severe manner and to brandish a threat, a plague or some other menace each time the Chosen People went astray. He realized that this was not the best way to lead His poor elect people back to repentance. He changed His formula, and modified His way with them.

Rather than hurl thunderbolts at them He offered His Heart: "Behold this Heart that has so loved men!" What cruelty not to give any other return than ingratitude, contempt.

It is striking in the Gospel that Our Lord is not so much concerned about demanding our fidelity as He is about revealing His own. He does not say, "Here is how much you must love Me and the way you should love Me." No, but "Greater love than this no man hath."

"To such an extent has Christ loved the world," marveled Saint Paul—to such an extent! Do you understand?

Christ reiterated His love and gave new proofs of His love much more than He expressed reproach.

There are few souls who can imitate this Christ-like magnanimity when they suspect or discover that someone has failed them. Yet we must all strive for it and aim at attaining the perfection of Christianity, the complete Gospel ideal.

Isabelle d'Este was forsaken to a certain extent by her husband, one of her biographers informs us. Did she shower him with reproaches? Did she send him upbraiding letters, violent literature? Nothing of the sort. With firm simplicity mixed with tenderness she wrote:

"... I am very well. Your Highness must not say it is my fault if I disagree with you, because as long as you showed me some love, no one could have persuaded me that you did not love me. But I do not need anyone to tell me to know that for some time Your Highness has loved me very little. However as this is an unpleasant subject, I shall cut it short and speak no more of it..."

Whether or not her husband returned to his duty after receiving this message is not so sure. There are some hearts that resist everything. At least his wife had chosen the best means to win him back.

Men's Virtues versus Women's Virtues

MANY MEN, still victims of an old prejudice, are very demanding when there is question of the moral life of their wife or their fiancée, yet strangely indulgent with regard to their own moral life. It is taken for granted that the wife must be pure and remain pure; she must come to marriage as a virgin and preserve the chastity of her married state. What of the man?

It is significant that women too seem to expect men to act differently, and to accept this double standard, as the reaction of the young woman in the following incident indicates:

Her husband was guilty of a flagrant betrayal of their love and had been unfaithful almost from the beginning of their marriage. The poor girl was discussing the situation with her father-in-law who was incensed at his son and raged against him, "If he carries on like that he is a blackguard, a vile monster!" And the wife had no other comment to make than, "He's a man!"

Questionable praise, we must confess, for the masculine gender! Christian morality does not subscribe at all to such standards. There is no double standard: one type of morality for young men and one for young women; one for husbands and one for wives. That man has a stonger pull toward the physical is possible; that he may be bolder and less restricted by delicacy or timidity; that because of his profession he must leave home frequently and consequently have more occasion to forget his wife and as the ugly saying goes "have his fling" is very true. But none of these reasons justifies or authorizes his misconduct.

An author who plays up his native city in his writing does not refrain from criticizing, and justly, those respectable men—the seventeenth century called them persons of quality—who in their own city enjoy an honorable reputation, figure prominently in their parish church, entertain the clergy frequently, but the minute they have left their city, forget their principles, take their morals lightly, read sexy novels which they lay in store at the station if they can do so unobserved and think nothing of sharing their hotel room with a chance woman acquaintance.

Let us allow for the author's satire and his outlook. But is it all false?

And when the little ragamuffin standing on the station platform heard the woman say to her departing husband, "Take care of yourself and don't forget me," wasn't it just the impudence of the rascal that made him say to her smartly, "Don't fret ma'am, he just tied a knot in his handkerchief!"

Out of sight, out of mind... May that never be true! Likewise may it never be said, "Out of sight, free from duty!"

Man's Fidelity

THE tolerance with which some worldly people regard the irregularities of men is scarcely credible. That is none the less their attitude. Everything is permissible for men. They are to be excused because of their temperament. "Nature gets the best of them, isn't that true? We must understand them and not be over severe."

How refreshing it is to hear a woman repudiate such unwarranted indulgence and condemn as should be condemned the liberties the world accords men in the matter of marital betrayal. Isabelle Rivière in *The Bouquet of Red Roses* gives us this satisfaction:

Agatha, the young woman in the story, picks up a volume of a contemporary writer; in the selection *The Evening with Mr. Teste* by Paul Valery, she came upon this opening paragraph:

> Stupidity is not my strong point. I have seen many individuals, visited several nations, I have taken part in various enterprises without liking them. I have eaten every day. I have gone with women.

She blushed with indignation and showed this last sentence to her husband.

"I find that statement more vile than the worst obscenity."

"Why, my dear?"

"Such utter disregard of fidelity! That complacent way of regarding man alone as the center of the world, and regarding the whole world, women included, as objects for his use, as just so many accessories. Don't you find that disgusting?"

"Yes... I believe it is the negation of all truth, of all love in any case."

Bravo! Let this vagabond Mr. Teste claim if he will that stupidity is not his strong point. He certainly takes the prize for presumption and cynicism.

Granted that woman is more *soul* than man, and he more *body* than woman, more alive to the physical, that does not authorize him to do as he pleases with the law of God and the dignity of women. Certainly if he expects to remain faithful without taking the necessary means, he will hold out only with great difficulty.

Watch and Pray. Here is a man who exposes himself to every risk, who seldom if ever prays, who receives Holy

Communion just at Eastertide or at very, very great intervals. Even if he has a high sense of honor and deep respect for woman's dignity, he will have great difficulty keeping his soul intact. We must not separate the demands of morality from the helps Our Lord gave us to observe them. To conform to the laws without having recourse to the helps is practically impossible. *Without Me,* said our good Master, *You can do nothing.*

What must we conclude then from the fact that man has greater difficulty than woman in preserving chastity? That he is free to dispense himself from chastity? Certainly not, but that he must pray more than his wife, practice more Christian prudence than his wife since he is more exposed to danger than she is both by his more vehement temperament and the occasions brought about by his business.

A Wife with Character

PEOPLE say that husbands do not like too strong a personality in their wives. Doubtless there are some sufficiently imprudent to prefer a simpleton or a doll, provided she is exteriorly alluring, to a woman of real worth who may prove to be someone to cope with. To such men, the otherwise incorrect but witty sentence might truly be applied, "Women know well that men are not so stupid as people believe, they are more so!"

In the history of Byzantium, an interesting incident is related. Queen Theodora had just come into power. Her son, the prince who would succeed her should have a wife. According to custom messengers were sent out to bring to the palace the twelve most beautiful girls they could find.

After the first elimination six remained from whom the future emperor. Theophilus was to choose his wife.

Holding a golden apple in his hand the prince began his

review. He was much attracted by a certain Kasia and just for something to say, he paid her this dubious compliment, "It is through woman that all evil has come to us."

"Yes," retorted Kasia, "but also all good."

Frightened by such quick reply, indicative of a quick temperament, Theophilus carried his golden apple to someone else.

A splendid example of masculine stupidity!

Happily the time when men reasoned that way is past. Those who are intelligent want to find in the woman they choose for their wife a person who is a real person.

Not one of those *blue-stockings* justly contemned by the truly wise, for forgetting the reserve which is the precious attribute of their sex, posing as intellectuals, acting mannish, using language which lacks refinement and foolishly aping masculine ways.

When women are not women, they are worse than men and they are ridiculous besides.

Man does not desire to find a duplicate of what he is when he looks for a companion! It is Eve that Adam desires.

But he wants an Eve who is not just a woman expert in trinkets and in whom veneer takes the place of mental and moral virtues; he wants an Eve who is an honest-to-goodness woman, and if possible, one of unusual character; one who can see the world otherwise than through the narrow dimensions of the ring she wears on her finger and does not concentrate all her attention on her jams and jellies or her next new outfit; a woman who thinks before all else of her home, but precisely because she wants her home to be attractive and she herself to be attractive in that home, seeks to enlarge her horizons and to be truly a real person.

Praiseworthy Vanity

A HUSBAND who is a man of sense as well as a good Catholic proposes this question: Ought concern for their appearance be something foreign to Christian wives? He answers the question himself:

> That would be simply ridiculous. I confess that I feel thoroughly enraged when I see women who act as if they were being very virtuous by their slovenly appearance and poor taste in dress. First of all, they commit a fault against beauty and grace which are God's gifts. But their fault is graver still: Have these noble souls taken care to consult their husbands and to assure themselves that he approves of this treatment? Let them not be surprised then if their husbands look elsewhere for satisfaction. Christian women must know once for all that to dress with taste and even with distinction is not a fault; that to use cosmetics is no fault either unless the results are esthetically to be regretted; that adornment as such is one of those questions of convention which is purely accidental and remains completely foreign to the moral order. Virtue owes it to itself to be attractive and even strongly attractive. The only thing that must be avoided is excess. There is excess when a Christian woman devotes all the powers of her mind to becoming as exact a copy as possible of the models in *Vogue* or *Charm* to the point of neglecting her duty. A woman who for love of dress would ruin her husband, neglect her children or even refuse to have them for fear of spoiling her figure would fail by excess.

This viewpoint is full of wisdom; it defends *right use* and at the same time condemns *abuse.*

One of the most ordinary vanities of women is the desire to look young. Husbands are in sympathy with this trait especially when years have rolled over the home. All women need do is purify their intention so as not to offer sacrifice to vanity; they should avoid exaggeration which makes them ridiculous.

They might just as well, for no one will be deceived except those who are willing to be. The world is penetrating almost to the degree of the oculist described in the book *The World as I See It*: This dignified gentleman, wise in the ways of the world, received his patient and listened sympathetically to her symptoms, asked the necessary questions, made his examination and gave his verdict: "Well, it's plain, you have cataracts. It's not a disease, it's sign of age. You told me you were forty-three: I wrote you down in my record as being forty-seven; but you have passed the fifty mark. Don't be disturbed by this."

If husbands have the right to demand that their wives try to keep themselves attractive, it is clearly evident that they in turn must do the same.

The wise advice to wives on the subject of personal appearance which was quoted earlier was followed by this equally judicious advice to husbands:

They have a duty to avoid becoming absorbed completely by their professional concerns. They ought to show themselves not only eager to be in their wife's company but attentive, even loving, and that, whatever be their age. There must be no false modesty or self-consciousness here: a husband owes it to himself to merit each day the love of his wife. Is it right for them to be willing to make the solidity of their home rest solely on the sense of duty they assume their wife possesses? Don't they ever fear losing her love or do they imagine such fears to be restricted to lovers only? Do they then want to treat their wife less considerately than they would treat a mistress?

Let husbands and wives in wise self-possession enjoy a happy, beautiful, and reverent liberty.

A Director's Counsels

In his book *La jeune Mariée*, Léon de la Brière quotes the advice given by a spiritual director to his penitent in the 14th century:

You ought to be attentive and devoted to the person of your husband. Take care of him lovingly, keep his linens clean and orderly because that is your affair. Men should take care of the outside business; husbands must be busy going and coming, running here and there in rain, wind, storm, and sleet; they must keep going dry days or rainy days; one day freezing, another day sweltering, badly fed, badly lodged in poorly heated houses and forced to rest in uncomfortable beds.

But they do not mind any of this because they are comforted by the hope that they will enjoy the care their wife will give them on their return.

How pleasant the thought of taking off his shoes before a cheerful fire, of bathing, putting on clean clothes, fresh shoes and stockings; eating well prepared meals that are properly served; of being sheltered from the inclemencies of the weather; of being obeyed; of retiring to sleep between fresh sheets and under warm bed coverings; good furs.

Remember the country proverb which says that there are three things which drive a man from his house: "a house without a roof, a chimney that smokes, and an argumentative wife."

Therefore, my daughter, I urge you to be gentle, agreeable and good-natured in order to keep in the good graces and the love of your husband.

Then all the while he is busy, he will have his mind and his heart directed toward you and your loving service. He will abandon every other house, every other woman, every other service. It will all be as so much mud compared to you.

Some very definite virtues are needed to follow out such a program:—a very high degree of *pure intention* to accomplish in a supernatural spirit the thousand little attentions required by human love; a deep seated *charity* that becomes more active and more vital by the tender affections of the heart for the beloved; a habit of order which has a place for everything and everything in its place; *skill in home-making*, that essential feminine talent of making a house a home, cheerful and agreeable, a warm and pleasant nest, and the desire on the part of the wife to make as many things as she can herself.

At the beginning of married life love alone without any special attraction toward renunciation makes such a harmony of virtues a possible achievement.

However, there comes a time in many homes when the spirit of renunciation must come to the rescue of love. Not that husband and wife no longer hold any attraction for each other, but they know each other too well to be under any delusions regarding their insufficiencies and they have to be able to pass over many imperfections. It is helpful for them under such circumstances to recall that marriage is a sacrament whose particular grace is to help the wedded couple live their life together.

Honest observers of Christian marriage recognize this: Catholicism has worked a great wonder, "it has succeeded in steadying the vagabond and insatiable sexual urge, it makes long cohabitation possible, it makes characters more supple and tempers dispositions; through constant effort and the joy of duty accomplished, it increases the moral worth of the individual giving meaning thereby to life and to death; it gives to society the most solid support upon which it can stand."

Friendly Argument

JUST as bickering, sulking, and domineering opposition should be avoided by husbands and wives, so free and friendly discussions should be encouraged as an aid to bind their souls in a closer union. Strife and rivalry motivated by self love is one thing, but sane and cordial disagreement or exchange of ideas is quite another. It is from the clash of ideas that light shines forth. And also warmth.

Writing to a young married couple, Bishop Dupanloup said to them:

> You were both astonished the first time I recommended argument to you—friendly argument—and still more astonished when I answered your statement, "we shall never argue," with the comment "So much the worse for you!"
>
> The truth is that in a society so intimate, so constant as marriage, if you do not feel free to discuss and even to engage in friendly argument, it is evidence of constraint between you; there is something which is preventing the free expansion of your souls.
>
> These little disagreements founded primarily on the affectionate observation of your mutual failings will not alter the peace of your home in the least; on the contrary, I believe that they will establish in it a more profound peace and more intimate union, because they will assure both of you of your reciprocal confidence.

Actually, as it is easy to see, the bishop was advising his spiritual children not so much to argue as to discuss. And if one insists on using the word "argument" it must be modified by the word "friendly." Then let them go to it!

Saint Louis was conversing one day with Queen Marguerite. She was complaining that the king did not have enough pomp in court functions and that he himself did not dress with the magnificence befitting official ceremonies. He thought, on his side, that the queen was taking some advantage of her position and that she gave way to excess in the richness of her dress.

"Would it really please you if I dressed more magnificently?" asked the king.

"Yes, I so wish you would."

"Very well then, I shall do so, because the law of marriage urges the husband to try to please his wife. But since this obligation is reciprocal, it is only right that you should conform to my desire."

"And what is that?"

"That you get into the habit of dressing as simply as possible!"

Well done! In friendly arguments such as this, charity as well as finesse and courtesy scores its point.

Don't think you must always be right. You ought to defend your point of view but you should not be hostile to the opposite viewpoint just because it's the opposite viewpoint and before you ever begin to discuss. Two minds are better than one—unless of course they're two negatives.

If the other person is right or it is better for the sake of peace to pull down your flag, then give in graciously and without bitterness.

Feminine Faults

WOMAN has a lively imagination; that is an asset. It can, however, soon become a fault; she readily builds up fanciful notions, and because an object is pleasant and flatters her taste, she seizes upon it as something worth having, confounding the attractive with the good, and salves her conscience with this false sense of value.

A critic could say with no little truth, "Every woman has three lives—a life she *endures*, a life she *wants*, and a life she *dreams about*; the first is made up of the things she does despite the fact they do not please her, the second is made up of the things she does because they please her and the third, of the things she doesn't do either because she can't or because even while desiring them she does not actually want them."

The third trait is the most interesting—this dream-life is the one that occupies woman the most. She plots situations to suit her fancy in which through the power of her imagination she is the heroine. The result is that she chafes at the impossibility of actually achieving what her imagination conceives or her sensibilities evoke.

Man, being obliged to plunge himself into things, to lose himself in occupations which if not more engrossing than home-tasks are at least more evident as to their consequences and much less conducive to meanderings of the imagination, is more given to hard-headed realism. He is in danger of living too much in the prosaic and of lacking verve; woman is generally not lacking in verve, but she easily lands in the stars for riding a myth.

Further, man, unless he is born talkative—and then he is truly obnoxious—is much less tempted to loquaciousness than woman. Knowing better than woman how difficult it is to be informed and being unwilling to talk unless he is informed, he is more discreet, less discursive; woman, less impressed by the necessity of being well-informed before speaking, begins by talking; she learns later.

Since woman's intuitions are much more rapid, she manages to talk on almost any subject without knowing much of anything thoroughly; it is a wonderful help to speak with ease because she is not hampered by the difficulty of being exact.

In addition woman has greater zeal, she is more apostolic, she has proselytizing in her blood. When Our Lord wanted to evangelize Sichem, it was a woman he sent—the Samaritan woman. And the work was well done; she quickly told her friends and acquaintances—all the people of the little village—what she had said to Jesus and what Jesus had said to her, even the admonition He had given her *"Thou hast said well, 'I have no husband,' for thou hast had five husbands, and he whom thou now hast is not thy husband."*

The love to talk is so strong in a woman that she does not hesitate to speak evil of herself to satisfy it.

Some cynic credits these cruel words to a child. Sympathetic friends asked the little one what his father's last words were. He said, "Papa did not say any last words; Mamma was with him to the end." It is too clever to be true.

It is a well known and incontestable fact that there are many women who possess exquisite discretion. Indeed, if men were not also inveterate talkers, would they find so much occasion as they do to speak unkindly of women?

The Psychology of a Mother

FRANÇOIS MAURIAC gives us a keen analysis of a phase of maternal psychology:

So did our mother appear to me: a creature above all creatures... It is strange to think that the most mediocre women and even the most wicked have been in the eyes of their little boy this almost divine being.

... The child must grow, withdraw from his mother; it requires separation for him to judge this creature of whom he was born. It is necessary for her to let this man, her son, try his luck, take risks, love a woman and take her to himself. All that seems simple and in keeping with the wish of nature. Yet, it is just that which gives rise to a drama more often than one would think.

... The hen drives away the grown chick who persists in following her but many women do not have that instinct. In their son they never see the child die; and this graying man that they wait on, that they scold, is still a little boy to them.

Further on he says:

As we advance in life, we perceive that man in his declining years has as much need of his mother as when he was a child. In truth, the child in us never dies; as soon as sickness attacks us and disarms us, the child is there again, that demanding child, who needs spoiling, confidence, who wants to be consoled and cradled. And that is why very often, the wife from instinct becomes a mother again at the bedside of this sick man; she assumes for the man whom weakness has reduced to a child the role of the mother who is no longer there.

Such is perhaps the greatest marvel of the feminine heart—the intermingling of maternal and conjugal love within it, so fused into one that there remains only this tenderness of the wife bending over her wounded and suffering companion; this tenderness of which poor Verlaine dreamed when he wrote these two lines:

> "How I am going to love you, beautiful little hands
> Clasped for a moment, you who will close our eyes."

Coleridge has said it well:

> A mother is a mother still the holiest thing alive.

Unhappily, what has contemporary society not done to "kill the mother."

In how many places, children are said to belong to the State; they do not even have to take the name of their parents; mothers are merely the material producers of the living persons which the country, the factories, and the army need. Their generative organs are considered. Their heart, not at all!

In other places maternity is so ridiculed that to have a family, particularly a large family, instead of being a glory, is an evidence of simple mindedness, old-fashioned ideas, and stupidity.

Again, selfishness has been developed to such a point that

while sterility may not be directly advocated, an immoderate limitation of births has been effected. To be tied down with children! No, thank you!

Before the war, Mauriac justly commented:

"Everything takes place in the world as if there existed a leader of gambling, a leader of the ball who feels that to fulfil his designs he must first of all *strike at the mother*."

And these last lines have become more timely than ever:

"In the world that it will be necessary to reconstruct, effort will have to bear upon this aim: *to restore woman to her true place*, to give her back her *essential mission*."

Courageous Mothers

EVERY woman, by the fact that she becomes a mother, is courageous, at least in regard to all that concerns her children.

She does not consider the trouble it is for her to watch at their bedside, to take care of them, to feed them, to help them; and if danger ever threatens them she will brave any peril to save them. Our Lord's example of the mother hen gathering her chicks under her wing is touching and at the same time far below the realities of maternal psychology.

Sometimes this courage grows to unbelievable force. It is enough to recall many instances of this during the war. Times of peace are not without their examples. Here is one that is profoundly beautiful:

At a certain high school located by the seashore, several students who had gone out for an afternoon of swimming were drowned despite the vigilance of the instructors. With which family should the faculty begin to break the bad news? One mother whose son had been killed in the war of 1914-1918, lost two boys in this tragedy. She had a profound faith, a valor without equal. The Father Superior knew her. He would begin with her.

She was admirable. Standing before the two beds, she uttered no complaint, no reproach. The priest wanted to thank her for her delicacy in the face of such grief.

But how was he to inform the other mothers?

"I will go," she said immediately. "They will not be able to say anything to me, for I have lost two."

When misfortune strikes someone belonging to me, do I manifest the same serenity, the same supernatural spirit?

In the course of a pilgrimage from the North of France to Lourdes, a poor child had to be taken off the train at Poitiers. His mother and he were going to petition Our Lady for the cure of his malady which was in its last stages. Mary doubtless thought it better not to let this poor child on earth any longer. Shortly after the train left Tours, he died. At the Poitiers station the waiting room was quickly arranged to receive him. The mother remained near the body of her little one while the necessary preparations were made. She was not weeping, she held the child on her knees, she was praying. "You would think it was Our Lady of Seven Dolors," whispered a sympathetic onlooker. It was true. She was not upset by the going and coming; she was absorbed in her suffering or rather she was dominating it; there was no outburst, no sobbing; she was praying. It was as if a halo of holiness surrounded her.

In sorrow it is not necessary to parade an impassibility which does not belong to earth. Our Lord wept over Lazarus. But it is essential to rise above the pain, to supernaturalize it; not to let it crush us; to understand through our tears that God is always good, and that if He makes us suffer, it is not to break us but to lift us up, to let us share His Calvary, to give us the means of sharing more richly in the Redemption.

O my God, I offer You my poor heart ravaged, bruised and aching. Crucified Jesus, help me in my crucifixion. I unite my tears with the Blood of Your wounds. May all serve for the good of my dear ones, for souls, for all souls.

Courageous Fathers

IF MOTHERS who have a profound faith can give evidence of a courageous zeal, fathers who are animated by solid religious principles can also offer examples of singular magnanimity.

A young Jesuit who had come from a large family was stricken with a sudden fatal illness. Hurriedly his parents were sent for. When they arrived their boy was already in his agony and died before their eyes. As soon as he had gasped his last breath, the father knelt down and leaning toward his wife asked, "If you will, dear, let us recite the Magnificat that God called our boy to religious life and that He took him at the age of Saint Aloysius."

Pierre Termier, the famous Christian geologist had a son. One day, the boy who was then fourteen years old, came home from school in gay spirits. He took the elevator to go to their apartment. There was an accident on the way up and the boy's head was badly crushed, causing instant death. The mother was overcome with grief. Her husband said to her, "Believe sincerely, my poor wife, that if God asks such a sacrifice of us, it is not for the pleasure of making us suffer, but for the eternal happiness of our child."

In how many homes where death has come because of the war has God been able to admire heroic resignation like this and superhuman joys in trial!

Assuredly, the designs of Divine Providence are mysterious. Why, why have all these young lives been snuffed out before they were able to attain virtues or enjoy the achievements of maturity? There is doubtless the *possibility for expiation;* who will ever know the power for reparation that all these holocausts will have in the life of a people called to offer them?

Then too there are individual reasons. How do we know what would have become of so-and-so or such a one among the young men of our acquaintance if they had lived? Being mortal, they have died. Too young, no doubt. But who knows if this death in their youth has not assured their eternity? We judge as the world judges—the only precious thing seems to be life on earth. Really the only precious thing is eternal happiness. Perhaps many of these youthful dead, had they lived in our world of sin, mingling with sin, would have lived in sin and died in sin. Is it not better, a thousand times better that they should have fallen at twenty in a magnificent act of generosity than to fall later at fifty or sixty with hell facing them?

Without even mentioning hell, what do a few years more bring to life if they must be passed—let us suppose they have been so passed—in spiritual insignificance and moral poverty?

To leave, if leave they must, is it not better that it be in beauty and in the exercise of heroic courage?

To be sure these noble thoughts cannot suppress the sufferings of fathers or of mothers. But in whatever situation we may be or whatever trial we must endure ought not faith always animate us? God never permits evil except that good may come. That is the truth we heard Pierre Termier recalling to his wife before the dead body of their son. I must tell it to myself in every trial and especially when faced with the bereavement of a dear one's early death.

The Lord gave and the Lord has taken away. Blessed be the name of the Lord; that is how saintly Job spoke. That is how I want to speak in my turn.

A Mother's Zeal

A MARRIED woman, the mother of a family, writes:

"I do not lack zeal; it is ardent, but is it well understood? I should like to lead all men to be good, virtuous Christians, but my position offers me so few occasions to put my zeal to work."

Is it really true that a wife, a mother, a woman who stays at home has so little opportunity for the apostolate?

There is first of all the good she can do her children by simply being near them and letting the flames of divine love which she nourishes within her soul penetrate them. Anyone who loves God and is eager for the salvation of his brethren cannot ever hide the inmost concern of his soul—this desire to glorify God as much as possible and to coöperate with his best effort for the sanctification of the world.

To practice the devotion of duty faithfully performed is no less efficacious than a more spectacular apostolate. To manifest by one's example that the Will of God holds first place, that caprice counts for nothing, and that true happiness is in faithful, generous, fervent service is an apostolate in itself.

To *bear witness* to a *great* religion before the children calls for zeal. The mother quoted before seems aware of this. She says, "To unfold religion to them as a vast system, which it really is, a system which envelops nature and humanity to unite them to God, cannot but give them a desire to know it."

So many educators and so many mothers fail miserably in this; they teach the children a religion without breadth, a religion which instead of delighting them repels them. That of course is the result of their not having sufficiently profound and sufficiently broad religious knowledge themselves. They have perhaps never read since they left school, no longer studied religious problems; they are satisfied to use their meager equipment into which erroneous ideas may have slipped and as a consequence they are incapable of answering difficulties or even imparting any enthusiasm to those with whom they speak.

Then there is the apostolate than can be exercised at home. Many wives regret that their husbands have not advanced farther religiously or that they are remiss in the practice of their religion generally because of a lack of intellectual Christian training.

Let them do all they possibly can to help their husbands and count on God to do the rest.

"I count on my daughters," continues the woman quoted before, to accomplish a task that I have barely begun although I believed I was working at it. Let them pray often for their father that God may enlighten him on the important obligations of Christianity, that the world and its prejudices may quietly withdraw from his soul in order to let the true light shine in it with full splendor. Charles is good, fundamentally good; it seems to me that the uprightness of his heart, his excellent qualities call for a more perfect understanding of the truth. He has good will, respect for religion, esteem for virtue but he does not have within himself all the resources necessary. It is not his fault. God will doubtless accomplish His work and my children will have the consolation of seeing their father become a good and perfect Christian; it is the desire of my soul."

And what about home-life? Is there no room for improvement? It is difficult, generally unwise to preach. The same holds true in regard to the circle of relatives, friends, and visitors who are often at the home. But a beautiful testimony of the Christian Faith in daily living will win hearts.

Is this not a very extensive field for apostolic zeal?

Domestic Help

A RECENT book on marriage is filled with splendid suggestions for happy home-life. One of its most interesting chapters is entitled "Those Who Help Us." It glorifies the domestic personnel, those who despite the beautiful derivation from the ancient word prefer now to be called *the help*.

It is clear first of all that their reason for existence is not that their employers have a right to lead a lazy life because the help dispense them from working. Those who secure help for themselves must work as well as their servants. Since the demands of motherhood or of education for the mother or father, or professional duties outside the home constitute heavy obligations which will not leave time for all the housework too, it is easy to understand that they will call in helpers.

The ancient Latin word *famuli* which was used to designate the servants who shared the life of the family, *familia*, strikes the right note. Hired help should not be slaves in the service of hard and overbearing idlers; they are an enlargement of the family for a common task in which all hearts and all activities performed together form but a single unit, with each person in his proper place, but in intimate cohesion with the rest, or ought we not say, "intimate communion" with the rest.

Thanks be to God, we can still find employers who do consider their servants in this light and also servants whose spirit of charity makes their task if not always easy at least always loved, servants for whom it is an honor to *serve*.

In reality, masters of the house as well as hired help have the duty to serve. The useless have no place at all in Christian society. Saint Paul says that they who do not work have no right to eat. But the same kind of service is not required of all. In an army, there are those who fight on the front line, those who transport food supplies and munitions, those who prepare the ammunition behind the lines or spend themselves in the numberless tasks the country needs done. All contribute to the good of the whole.

To serve in the more humble positions requires a greater virtue, above all when this service requires subordination to those who have authority; we will never praise those too much who accept the employment of serving others, not with jealousy in their hearts and only because necessity forces them, but with humility and charity.

Those who are obliged to have domestic help ought to hold them in high esteem. They would of course fail in their duty if they let each one have his own way in the running of things; in domestic society as well as in every other society, there must be authority to be respected.

Employers must not demand tyrannically more than is fitting; they should give sufficient recompense for the services rendered. They need not think they have fulfilled their whole duty just because they pay a just wage; in a *family* all have rights, each one according to his position has a right to the affection of all. Employers who are parents must insist that their children be respectful to the help. The help should be invited to live in the atmosphere of the home and while high moral standards must be required of them they should be allowed liberty in their religious life.

A family is a domestic community. The zeal of all must be aroused for the well-being of each and in such a way that God may be glorified to a maximum degree in this nest where the great rule is understood to be not the code of the worldly spirit but the peaceable demands of the Gospel.

Love Out of Bounds

Here is a married individual who has not found in marriage all that marriage seemed to promise or here is one who so far has had perfect happiness. But one fine day there comes into the picture the perfect creature, the dream-person—the ideal.

Oh, to be sure, there is no thought of renouncing one's home, but one dreams of a friendship of a very special kind ... intellectual exchanges ... There will be bodily separation but as high a degree as possible of soul union. They do not wish to fall. They will not fall. Is such a noble friendship forbidden?

A noble friendship is certainly not forbidden. But is that the case we are considering or is it not rather a dangerous friendship of which we speak? When beauty—let us suppose it is not just an imaginary ideal—does not coincide with the good, can there be anything else possible but seduction and fatal risk?

After all, have you not promised to another the entire gift of yourself. Love does not consist only in the material gift of the body but also and still more in the gift of the soul and of the heart. What then does this mean? Do you think you can divide the divine arrangement? Reserve for your marriage partner the traditional gift of your flesh while you are withdrawing the very part that gives honor and dignity to this tradition—your interior affection and fidelity.

Your partner in marriage has a right to your whole being. The day of your marriage you indicated no division; therefore you are in contradiction to what you have promised, to what God demands and to what your partner expects. Would either of you have accepted the other if you thought the endurance of the bond was based on whim and that an essential reserve was contemplated? Does not marriage involve at one and the same time the body and the heart. There can be no thought then of a simple material fidelity.

Reverse the roles. The temptation which you are experiencing—because it is a temptation and a sly temptation at that—is not experienced by you but by your partner. What would you think of giving in to it then? Would you be willing to accept the situation for yourself that you are tempted to impose on your partner?

You say "we shall never go so far as to be intimate." Are you sure? How can you guarantee that after a primary infidelity you will not fall into a secondary infidelity? And what assurance against surprise have you? If you boldly walk up to danger, do you believe divine grace to be obligated to save you in spite of yourself? How many who like you claimed to be strong and sure of themselves have fallen! All the sins of infidelity in marriage begin like this.

Surely if at the first attack, this perverse love would reveal all its batteries the noble soul would revolt. But it doesn't. It ingratiates itself, slipping in decorously and gently. Patience! It will turn sensual and you will be tricked!

Besides, suppose you do keep your senses in control, are sins of action only to be condemned? What of sins of thought? Of desire? Our Lord said, *that anyone who even looks with lust at a woman has already committed adultery with her in his heart.*

But you say, I shall accept only what is elevated, noble, in this friendship. So you say. But that you will not do because it is practically impossible. Let us just admit your hypothesis for the sake of discussion. All right, it is true for you. Is it true for the other person? Can you say positively that your imprudence will not arouse in him or in her troubled thoughts and desires? You are not an Archangel; the other person is no Seraphim. Well then?...

No! no! Away with lies and false reasoning! Lord, put order into my love. Grant that I may love only according to Your law.

The Folly of Love Out of Bounds

I HAVE meditated on the ethics on this kind of love. Now I shall consider a few examples of its consequences to convince myself of the right attitude if by chance I still need convincing.

Countess Potochka relates in her memoires that during the occupation of Poland by Napoleon she paid too much attention to a young French officer. Her words are interesting: "Faithful to my duties, I would not even consider the possibility of a sentiment that I should have avoided and I contented myself with denying the danger." How many in similar circumstances do just that!

"It seemed permissible to me," she continues, "to entertain friendship for a man who possessed all the qualities one would have desired in a brother." She emphasizes the next point, and it is a current delusion: "I forgot—and this was the greatest of my wrongs—that a young wife ought not to have any other confidant, any other friend than her husband. But then, why did not my husband make me remember it?"

If women can profit by meditating on the whole text, men ought to memorize the last line of it. It is unfortunately only too true that the infidelities of many wives have as their explanation, let us not say excuse, an initial fault on the part of the husband. Likewise the failings of many husbands in regard to marital fidelity have been prepared for at least by the bungling of their wives. Some men and some women try to justify their conduct on the basis of their particular situation.

"We are no longer in the ordinary conditions of marriage. We live fraternally and are consequently more free in our interior life since we have found through experience that a union of souls between us is not possible..." There is only one answer to such a statement: Even when by mutual consent, because of a lack of soul-union, husbands and wives live without practicing bodily union, they still have no right to infidelity of the heart. Such infidelity in addition to being against God's law is opposed to the divine institution of the family.

I saw in the preceding meditation how it is against the law of God.

How is it against the divine institution of the family?

The family is a couple and not an assembly of three persons. *They shall be two in one flesh.* To yield themselves to a passionate love outside of marriage can only augment and accentuate the distance between the husband and wife and introduce an element of damnable licentiousness. And if this new love does not satisfy you, will you have recourse to a third, a fourth? Where will you stop?

Throw away your novel and start living your duty! It is austere perhaps, but it brings its reward with it. Never will an upright soul find peace and happiness in a love which his conscience condemns, which it cannot do otherwise than condemn.

The Prayer of the Married

OF PRIME importance to the married is their prayer together—that precious time in which the two souls united by the sacred bonds of marriage fuse their aspirations, thoughts and desires, forgetting to discriminate which are their own individually and present themselves to God, each mindful of the other, offering themselves in a unity that is continuously strengthened by a mutual love which increases tenfold every day.

Then when God has sent newcomers to the home, there will be prayer in common, each of the little tots and each of the older children will join in the prayer of father and mother and all will recommend to Our Lord the sanctification of the whole assemblage.

If ever circumstances such as war, travels, duties of state require a temporary and perhaps periodic separation, there will be the prayer said at a distance by each of the two hearts torn apart by the goodbyes of parting and the prolongation of the absence—a prayer in which each under the eye of God strives to live together the same moment of life and pleads for the courage to continue the trip in unison to heaven.

Nor is any of this kind of prayer prejudicial to solitary prayer; when one of the two is engaged in the duties of his state or in some apostolic activity, the other more drawn to prayer, can in the silence of the soul seek to acquire from God for both of them and for the whole family, opportune graces. Prayer at such times will not only be prayer of petition but even more—an elevation of the soul to God to adore Him, to keep the Good Master company. There will be few words or specific reflections, but a gift of the heart, a search for union through intimacy of the soul. Or when one participates in the Liturgical prayer of the Church, there will be union of heart with the whole Church, a warmer and more fervent share in the Communion of Saints. The soul at the center of the world joins in the *Sanctus* of the numerous Masses that are being celebrated, and shares in the Great Prayer of Christ for the world.

There remains another form of prayer, the conjoined

prayer of the *parallel union* of *their two lives,* not through any words or special acts, but by the consecration to God of the deeds of all their days, the wife at home, the husband in his office, or store, or shop. *Pray always,* said Our Lord; He did not mean that we must necessarily be always in the act of praying but in a state of prayer which means to so act that one's whole life rises as a prayer because of the offering made of it to God and frequently renewed. The state of prayer is the state of elevation, the explicit or implicit gift made to God of all the minute particles of each instant's activity.

Toward the end of his life, Saint Francis de Sales, overwhelmed by the occupations of his ministry and the responsibilities of a large diocese thought he was obliged to curtail somewhat his extra prayers of devotion. "I am doing," he explained, "what is the same thing as praying."

Mental prayer and vocal prayer are not always possible to the same degree for all, although all must assure themselves of at least the minimum, as the vital prayer of maintaining union with God.

Prayer Together

IF Our Savior's words, *Where two or three are gathered together in My Name, I am in the midst of them,* apply to strangers and persons indifferent to one another, how much more significant they are for two beings destined to be but one heart and one soul! No society can better draw down the graces of God through prayer than the society of man and wife. Already united by so many bonds, what a truly community-union does their conjoined prayer effect!

General Reibell who was asked to write the preface to a World War book took leave to strike this personal note: "There are two habits to which I remained faithful during our expedition: I kept a diary of each day's events and the reflections they aroused in me; then I read a chapter of the *New Testament* and a selection from the *Imitation* in the order my wife and I had agreed upon before parting; in this way we prepared a meeting place for our intimate thoughts across the distances which separated us. If, as happened on rare occasions, I was obliged to neglect this double obligation for a day or two at the most, I made up for it the following days, bringing myself up to date both in my journal and in my reading. When I completed the reading material I began over in the same order as before until the end of the double set of three hundred sixty-five days of our African campaign."

The husband in this case is the one who took the first step. Frequently the lead in the spiritual is taken by the wife. Often husbands are grieved to the depths of their being because they see that their wives do not draw the family to God.

Whether the husband or the wife takes the initiative matters not so much; what does matter is that a Christian family should advance spiritually to the degree of performing together the essential acts of religion.

There will be times when real necessity obliges husband and wife to fulfil certain religious exercises separately; for example, if the wife is nearing the time of her delivery or has just given birth to a child, or if for domestic reasons they must attend different Masses so that someone can be home to take care of the personnel or watch the children...

Aside from such cases, it is desirable that they should perform as many of their spiritual duties as they possibly can together; theirs is to be an association. Let them pray together beside their bed, exchange intimate thoughts after an inspiring and spiritual reading done together, say grace before and after meals together and so on through the other opportunities for prayer in their life.

One of the two may have a greater taste for prayer than the other and there is no reason why it should not be satisfied, no reason why the claims of grace and the attractions of the soul should not be followed after the spiritual exercises which should be done together have been fulfilled; duty of state must always come first, must be safeguarded.

In this way independence of soul is assured along with close cooperation, in a worship by two with souls united.

Prayer for Each Other

A FATHER and a mother willingly pray for a son in danger, a sick daughter, a child in distress. But not so frequently do husbands and wives pray for each other. Yet that would be the way they could most easily obtain the graces necessary to achieve their common desires and fulfil their common mission.

How beautiful it would be if, during their evening prayer together, there could be a pause such as the one for the examination of conscience during which time each would pray silently for the other, recommending to God all the other's intentions sensed, guessed, and known as well as those that only God the Master of consciences could know.

Even more beautiful would it be if they would receive Holy Communion together frequently so that each of them could speak more intimately to Our Lord about the needs of the other, begging not only temporal but spiritual favors for this cherished soul.

Cana Conferences are becoming more widespread. Here both husband and wife listen to the same discourses, make the same meditations and are called upon to form the same resolutions. They are not expected to make their retreat as two married celibates but as a couple together, to be sanctified conjointly.

They will in their Cana Conferences experience at times no doubt a little sly joy,—quite pardonable to be sure,—at hearing the very things they have been trying to convince their partner of, stressed energetically by a qualified speaker and with every chance of being effective since at such times the soul is more receptive.

They both become compromised in the eyes of the other; neither has any excuse in the future for going off on a tangent.

A further advantage of Cana Conferences is that the couple can more easily advance in holiness if their striving after it is synchronized. In many homes, the wife can manage to slip away for an annual retreat which has become habitual for her while the husband according to his reasoning can never find the time for these periods of recollection. As a consequence there is a sort of spiritual cleavage between them. They do not advance equally with the consequent danger that to one the piety of the other may seem too rigid or too absorbing.

Let the wife, have, if she will, her additional practices of devotion to supplement the couple's united prayers; if she is intelligently pious they can only serve for the good of the home. But it remains true that her efforts ought to be directed less to surpassing her husband in spiritual exercises than to elevating his spirituality to the heights of her own, assuming that hers is perfectly balanced, warm and vibrant.

Certain timidities must be overcome. At the beginning of married life, the husband will accept everything from his wife. He expects her to surpass him spiritually and above all he expects her to draw him forward. Let her then use her power prudently, intelligently, delicately in virtue of her love. Let her not be motivated by the desire to count her fine successes but to spiritualize her home. Her husband can only be grateful for it. He will welcome her influence, profit by it, follow it.

Marriage and a Life of Prayer

IT IS a mistake to think that only priests or religious can attain to a life of profound payer.

A religious priest, the biographer of a young girl of the world who had been an example of magnificent fidelity and the recipient of singular graces from God, recounts that one of the theologians who examined the book expressed great admiration for the young girl. "People believe," he said, "that the great graces of contemplation are scarcely ever found in the midst of the world. I have found in cloisters and monasteries and among the clergy, souls who have received astonishing graces of light and of ease in prayer. I can therefore speak from experience. However, the two souls who seemed to me to be the most favored were neither priests nor nuns but two persons living in the world, two mothers of families." He added, "They were far from being complacent about the favors they received; they believed them to be quite natural and never dreamed that they themselves were singularly privileged."

And all that while living in the world as married women!

Then we have the example of a doctor, an excellent practitioner in a large city, much in demand because of his great skill and superior knowledge. Note his deep life of prayer as revealed from the following quotations from some of his letters:

I recollect myself in the course of my professional visits, going from one duty to another, those duties which present themselves to me so clearly as acts of charity to my neighbor in whom I have the impression of ministering to the suffering Christ.

In the interval which separates one act of charity from another, there spontaneously wells up in my heart irresistible movements of adoration, a necessary worship of praise, a humble and self-abasing offering of my impotence, a very real pain at being separated from the Well-Beloved of my soul, and, in the midst of it all, a consoling peace and a strong leaning on God who lifts me above depressing physical fatigue and wearing privation.

Another time he wrote:

The sight of souls so little concerned about God causes me pain and heartache. I should like to see all creatures praise God, concern themselves solely with Him and refer all to Him. I have great difficulty lending myself to the thousand little things of *here-below* which have no direct connection with God.

This interior union with God in no way hindered his exterior ministry. With what soul power did he accomplish it!

In the midst of overwhelming activities, an impression of profound solitude enfolds my soul. Action is no longer anything more for me than the accomplishment of duty, for the only duty of my life, leaving out of the picture any consideration of this frightful *I* and accomplishing everything for a single purpose always present, always engulfing me—God.

One might say that there is substituted for the egoism which is proper to me a power which is foreign to me but which draws me on while exercising over my will a force which impels and which is ever new.

In his last letter dated August, 1936, we have these thoughts.

It has pleased God (I should never think of asking Him for it) to grant me six months of immobilization because of a cardiac lesion. A Garden of Gethsemani? Amen.

I was formerly taught what adoration and thanksgiving mean. Now I am immersed in adoration and thanksgiving. I have been taught that we fulfill the highest apostolate in the place where God for all eternity wants us to be. Therefore, I say three times over *Amen* and *Thank You*, my God.

Choice Graces

PERHAPS on reading the beautiful selections from the doctor's letters I have somewhat envied his union with God. Perhaps there arose in my mind the question: "What would I have to do to achieve such close intimacy with God?"

First of all, I must remember that such a degree of union with God is in the domain of gratuitous gifts. Our Lord gives them or does not give them as He sees fit. That is His own concern. In themselves, these gifts are no forecast of sanctity in the person who receives them. Someone can be quite perfect and never receive these favors; a person can be most faithful and attentive but either because of special difficulties of temperament or of capacity or because of God's permission he will never receive like gifts.

By the very fact that they are gratuitous, they are inherently out of proportion with human efforts. They are liberalities of God that we are powerless to merit in the formal sense of the term. I am walking along the boulevard; I meet several poor persons along the way; I give something to the second not to the first, to the fifth and not to the fourth. To none of them do I owe a thing. I have bestowed a favor pure and simple and no one can lay claim to my bounty as his due.

So too with the special favors we are considering. They manifest the munificence of God and do not prove the holiness of the recipient.

It is evident though that if God is free to bestow extraordinary graces according to His own will, in general, He dispenses them to those who by their generosity have given assurance beforehand that these favors will fall on good ground. If by right they are purely gratuitous, in fact they most often recompense a generosity that is particularly ardent, a devotedness and a striving that has been heroically maintained.

In practice, I should let God play His hand. He is well-versed in what He is doing. I should not presume to dictate to Him the method He should follow. I can play my hand too. His very own specialty is liberality; mine should be generous love. I ought to be bent on giving, not on receiving.

If in the course of my life of striving, God is pleased to give me a keener relish of Him, an understanding of Him beyond my knowledge of His perfections, a love for prayer and for sacrifices He will have free sway in me. I shall praise Him with my whole soul; but it is not to win these favors that I intend to push my fervor to its peak.

If, on the contrary, He lets me on the level of common prayer and the ordinary state of the general run of people; if He even abandons me to a spell of aridity—a common trial of earth—either for periods of time or perhaps permanently, I shall cast myself upon His love and beg Him to insure my faith in Him and to preserve my fidelity. I know what I am worth—not very much.

The soldier ought to serve. If his Captain notices him and puts him on the list for the Legion of Honor, fine! A red ribbon, however, adds nothing to the value of a man. He is worth what he gives and not what he receives.

I shall strive to give much.

TRAINING

The First Years

In his book *Something of Myself for My Friends Known and Unknown,* Rudyard Kipling uses as the keynote for the first chapter, the following quotation: "Give me the first six years of a child's life; you can have the rest."

How parents ought to meditate on those words!

Why did Rudyard Kipling speak in this vein?

Before these first six years there is of course the question of heredity. Every man is an heir and every man is an ancestor. Children do resemble their parents. We have considered this before.

There is a second kind of hereditary influence—the formation that is given even before marriage by the father and the mother. "When does the education of the child begin?" Napoleon was asked. He replied, "Twenty years before its birth in the education of its mother."

From its mother? From its father too. But the mother is unquestionably a prime influence since until the child is at least six the principal care of the child is in the hands of the mother.

What a mistake to let a child give in to all its whims!

"But he doesn't understand," people say. "You can't reason with a baby in the cradle."

No, of course not, but from the cradle on, the child can be taught many things well. Not by reasoning but by habit-formation.

Here are two mothers; both of them have a baby. Naturally both babies cry when they want their desires known. In one case, the mother who knows that all the needs and legitimate wants of the baby have been satisfied, lets it cry; it should like to advance if it could, the time for its bottle. No, it will be served at the right time, not before. The little one soon perceives that no one pays any attention to its demands and ceases its tempestuous howling.

In the other case, the minute the baby begins to cry, the mother dashes to soothe it. She cannot resist her baby's cry. Instead of rearing it for itself, she rears it for herself, because she suffers too much from hearing it call or because its tears unnerve and disturb her. She gives in. She is lost. The little one is going to become frightfully capricious. Later she will not be able to control it. "Cry away my little man; you don't need a thing," would be a more wholesome attitude than yielding, provided of course, she knows that the baby is all right and that her conduct is not motivated by laziness but by a true desire to train the child.

That is only one detail. But in everything she should be guided by the same principle—the true good of the child. Then at six years it will know how to obey. And if the mother follows through progressively with the development of the child, helping it to use properly its young liberty, she has the game in her own hands. All is not finished. It might be more correct to say that all is beginning; nevertheless the mother has successfully come through a vital stage. Up to this point it is properly called training, a most necessary period indeed. This training will develop into real education. If the early training has been lacking, the succeeding education becomes almost impossible; for how can one erect a stable structure on a volcano; how build a firm will on a nature perpetually wavering and swayed by caprice?

Kipling was right. In the light of the truth he expressed let me correct, if necessary and if there is still time, my method of acting.

Love for Children

It is essential to love children enough:
1. To be willing to have them
2. To be able to endure their demands
3. To be able to supernaturalize one's love for them.

1. *To be willing to have them:* I meditated on this point when I considered the law of fecundity and charity in marriage.

2. *To be able to endure their demands:* Very little children have no defense and no power. Someone must always come to their assistance. Happy those who can guess these needs of theirs. Mothers generally know the secret of that. But just the same the baby will cry, become restless and set up a howl. Every baby in the cradle is a revolutionary in the bud; the best established customs ought to give way to its caprice, or so it thinks, and if its desires are not obeyed, it storms and puts the house in an uproar.

Furthermore the child is born cunning. It finds out very quickly the best ways to get what it wants, not through reasoning but by intuition. Such an action, such an attitude produces the desired result; the opposite way of acting does not work. There is no more limpid logic to be found anywhere.

Nor any more transparent pride. It knows itself to be the center of the household and is not ashamed to act the part. It is a monarch. Papa and mamma, brothers, sisters, and all the other members of the household make up its court, each one dancing attendance to its thirty-six wills. Furthermore, it distributes as rewards the favor of its broad smiles.

Later it will have to play, jump about and run; to break things will be a delight; so too will it be fun just to sit still and listen to a story. The little girl will be taken up with the care of her doll and if her elders have bought her a doll that says *papa, mamma,* they need expect to hear nothing else all day! The little boy will play soldier or train or if he has received a drum or whistle for Christmas, the household will be well aware of it!

Parents should take serenely and as a matter of course the baby's pranks and outbursts, working at the same time toward a wise training, the prelude of a wise education. They should expect their growing children to make noise, to be curious, to want to touch everything; furthermore, they need not feel obliged constantly, to put a damper on their romping and their noise; whenever and wherever it is necessary they ought to explain to the children what they may do and what they ought to avoid.

3. *To be able to supernaturalize one's love for them:* Parents should strive to love their children not only because of their natural charm but for higher and truly divine reasons. "I love my children so much," parents say as if they were vying with one another; mothers especially are likely to talk like that. It makes one want to warn them, "If only you could love them a little less but love them a little better." Or rather, since we never love too much but badly, "Love them as much as you wish but for their sakes, not for your own."

For their sakes: Therefore do not give in to all their caprices; do not try to spare them every effort; do not treat them as little idols; do not teach them pride and vanity even from their earliest years.

For their sakes: Therefore be alert to know what might harm them not only in what concerns their body but also in what might even remotely concern their soul.

For their sakes: Therefore, try to discover behind the human silhouette of each of these baptized souls the Holy Trinity dwelling within them and the likeness of Christ; do not rest satisfied until all your training and education is directed to make of them truly holy tabernacles of the Most High and authentic continuations of Christ.

From Three to Five

AT THIS period of their life, children have not in general arrived at an awakening, at least not a complete awakening, of their moral sense. They are midway between the unawareness of their first years and a completely rational contact with life; their principal occupation is play—the little boy will be busy building and tearing down; the little girl will be busy scribbling away at indefinite designs or dressing and undressing her sawdust doll, the first in a series of many dolls.

They will have just the beginning of a contact—depending upon their family, their mother particularly—with the invisible world. They will learn their prayers, know that there is a God who is good and they will hear about little Jesus. They will also know that there are things that are forbidden, but they will not as yet see the wickedness of sin; they take what belongs to mamma without knowing that they are stealing; they do not always tell the truth without knowing really that it is an evil thing to lie and when they do speak untruly it is much more through an instinct of self-defense than through innate perversion. They would go to the end of the world for a kiss and much further still for a piece of candy. But if they must give up the piece of candy to a little brother or sister, they will do it with not too bad a grace but they will see to it that they get a lick of it themselves before parting with it; after all, aren't they being quite generous already? And if for Christmas mother has suggested that they sacrifice some of their sweets to little Jesus, they do it eagerly but see nothing wrong with coming back quietly later *to eat up their sacrifices.*

It is important to capitalize on this marvelous period of the child's life.

Since the child loves to imagine, it is necessary to suggest images to its mind and since the child needs to be educated, these images should be elevating. That can be done very early by using the lives of the saints, the life of Mary and of Jesus. Why not? How many details of Scripture are most picturesque and quite within the grasp of the child's mind; this is especially true if the Gospel episodes have first come by way of the mother's heart; she will know how to awaken without straining, instruct without fatiguing, and adapt it all to the mentality of the child.

A prime guiding principle here is *Never anything inexact!* Children at this age are extremely docile. "Papa said it or Mamma said it," makes it sacred. Therefore, great attention to the stories they are told, to the allusions made or the conversations held in their presence.

At this age the child is inclined to refer everything to itself, but very likely to be disinterested in goodness. By nature it is selfish; it has a terrific sense of ownership; will share nothing; wants everything. Since it has numerous needs and knows itself to be little, it seeks to surround itself with the greatest possible number of things to its own advantage. But if little by little it is taught to look about to see that there are others less privileged, that to give up things for love of another is something fine, it will be found capable of remarkable generosity.

The child at this age has not since the time of its baptism become incrusted with the shell of negligence and the faults an adult might commit; simplicity is inherent in it; it is pure; it has infused Faith and the Holy Spirit in its soul is at ease.

But it is essential to avoid scandalizing the least of these little ones, giving them the example of evil, of impurity even material impurity, of lying, of anger.

Further, the child is readily distracted, forgetful, has its head in the clouds. You speak to it and it listens or does not listen as fancy strikes; it follows its own thought and interior emotion. Your commands fall on its ears like water on marble. You must catch its attention, reiterate your suggestions or commands without impatience on your part or fatigue for the child.

Constant attention is necessary to train them in manners, in proper sleeping habits, in conduct at table; to check the first symptoms of greediness, laziness, lack of discipline, sensuality. The child is still thoughtless but the educator must not be. Long explanations are not needed; a word, a simple look go a long way and speak volumes at times.

Parents should never lose courage even if the results are imperfect. Let them examine their methods and change them if necessary. Let them see in these little ones only Christ—*Whatsoever you do to these, the least of My brethren, you do unto Me.*

The Art of Giving Children Faults

THERE are two great means of developing faults in children: First by giving them a bad example; second, by spoiling them.

1. *Giving them a bad example:* All men are imitators; children are more exposed than others to the appeal of imitation; they love to imitate adults, and by preference those within their immediate circle particularly their parents who appear to them as exceptional beings in whom there is nothing reprehensible.

Is the mother vain? The daughter too will be vain; she

will speak, act, dress, not for an ideal of beauty in keeping with her condition, her station, but for the favorable opinion of others. She will strive to surpass all her companions, her friends, by the cut of her clothes and the extremes of style; she will attach a considerable, yes even an exaggerated, importance to the tiniest details of her costume; she will suffer a severe attack of jealousy when she believes someone outshines her.

Is the father proud? Does he try to exaggerate his good points and belittle those of others or refuse to recognize them? His son will be a snob, disdainful of others, self-sufficient, pretentious, arrogant, obstinate and will manifest no understanding whatever as far as others are concerned.

Are the parents loquacious? Contentious? Sharp in their speech? Their children will be intemperate in speech, quarrelsome, envious.

Are the parents deceitful? The children are in danger of becoming liars. Are the parents generally indiscreet in conversation, passing judgments thoughtlessly? The children already too much inclined to judge everything from the height of their grandeur will pass snap judgments, unjust and untimely criticisms.

Do the parents manifest their love of ease, of wealth, even a thirst to acquire riches by any means? The children are likely to be selfish, attached to their own comfort, cheaters on occasion.

2. *Spoiling them:* Some parents are too harsh and do not encourage their children at all. Others, by far the greater number, are too indulgent, flatter their children, satisfy all their whims.

Parents who spoil their children do not seek their good, love them for their sakes. No, it is a form of self-love; the parents seek themselves in the child. Such parents cannot put firmness into the education they try to give; they cannot punish when necessary; prevent escapades; secure obedience; they cannot defend themselves against any caprices.

"But if I lack kindness," you say, "my child will withdraw from me; in difficult times he will avoid speaking to me; I shall not have his confidence. If on the contrary I have multiplied my kindnesses to him, he will remain open, I shall keep a hold on him."

There is no question here of failing in kindness; it is a question of forbidding oneself any weakness. Far from having to fear the loss of the child's confidence, if one is judiciously firm, the parents shall win the child's confidence because they are wisely strong. When the children understand that in the marks of affection their parents bestow on them they are not seeking something personal but only the good of their children, they will be quick to realize that in the severity their parents inflict on them, there is likewise no trace of caprice but only the desire for their good as before.

It is precisely that realization which has educative force— this contact with strong and detached souls.

The Untimely Laugh

A FAMOUS French critic relates this incident about one of his colleagues. "He was only five years old and he had committed some misdemeanor. His mother who was busy painting put him outside her studio as a penance and closed the door to him. Through the closed door the little fellow using his most earnest and pleading tone begged for pardon promising not to be naughty again. His mother did not answer. He made so much ado that she opened the door and on his knees he crawled toward her, pleading with her as he came, in a voice so earnest and an attitude so pathetic that by the time he arrived before her, she could not refrain from laughing. Immediately he stood up and changed his tone, 'So,' he cried, 'since you are making fun of me, I will never ask pardon again.' And he never did."

To appear amused at an act of generosity on the part of a child is the best way to make it lose forever a taste for generosity. Beyond a doubt, the mother was not laughing at the sentiment that stirred the soul of her child, but only at his heroics in expressing it. But the child could not distinguish. She laughed; therefore she laughed at him; if she laughed at him, he must have seemed ridiculous; never again would be put himself in a ridiculous attitude. His little conscience is geometrical. His reasoning is utterly simple but it is in keeping with his age.

Can anyone ever measure how much a poor child who has done wrong has to overcome himself in order to ask pardon? He blunders and then what happens? Can't you see? He is wounded by the pain he gave his parents, tortured perhaps by remorse, frightened by the prospect of punishment. His request for pardon is expressed in sobs and long drawn out breaths. But he is truly sorry. Born actor that he is, it is possible that he might deliberately exaggerate the outward manifestation of his repentence, but is it true? Most often the child is honest and except where there is direct proof to the contrary, his action is sincere, expressing exactly what he feels.

How disconcerted he is then when his repentence is met in a way he so little expected and so misunderstood. Sometimes the child merely wants to confide a secret or in his simplicity he asks a question without realizing its import or he expresses an enthusiasm he hopes to have shared or a desire to be generous that he longs to have approved, but if he sees that no one listens to him or that his elders appear to smile at his beautiful dreams or his requests for explanations, he learns to close up like a clam; no one will ever know anything more of his little soul; he will keep his thoughts secret and will try to find for himself the answers to the troubling questions that torment him.

There is another kind of ill-timed laugh, the laugh of parents or others at the morally bad actions of a child.

In considering the behavior of children, careful distinction must be made between two kinds of acts: those which have no moral import such as skinning their knees in a fall while running, soiling their clothing through inattention, turning over an inkbottle through clumsiness, and those which do have moral significance such as stealing, lying, disobedience and lack of respect.

It sometimes happens that people are extremely severe and make much ado over the acts in which no moral responsibility is involved, but they joke or laugh at words and acts that are morally wrong. Nothing so deforms the consciences of children. They learn to consider as serious acts those over which their elders have made a scene but which actually are not serious at all; to consider as insignificant those acts which made others smile but which are morally quite serious.

All this means that as a parent, as an educator, I must be watchful over my smiles and my laughter. I cannot be inopportune in their use.

Love versus Maternal Instinct

A MOTHER of a family, herself a noble and spiritual educator wrote:

We never succeed in making of our children all that we should like to make of them; and sometimes we do not accomplish anything of what we thought we could accomplish. The role of educator in theory offers many charms but in its fulfillment how many thorns! Not to become discouraged is in itself quite an achievement.

The most important virtue to engender in the souls of children is confidence.

Children always have faults; they develop with age; when one fault is destroyed, another appears. What ought to be developed first is confidence; a confidence which will make them docile solely because of the conviction that there can be nothing better for them than the arrangements of the persons who are training them; but when they seem to torment them or cross them, they truly have their good at heart. The most agreeable training is not always the most salutary. Far from it! Adversity and contradiction are useful for all ages but particularly for the young, to correct their violent tendencies and strengthen their undeveloped wills. For those who consider everything from God's viewpoint, adversity gives the final touch; it adorns as with gold one in whom virtue is deeply rooted. But how can one call upon this harsh instructor to teach one's very own children? Mothers are too tender to be perfect educators or rather their tenderness has about it too much sensitivity which, we might say, aggravates the eternal conflict between the spiritual man and the carnal man. Maternal love is often too much hampered by maternal instinct which protests and prevents the forceful action that ought to be taken.

This distinction between real maternal love in the full sense of the word and maternal instinct should be maintained; the author of the preceding lines is alert to the difference and concerned about not confusing them; one of her daughters had a particularly difficult temperament; the mother encouraged herself to exercise the necessary firmness with her just as with her other children:

I shall set myself the duty of not being weak, too easy, of not giving in to all their desires. I shall try to give them the reason for my decisions, but I shall believe that I do them a service by putting some obstacles to their desires. Kindness will dictate my conduct; I hope that kindness will render it bearable for them.

If I fear the opposition of a strong character and the tendencies of a spirit which promises to be frank and curious in Laurence, I fear in her sister the faults arising from an easier temperament which is avid for praise. Will she be able to hold her own with the firmness I should like to see her acquire? My God, I cannot foresee that; I place her interests as I place my own into Your Hands.

That is the way to act: To try to adopt toward each child the method most likely to succeed, and when that is done, to trust the rest to Divine Providence.

Training in Obedience

THE father is the father; the mother is the mother. Each one's role is different; together they must harmonize.

This is particularly essential when there is question of the exercise of authority over the children.

The principal authority is centered in the father; the mother who is associated with him, shares this authority. Both have therefore according to their respective roles the mission to command; the father in a way that is not more harsh but more virile; the mother in a way that is not more easy-going—she ought to demand the same things the father requires and with the same firmness—but more gently expressed.

Parental action must be common, harmonious, coordinated, directed to the same end. Extremely unpleasant conditions are created if the mother for example tolerates an infraction of an order given by the father.

The father on his part should avoid too great sternness,

an uncalled for severity of tone or what is worse, cruelty. The mother should guard against weakness and insufficient resistance to the tears of the child or the cute little ways it has discovered for avoiding punishment or side-tracking a command.

She ought to be particularly cautious not to undermine paternal authority either by permitting the children to disobey his injunctions or, under pretext of tempering the father's severity, by countermanding his orders. It is from the father himself that she should secure the necessary relaxation of requirements if she feels he is being too rigid; never should she on her own change a decision that the father has given. Otherwise the children will soon play the father and mother against each other; they will know that they can have recourse to mamma when papa commands something and they will be able to disregard the order. Father and mother both lose their authority in this way to their own great detriment. The wife discredits her husband in the eyes of the children and herself as well. Never should the children sense the least discord between their parents either in regard to their principles or their methods of training. Quick to exploit the rift, they will also be quick to get the upper hand. It is the ruination of obedience. The mother can blame herself for working forcefully for its destruction.

She is perfectly justified in trying to make the execution of the father's orders more agreeable; that is quite another thing. But in this case she must justify the conduct of the father and not seem to blame him by softening the verdict.

Husband and wife are but one; he, the strength; she, the gentleness. The result is not an opposition of forces but a conjoining of forces; the formation of a single collective being, the couple.

Another point in this matter of obedience: Never let the

children command the parents. How many parents, mothers especially, betray their mission! Parents are not supposed to give orders indiscriminately but wisely; when they have done this, they should not go back on a command. To command little is the mark of firm authority; but to demand the execution of what one has commanded is the mark of a strong authority.

There should be no fussiness, no irritation, only calm firmness. The child, who becomes unnerved, and certainly not without cause, before a multiplicity of disconnected orders that fall upon him from all sides, submits before a gentle and unbending authority. Calmness steadies him and unyielding firmness unfailingly leads him to obey.

Children Who Command

IF THE training of the children from babyhood has been well done, there is the happy possibility that the parents can really be masters in their own home later on. Not that they need to exercise a fierce militarism; they should rather inspire a holy and joyous liberty; but when they give a command, the children must know that there is nothing for them to do but obey.

They will give few commands, avoiding such perpetual admonitions as "Stand up straight! Don't slouch! Do this. Don't do that," which irritate children to a supreme degree, weaken authority, and in time nullify the effect of any effort to command. In the whirlwind of commands and prohibitions in which they are caught, children can no longer distinguish between important issues and details. Not having the strength to observe all the directions they receive, they decide quite practically to observe none except when a painful punishment impresses them with the need to obey.

Although the parents should give few commands, they must abide by what they have commanded and see it through. If children note that it is easy for them to wear out the patience of those who issue commands or prohibitions, and that sooner or later they will have the victory, they will unconsciously or even through a perversity that will always increase, set about to manoeuvre more and more triumphs for themselves.

"Leave that door handle alone!" Fine. The child hears the command. A second later he is at the handle again. Again he is told to leave it alone. The child resigns himself and for some time does not go near the door. Will he make a third attempt? Why not? After the second injunction mamma generally says no more. As a matter of fact, he renews his disobedience. Mamma lets it pass. She is conquered.

She will be conquered forever.

That is just one example of ten thousand where training falls short.

But when children know that what is said goes, the temptation to defy a command does not so readily come to them; or if should it come and they yield, they know their parents will not let their disobedience pass and that they will pay the penalty; they know too that the punishment will be in proportion to the offense, neither too little or too much but exactly proportionate; they take it for granted.

Away with all fussiness however! Let children exercise some initiative. How many parents forget that they were once young and as a consequence what it means to be young.

In his book *My Children and I*, Jerome criticizes in a humorous fashion the exaggerated notions of some parents who do not want to recognize the power for frankness in boys and girls of twelve, fourteen or sixteen years.

Veronica, one of the young daughters of the home, finding that the discipline of the house was too rigid protested with the comment, "If grown-ups would be willing to listen, there are many things we could explain to them."

She decided to write a book in which she would give parents some wise advice. "All children will buy it," she said, "as a birthday gift for their father and mother."

Veronica was doubtless somewhat presumptuous but not stupid. People can learn at any age.

Even from their children.

Even when their youthful lessons are developed from impertinence.

It is better, of course, not to need their lessons.

Training in Docility

Many parents complain that they can no longer get their children to obey.

Is it the fault of the children? Is it not rather the fault of the parents? A failure in obedience because of a failure in authority?

To command requires as much abnegation as to obey. If a person commands to satisfy his need of imposing himself on others, to satisfy his vanity, to prove his power to himself, he has missed the purpose of authority. Authority does not exist for itself but for the good of subordinates.

Parents can go to the other extreme and let their children to their whims and fancies in order to escape imposing any inconvenience upon themselves, allowing everything to pass and even refusing to forbid what they should forbid. That too is a failure in their mission. To have authority is to have the obligation to exercise it—according to the circumstances and without exaggeration certainly—but it must be exercised and not held in abeyance; that would be a betrayal of a trust.

Authority is to be exercised; to be exercised within the limits of its control; that is its function. If through laziness or poor judgment authority is not exercised or is badly exercised, how can we be astonished that obedience is lost?

Authority supposes a soul at peace, a courageous soul, dominated by a sense of duty, devoted to the interests of the subject, free of capricious impulses and that sentimental concept of love which is often found in mothers who confuse tenderness with idolatry.

Parents and educators must arm themselves with courage to dare to take a stand against the caprices of their child. They must have keen judgment to know in which instances they should command or refrain from commanding, to be able to adapt the order to the capacity of the subjects, to be able to understand the subjects' desires and satisfy them, to oppose their whims, their impetuous desires and disordered impulses.

In all this there must not be the shadow of oppression. Parents should realize the children's need for distractions, activity, learning, and loving. They ought to satisfy them in everything that is legitimate. That will provide a generous principle by which they can refuse them what is not legitimate. In everything the parents should act with a balanced mixture of gentleness and firmness.

Certainly they should not govern their children in a way that suppresses their initiative. Their problem is not to develop paragons of perfection, children who are exteriorly docile but docile through passivity.

Parents should as often as possible insist that their children make their own decisions, assume their little or great responsibilities; but at the same time supervise and watch over them unobtrusively; be ready to help them if need be when they hesitate or arrive at imprudent decisions.

This implies that the parents strive less to develop a satisfactory exterior behavior than to fashion in the child a conscience that is exact and clear in the knowledge of its duties; it is essential that when a child obeys he does so not because of external constraint but through obedience to the law of duty, to the inward law formuated in the depths of his soul by God Himself.

The formation of the child's conscience is therefore inseparable from his training in obedience. Let the child know that he must obey only because he must above all obey God; parents and educators are only the intermediaries of God in his regard. Punishments which must follow wrongdoing will never be for him the indication of his parents' excitability or moods but always and only the justification of a moral principle that has been violated.

Intelligence and Firmness in a Mother

CAN the mothers who are real educators be counted by the hundreds? Many see what ought to be done but do not have the courage to require it or rather to impose it on themselves to see it through. Others again have sufficient firmness of character but lack keenness, insight, psychology.

Madame Marbeau whose son was to become bishop of Meaux possessed the rare balance of intelligence and firmness.

One of the brothers of the future bishop had been naughty and troublesome at school and was sent home by way of punishment. At home he was obliged to recount his escapade. The child was difficult and it was not his first offense. Madame Marbeau marched him up to his room, closed the door behind them, took a switch and ordered the boy to take off his coat and a few more things. "My child," she said, "you are dishonoring your name. I am going to whip you for it so that you won't forget it. It grieves me to do so. I have a heart ailment and could die of emotion... at least my death would remind you not to offend God."

When her children were old enough to be able to take responsibility, Madame Marbeau gave each of them a watch, accompanying her gift with the wish "May all the hours of your life to the very last, mark the good you do. May you never have to blush for one of them."

She encouraged the older ones to offer sacrifices to bring blessings on their future home, "Offer that up for the one whom you will marry."

A mother ought to be willing to make her child shed tears if that is the only way to instil a lesson which other means have failed to inculcate.

Surely, the whole art of educating does not consist in the art of being severe; some parents are too stern and they create a depressing and disheartening atmosphere in the home; that is the other extreme of indulgence. Exaggerated repression and excessive weakness are both harmful. The one who must be most watchful against excessive weakness is the mother, to whom is attributed the quality of kindness as an almost natural instinct and whose whole vocation is bound up in kindness. In their early days the children will be tramping all over her feet, but when they grow older they will trample on her heart.

The child should be encouraged to the complete accomplishment of his duty; nor should the parents take over to spare him the necessity of effort; they should rather stimulate him to furnish his own effort. He should be given a taste for fundamental honesty very early in life, the understanding that time is money advanced to us by God to enable us to purchase not only our eternity but the grandeur and beauty of our present life.

Then at the opportune time the child should be directed to consider his future. After making of his present home an invaluable training center, let the mother use the thought of the future home he will establish as an incentive to needful renunciation and self-denial. Should a son or daughter give indications of a special attraction to the virginal state in a consecrated life, with what care should the mother watch over them. What a grace for the family if their dreams should be realized! But such graces are bought! By the sacrifices of the children. By the sacrifices of the parents above all, but primarily of the mother.

These are not the only characteristics of a solid training but they are important characteristics. Let me examine myself on them. What judgment must I pass on myself?

Picture Study

MOTHER has gathered her little world around the table. She has chosen a supply of beautiful pictures; there are all sorts of them.

"Now suppose everyone keeps still. Look well at these pictures and make your choice without telling it... Then in a few minutes you may each tell me in your turn which one you prefer. If you explain well why you prefer it you may have it to keep for yourself. All right, let's start. Is everyone here? Take time to think carefully. When you have all made your choice we shall begin to speak."

Soon little hands were busy fingering the pictures; indecision was evident on the children's faces. Finally their choices seemed to be settled.

"Very well, Peter, you begin."

Peter had been attracted by a troop of soldiers marching behind the red, white and blue:

"Because it has the flag of my country," he said.

What a beautiful lesson to develop, the lesson of patriotism, a lesson in humanity. Why should we love the world; why too should we prefer our own country? We should prefer it to the point of defending it if it is unjustly attacked. What is a just war, an unjust war? Is it sometimes permissible to kill? What is the duty of the leaders in war? Why should we salute the flag?

And all listen to the simple lesson so marvelously and expertly explained drawing great profit from it. A true course it is in philosophy, civics, international ethics, and will-training.

Little Louise decided on a picture of a beautiful baby by Reynolds, a pink, chubby baby with curly hair. She gives her reason in a tone of voice that reveals her budding maternal instinct, "I want it because it looks like my little brother."

And Mother seizes her opportunity to explain the mother's role, her joys, her difficulties, her responsibilities.

Jeanne, a robust girl, not blessed with much imagination shows great admiration for a very ordinary postcard representing two children in the country, standing before a rustic home at an outdoor fireplace roasting potatoes and chestnuts . . . She chose it because "it shows what we do on vacation when we have no more homework to do."

This brings forth a little homily on energy at work, coupled with praise for the honesty of the child; the motive of choice alone is blamed as indicative of no great zeal for study.

Paul, whose stuffed pockets seem to contain a whole workshop—string, broken springs, rubber bands and other odds and ends has been waiting a long time to explain his choice: "I like this airplane which is going to take off; see the pilot has put on his cap; he is going to take two passengers. I want to be a pilot when I get big..."

How many correct ideas to develop, enlarge and enrich; how many inferior sentiments to uplift; how many social principles to instill according to the capacity of these little minds and consciences so newly formed; how many futures to map out and how many vistas to open up.

There is nothing austere or forbidding here. It is life presented in beautiful simplicity. All the mother's explanations are within the children's grasp, but how richly instructive and informative! They had so much fun. And they learned so much.

Impartiality

ONE great principle of education that is of prime importance is that there must not be two systems of weights and two systems of measures in the family; it is necessary to treat all the children impartially.

The celebrated Carmelite, Mary of Agreda, whom Phillip IV of Spain did not hesitate to take as his confidante and advisor in matters of state and the government of men because of her spiritual insight and virtue, wrote the following advice to him on October 13, 1643 after she realized, either through spiritual lights or human reports, that he was inclined to yield to the ascendancy of a certain individual in his court:

It would be better to put all (your counsellors) on the same level by listening to all of them so that each one believes himself to be your favorite without Your Majesty's according more to one than to the other. Thus God has placed the heart in the center of the body that it may vivify and stimulate all the members equally; the same sun lights us all without any distinctions.

This rule which Mary of Agreda gave Phillip IV for the government of Spain is very valuable within the family.

One or other of the children must not get the idea he is preferred; he will be tempted to abuse the situation. Above all, the other children must have no cause to believe that one of the members of the family is the object of special predilection.

All ought to believe that they are, each of them individually, the privileged one; and that because actually and not as a pretense the father and mother make no distinctions of person but give to all their maximum love.

If any exception must be made let it be for that one who is least gifted, the most sickly, who has the least defense. In such a case only will the other children pardon partiality.

Generally, however, such advice need not be given to mothers. As Bishop Dupanloup explains, maternal love is so wide and deep that there is in it an innate and magnificent contradiction.

If her child is beautiful, richly endowed, how the mother cherishes it! If on the contrary, her child is puny, deformed by nature, she has treasures of affection for it such as she has for no other.

Here is the beautiful passage. It is taken from a volume which has not gone out of date; how many married people and parents could profit greatly by reading it and meditating on it: The name of the book is *Letters of Direction on Christian Life* and the particular sections referred to now are the passages on *Marriage, Motherhood* and *Conjugal Fidelity:*

Maternal love possesses two contrary impulses which are characteristic of it. We could not measure either of them, nor could we pass them by in silence.

The mother loves her fortunate child, the handsome child, the prosperous child, for its happiness, its beauty, its prosperity;

there is in this a just pride which belongs to maternal love and does not sully it. At the same time, the mother loves her child who suffers, who is listless, who is deformed because of its suffering, its languor, its deformity; and her love goes to terrifying extremes.

One must see a mother looking at her infirm and deformed child... It is as if she wants to fill up all the voids of that being, that she wants to enclose it within herself so that curious and unkind looks cannot reach it.

If she has a wayward child, it is this one she loves in spite of herself; if she has a sick child, it is toward that one she directs all her concern, and on the contrary should her child be a hero... how happy she is!

Difficulties of Christian Education

IN ORDER to make a true Christian of a child, four difficulties must be conquered:

1. The child himself.—He is light-minded, superficial, completely exterior. The invisible world seems unreal to him. Doubtless, the infused faith received at baptism gives him a kind of aptitude for perceiving divine realities; and the educator will not fail to utilize and develop this aptitude. It still remains true that the child for whom the world of images alone has value is in grave danger of progressively losing interest in the Kingdom of God to give more and more attention to what Our Lord calls *all these other things*.

Furthermore, he is on the threshold of life and that life is the present life; he feels strong; death is far away. His very existence appears to him as something almost eternal. He dreams of marriage, thinks of a career and is immersed in distractions. He thinks very little about his soul if he thinks of it at all.

2. The family circle.—The family encircles the child with a certain general atmosphere of ease, of comfort, of

forgetfulness of the essential. The practice of Christianity within the family may be very weak; there may be a complete absence of good example. An exaggerated liberty in regard to reading may prevail; the newspapers and magazines brought into the family are perhaps most unchristian, utterly pagan in tone. And as for the religious observance of Sunday, it is reduced to a minimum and that minimum is merely routine. True piety is definitely lacking; so too is any semblance of regularity in rising and retiring; a shameless preoccupation with frivolities crowds out everything else. The development of a spirit of sacrifice and the formation of a religious spirit receives scarcely any attention.

3. Schools.—Let us consider only those schools in which religion is recognized. To whom is the religious instruction confided? How well is education to the supernatural safeguarded? Even in institutions where exercises of piety are held in esteem, is sufficient effort made to combat routine, to avoid blind imitation and to vivify religious practices? Is sufficient care taken to explain doctrine thoroughly? Is not a great deal of precious time lost in problems of apologetics while the children have very little acquaintance with the substantial realities of the deposit of faith? Is the teaching of Catechism carefully centered about the dogma of Grace and of Incorporation in Christ? Are the truths of faith made to live by being presented in relation to modern life, adapted to the needs of the young people and the needs of the time?

4. The general easygoing attitude of society.—Father Gratry used to say that young people had difficulty escaping the two trials that their social environment imposes—the trial of fire and the trial of light.

—The trial of fire. By that Father Gratry meant the test of pleasure, the test of the senses. The great means of information are sometimes transformed into means of corruption.

Reading, unbridled freedom, certain types of amusement finish the destruction. The world ridicules the chaste; materialism at times gross, at times refined, threatens to penetrate all of life especially now that the constraints of the war have been lifted.

—The test of light. This, Father Gratry explains, is contact with pagan mentalities, with philosophies of scepticism and agnosticism as noisy as they are baseless but none the less alluring in an age of independence and awakening passions.

All these conditions point to the importance of a virile training of the individual from childhood; the need of a healthy and uplifting family life; the value of a solid intellectual formation that is thoroughly Christian; the necessity of a purification of the general atmosphere.

The children of today have been compared to "an invasion of little barbarians." We must civilize these barbarians if we want to prevent the arrival of barbarism or a return to barbarism.

Supernatural Mothers

CHESTERTON expressed himself as well satisfied that education is entirely confided to women until that time when to educate becomes entirely useless—for, "a child is not sent to school to be instructed until it is too late to teach him anything."

In other words, education depends on the training given during baby days and early childhood and such training is the concern of women. That is a certain fact. It is also a serious fact. Because at once there arises the problem: Are all mothers charged with educating their children capable of it?

Some women excel in child-training. And often they

are equally successful in handling their children once they are grown.

How solicitously these mothers watch over their children even in their babyhood not only in concern for their bodily good but for their soul as well, warding off from them whatever could be a source of trouble later. With what love of God they profit by their babies' first glimmerings of reason to teach them how to fold their hands in prayer and lift their hearts to God. How zealously they prepare them for their First Holy Communion, speaking to them of the marvels of the Eucharist, encouraging them to generosity and love of Jesus Crucified.

Without any thought of self, but with joyful and supernatural austerity, they teach their children to make sacrifices, to think of others; with what divinely inspired skill they show them the immense needs of the world, make them think of little pagan children who have no Christian mother or father or brothers or sisters who have been baptized.

"Children are serious-minded, and to keep a childlike soul means precisely to continue to look at life with a serious attitude," says Joergensen. Mothers with a supernatural spirit, whether they have read Joergensen or not, seem to use this idea as a guiding principle and by it help their children to preserve while growing up, the juvenile depth of their serious outlook on life.

Even when their children are grown, how they help them to develop this serious attitude and protect them from losing it or submerging it in an atmosphere of worldliness and frivolity! How earnestly they try to give their children true Christianity grounded much more in love than in fear; they do not constantly terrify them with the idea of sin; they lead them even more by example than by word, to look upon God as a God of mercy and not as a sort of "super-parent who is always dissatisfied, severe, angry, ready to forbid and to punish."

Living a life of divine familiarity themselves, these mothers have learned the great mystery of "God nearby," of God residing in the depths of the soul in grace, a God whose dearest wish is to draw us into closer intimacy with Himself.

It has been said that "there are two ways of giving the consciences of children an intense sense of the privation of God"; either by default, by never putting them in His presence; or by excess, by putting them in His presence in such a way that He becomes a nightmare to them from which they flee as soon as they realize that the whirl of life helps them not to think of Him."

Supernatural-minded mothers would never fail in the second way. If their grown boys and girls remain in the state of grace, it is through a holy pride, an interior joy, the result of having been impregnated early in life with the conviction of God's nearness, with the determination to remain forever living tabernacles of the Trinity, *other Christs*.

Honor to these mothers, true educators!

Education to the Supernatural

THIS does not mean education to piety. In Christian families this is properly provided for: The children are taught their prayers, how to go to Confession, how to prepare for Holy Communion, how to assist at Holy Mass and other church services, how to say the rosary. All this is fine, but perhaps it is not the essential!

The important thing is to teach the child who he is, who God is, and how God wants to mingle His life with his by coming to dwell in him, consecrating him thereby as a living tabernacle of the Most High. When the child knows all this not merely as bookish knowledge but as knowledge lived out and often recalled, exercised by his faith and his young good will, then and then only, will there be a solid foundation on which to build religious instruction, to justify and demand exercises of piety. It is absolutely essential that before all else the child be informed of the divine riches which his baptism brought him. It must be explained to him that the day he was carried as a little baby to be received into the Church, God came to take possession of his soul.

He should be taught that when people come into the world they do not possess this divine life. God gave it to Adam and Eve in the beginning but they lost it. Right here is a splendid opportunity to explain the greatness and goodness of God, the marvel of our supernatural life, how God created man greater than nature, how He wanted to make all of us His children. The little one knows well what a father is. Explain to him that God is our Father in order to give him what is essential in all true piety, a filial spirit and an understanding of how true it is to call God, *Good*.

The story of creation fascinates children; so too does the story of Adam and Eve and the Fall. What a lesson for the child is the example of the terrible punishment incurred by disobedience! ... The divine life is lost! But God still loves His poor human creatures just as mamma and papa continue to love their child after he has done wrong. And what is God going to do to give back this lost supernatural life? When one commits a fault, he must make up for it to obtain pardon. Who can make up for such a fault? God asks His own Son to do it. His Son will come down to earth. And then follows the beautiful story of the Christmas Crib and the timely application of these truths: How we should pity those who do evil and if we can, help them get out of their misery, their bodily and spiritual wretchedness!

Not only will Jesus live upon earth with us but He will die for us after living more than thirty years over in a little country where we can find many souvenirs of His stay—the little town of His birth, the workshop of His fosterfather, that noble carpenter named Joseph, the villages that heard Him preach to all, and especially to children, on how to get to heaven, the place of His death upon the Cross, that place of suffering where Mary His Mother stood beneath His instrument of torture... All that, all that so that John, Paul, James, Henry, Peter, Louise, Camille, Leonie, Germaine may be even while they are still on earth, little—and yes very great—living tabernacles of God who is Goodness itself; so that later in heaven they may be with the God of their hearts forever.

Religious instruction is not sufficiently centered; it is not centered about the central mystery of Catholicism. Even the cathechism with its divisions of Dogma, Morals and the Sacraments—divisions that are perfectly logical and understandable but more adapted to theological authors than to the souls of children—can, if we are not careful, make one forget the beautiful wholeness of Christianity which is superbly majestic in its architectural lines, clear, and pulsing with life.

Education to the Supernatural (2)

IT IS clear that everything centers about the dogma of grace and our supernatural elevation. The best way to develop this idea with the child is to use the technique of an object lesson and explain the rites and ceremonies of baptism to him. That will be a little drama in which he has been the hero, and consequently, it will hold tremendous interest for him. It is something about himself, it is his own story he hears; he will be delighted.

Describe the ceremonies graphically for the little one. As soon as feasible, take him to church. Before showing him the tabernacle, the Eucharistic dwelling, take him to the baptismal font: Here is where you became *a living tabernacle of God*. At the words of the priest, "Go out of this child, unclean spirit; give place to the Holy Spirit," the devil was forced to leave you, because of the power Our Lord gave to His priests. Then the Holy Spirit came to dwell in you. And since the Holy Spirit is one with the Father and the Son, God in His fulness came to dwell from then on in your heart—yes, there are three Persons, but there is just the same but one God; there are five fingers but they make only one hand—and that one God in all three Persons dwells in you.

God does not have to use an airplane like the one you saw landing from its flight the other day, but He does come down from heaven to dwell in your soul; He came into each of us, Papa, Mamma and in you, in Henry and James and Pauline, in Genevieve and little Louise. He comes on His own without anyone else sending Him and His coming is very real. Besides all this, His dwelling in all of us does not keep Him from continuing to dwell in heaven, too. He is all-powerful; it causes Him no difficulty to be at several places at once. If He who exercises His power everywhere, comes especially into the souls of the baptized, it is to dwell there in a dwelling of love. When your godmother or your grandfather come to spend a few years at your house, how happy you are! It is to give you pleasure that they come; and they bring with them goodies and lovely presents.... God does the same thing when He comes to stay in you— He brings presents with Him; we call these gifts graces; that means favors, gifts He is not obliged to give but which He gives just because He is so good. Good, did we say? Extraordinarily good! Much kinder than godmother or grandpa; kinder even than Papa or Mamma. He is the One who made the kindness and goodness of fathers and mothers and of all good people on the earth. Think how much greater is God's goodness since He possesses all this goodness put together and a great deal more besides!

But then if God is like that, how ought James and Joseph and Henry and Isabelle and Louise and Madeline behave themselves? Well, first of all, they should never do anything that would chase God from their souls; to do that is what we call mortal sin; mortal, because it forces God to leave just as if it killed Him. God cannot die, but it is just as if the person would say to Him, "I don't want anything more to do with You; if I could do away with You, I would do so!" That is why mortal sin is such a vile thing.

And it is not enough for you to keep from driving God out of your soul; no, there in the depths of your heart, you should try to keep Him company. Don't you think so? How sad that would be if He would be there within your soul and you would not pay any attention to Him, and seem to attach no importance at all to His Presence. That would not be very nice. You ought to visit Him there within your soul, in the morning, in the evening and often during the day; speak to Him; tell Him that you love Him very much. He who loves as a real Christian, a truly baptized soul, keeps God company since God is with him all the time.

Education to the Supernatural (3)

SINCE God is always present in the soul of the baptized person—provided that person has not driven Him away through mortal sin—with what respect should he treat not only his soul but also his body!

Mothers always dress their little ones in a beautiful white dress for their baptism. This is to show that later they ought never cover their souls with stains of sin. If muddy spots on lovely white material is ugly, how much uglier are sin stains on the soul!

That is also why the priest after bringing God into the soul of the tiny baby by saying as he pours the water, "I baptize thee in the Name of the Father and of the Son and of the Holy Spirit," hastens to add the injunction, "Receive this white garment and carry it undefiled to the Throne of God." The whiteness of the garment symbolizes the purity of the soul.

When we have to appear before God at the end of our lives, what will He ask us? "Have you been faithful? Have you always respected the beautiful virtue of purity? Or is your soul stained by sin? Have you committed sins? Mortal sins? At the moment death struck you down, did you have God in your heart or had you driven Him away as if you wanted nothing more to do with Him?

"You drove Him away? Ah, well, since that is how it is, I want no more to do with you: I too will drive you away, begone!"

It is just as a father might call before him his child who had insulted him or tried to kill him; he would say, "I no longer look upon you as my son. You are not worthy to remain in the house. Get out! I will never speak to you again, I will never love you again!"

How dreadful to be driven away by God because we tried to kill Him with sin in our soul; because we tried to drive Him away...to drive Him, God who is so good, from our heart!

We must indeed pray that such a thing never happens!

If we want to die without stain of sin upon our soul, we must live without staining our soul by such ugly defilements. Now since God dwells within our soul and since our soul is enclosed within our body, then we must also keep our body pure. We must never use it to commit sin. We should always look upon it as a kind of church in which God dwells. What would we say of naughty boys who would throw pebbles into the window of the parish church or mud from the street on the decorations or the altar inside? It would be an insult hurled at Jesus who stays there in the tabernacle so that we can go to Him to tell Him that we love Him and that we are happy to be with Him.

A little baptized child is like a church, but a living church.

Jesus and the Child

How should we introduce Jesus into the life of the little one? Marie Fargues, a one-time educator, suggests the following psychological procedure: "You love Jesus very much, don't you?" the mother asks the little one in a tone of voice that calls forth a fervent "yes." Mamma must love Jesus to speak as she does. Therefore, Baby loves Him, too, and he wants to show it. He will clutch the picture of Jesus that the mother holds out to him, and kiss it with much ado. A statuette, a crucifix, a medal—these objects offer no direct interest to the child other than their polish or their color; mamma's face is certainly softer and more pleasing. But if one is to embrace, there must be something to embrace; and how can one show that one loves without embracing. That is the sole reason of existence for the statuette, the picture, or the medal of Christ as far as the baby is concerned. People don't embrace just anything, like papa's paper or the sugar bowl; these things have other uses. But the things that are connected with the Name of Jesus, these things one kisses for love of Jesus.

But Who is Jesus?

Who is Jesus? A baby does not ask that question. Jesus is a fact, like papa or mamma. And the little one is not in the least disturbed about giving the same name to quite different objects, a medal, a picture, or a crucifix. For, in the beginning, the picture, the medal, or the crucifix, is Jesus. It will take time for the little one to understand that these things are merely representations of Jesus.

Little by little, the child will begin to distinguish the person from the representation and will begin to build up a more correct concept: Jesus is at one and the same time, the One who is represented on the medal, the One who lives in the tabernacle, the One who is on the crucifix, the One who is on the picture, the One who lives in the church, and the One who is in mamma's heart after she goes to Holy Communion.

From then on, the clarification can be continued by helpful statements or questions: "Yes, Jesus is here," or "Jesus did that" or, if we are in church, "Where is Jesus?" At Christmas time when the little one pulls on mother's sleeve, insisting, "I want to go over and see little Jesus in the pretty crib," a splendid opportunity presents itself to explain the difference between the figure of Jesus in the crib and Jesus present in the tabernacle.

The transfer from the concept of Jesus to that of God is evidently a delicate step. The mother has told the child that God is everywhere, sees everything, but that He has no body. Now Jesus has a body. All that is not very clear to the child. Little by little, it will become so.

God is at one and the same time, the Father, Son and Holy Spirit. There is God the Father, God the Son, and God the Holy Ghost and they have existed from all eternity. It is the Son, however, who became Jesus when the

Blessed Virgin gave Him a body, and He walked among men on earth.

Thus the little one through acquaintance with Jesus rises to knowledge of God. That God should have become man, is not at all astonishing to the child, and still less astonishing is it to him that Jesus had a mother.

Thus, bit by bit, things are seen in their proper relation. There cannot be complete clarity all at once. However, by means of successive bits of information, and above all by successive attempts at prayer, the little one enters into contact with Jesus; this contact is more of the heart than of the mind.

Historical and doctrinal ideas will be added later to complete the child's concept. Even at this early age he has become acquainted with the Triune God and the Incarnation. The cross, too, has been revealed to him. It is a delight for the child to hear the story of Jesus' life, and, in the retelling how many ideas can be given, how much curiosity satisfied, how many lessons taught!

Since Jesus loves children so much—and we know that He does from the gospel story of Jesus blessing the little ones—since He has loved people so much and done so much for them, should not little John, or Lucy, or Alice, love Jesus, too, with all their heart; should they not learn from Him how to make a generous sacrifice when the opportunity presents itself?

The Father Who Doesn't Pray

LITTLE Paul who is only four-and-a-half years old, is kneeling beside his bed saying his night prayers; they seem to be very long.

"Haven't you finished your prayers?" asks his nurse.

"Yes," answers the child slightly embarrassed.

"Well, then, what are you doing now?"

The child blushes and murmurs timidly, "I say two of them every night—my own and papa's. I heard him refuse mamma when she asked him to say his prayers; so now I am doing it for him."

Precocious, would you say? Maybe so. But have children not often startled us with their penetration?

How foolish are those parents who believe they can fail in logic before their children! How little do they know of the workings of those little minds and those little hearts! How little do they know how these little ones can put to use what they hear!

Lady Baker, a convert, writes in her book *The House of Light* that when she was a child of about eleven years, she overheard a conversation between her father and her mother on the subject of religion. The father was saying, "I heard a good sermon today; it pointed out how the Reform was a great mistake and that England would have been much better off without it...."

"Be still," interrupted his wife in a scandalized tone, "be careful before the children."

"I was sent off to my studies," continues Lady Baker, "and I heard no more of the conversation; but I took to dreaming over these strange words."

That very evening while taking a walk with the maid, she asked to visit a Catholic church. From that date, she says, there was born in her the desire to study the beginnings of the pretended Reform and to change her religion later should this study prove that what her father had said was true.

It may be that I have not lost the habit of prayer, thanks to God's grace, but it could easily be that I do not let my children see me praying often enough. To pray, and to let one's children see that one prays, are two different things.

It is not enough to pray as an individual only. My duty as head of the family is to pray in the name of the family, in the sight of the family, and with the family. My boys must know that their father honors God; they must see that he conducts himself respectfully before Him; they must learn from his example the great duty of adoration and worship. Prayer, at least evening prayer, should be said in common.

In many families where all gather together at the end of the day to honor God, it is the mother who leads the prayer until the time comes when each child will be able to take a turn. It would be much better if the father would take the lead. It is the function which belongs to him, a function which is almost priestly in character.

Should it ever happen that I have occasion to pass unfavorable judgment on a churchman, or on some religious incident—although it could seldom happen that such an action would be my right—I must take care as to who is listening. Children don't miss anything... let me give that some thought.

Table Prayers

A CELEBRATED economist, LePlay, wrote "Until I can say grace at meals without astonishing any of my guests, I will not believe that I have done enough for the return of good habits." Grace at meals seems to be a simple detail. Are we not perhaps attaching too much significance to it?

Consider it a detail, if you wish, but it is a detail which proves much. René Bazin relates how edified he was while visiting in the north of France as a preparatory study for one of his novels, to observe how the family of an industrialist, in Roubaix, had said grace faithfully before meals, assigning each child a day to lead.

Another author relates the profound impression made on him by his visit to the home of an outstanding businessman in Antwerp. Before and after dinner, the eight children stood with their parents around the table while the father devoutly recited the meal prayers.

Where the practice of saying grace is found in a family, there is also found true family life blessed with children and with solid piety; there will be no selfishness; instead there will be found a love for tradition, respect for authority, and an undisputed reign of Christ over the home. The saying of grace may be a small thing, but it is an indication of great things.

The Christian family will not be restored, nor will it be maintained, without the restoration and the maintenance of Christian practices—the noblest practices surely, and the most obligatory, but likewise the most insignificant in appearance. However, are there any which are truly insignificant?—

—But these things will embarrass our visitors.

—Nothing forces them to pay you a visit, and if they want to do it, they undoubtedly respect the customs of the house, the crucifix on the wall as well as the tint of the wall, the normal acts of Christian life as well as the menus prepared for them. No one is obliging them to adopt your conduct, but they can at least accept it while they are with you.

The real motive, if you are truly honest, is not charity for others, but human respect and a concern for yourself. You are afraid; you do not dare.

Your visitors will be either Christian or non-Christian. Why among Christians should one blush because of Christ? If the guests are not Christians, will they be astonished at Christian acts, knowing the atmosphere of the home and the character of those who dwell in it?

In addition to grace at meals, another beautiful Christian custom for the home is the evening blessing given by the father to all the children: As each child comes to give him a good-night kiss, the father lays his hand upon his head or traces a little cross upon his forehead. What an advantage for the children who see in their father a quasi-religious—as they really should be able to do. What an advantage for the father who will as a consequence be more conscious of his office. Imagine what his thoughts must be as he blesses his children in the evening if, during the day, he has done something for which his conscience reproaches him!

"We shall make our brethren Christians again," sing the *Young Catholic Workers.* "We shall make homes Christian again," should be the song of married Christians. To do that, they must begin with their own.

Children and Christmas

IT IS easy to understand how enraptured children can become at the contemplation of a tiny Babe in a manger. To have God reduce Himself to their own status, to become a child like them, to need a mother, what more could they desire! They feel on a footing with Him. The Almighty is of their stature!

We are told that on Christmas Eve, Saint John of the Cross used to carry a statue of the Infant Jesus in procession about the monastery. The procession would stop before each monk's cell asking hospitality for the Divine Babe. The cells, like the hearts of the monks, would open to faith and to love. Only then would the statue be carried to the Crib and the Divine Office begin.

Children share the simplicity of these holy monks. Nothing attracts them more than the Crib.

This very attraction makes it imperative that they learn about it correctly.

Care must be taken not to mix in with the gospel mystery

any details which the child will later come to recognize as false. What good can come of representing Santa Claus almost as God the Father who has given us His Son? Why let children believe that it is the Infant Jesus Himself who comes down the chimney to bring them presents... only to hear some day, "You know, mamma, this is the last time I'm going to believe in Little Jesus who comes down the chimney with presents."

If we mix the false with the true, it is no wonder the child will not be able to separate legend from doctrine later on. The Gospel is sufficiently *extraordinary* in itself without our adding any of our own creations to it. If we do, we may well fear the child will become disgusted later at being deceived and reject everything.

Any charming legend or pious little story we may want to tell them when they are very little should be kept quite distinct and handled very differently from the dogmatic truths and authentic historical facts we teach them. Let us not introduce fairies into the story of Jeanne of Arc's childhood, nor put the legend of Saint Nicholas rescuing little children on a level with the realities of the Redemption, with the facts of Our Lord's saving us from hell.

If, therefore, we are to capitalize on the child's attraction for the marvelous, let us avoid abusing his credulity; above all when dealing with the lives of the saints, with the Blessed Virgin and with Christ, let us not mix the false with the true. Let us always keep on a plane apart those truths which are to be forever the object of ineradicable belief.

There is, however, a positive suggestion to offer: Explain to the child how Baptism has made him a living Crib; not a wooden manger padded with straw, but a living Crib; not a crib where only little Jesus lives but a Crib where the Three Persons of the Holy Trinity dwell, the Three Divine Persons. Here, too, is splendid opportunity to show the child the difference between the two presences—the presence of God in the soul through grace and the presence of Jesus in the stable through the Incarnation.

Eucharistic Education (1)

A FATHER wrote the following incident to a friend:

"You are acquainted with my little boy. The other day his sister who is fifteen asked him, 'Bernard, what is the difference between Holy Communion and blessed bread?' That could have been a stickler for a little fellow only six-and-a-half. 'Oh,' he answered quickly, 'they are not at all alike. Blessed bread is just bread and Holy Communion is our good Jesus.' The child has never had formal catechism lessons, but he has observed about him the practice of Christian life; he has heard his mother tell him upon returning from church that she had received Holy Communion; that is all."

However the child acquired his correct ideas, it is evident that with a knowledge of this kind he is ready to make his First Holy Communion.

The Church requires the child to know the difference between the Blessed Eucharist and ordinary bread. Relative to this point the bishops of Belgium state in their *Practical Instructions* that "the child has sufficient knowledge and has met requirements if he knows *according to his capacity* that in the Eucharistic Bread there is the true living Body of Jesus Christ with His soul and His divinity, glorious as He is in heaven."

By way of supplementary explanation the *Instructions* add:

"It suffices to have him know that Jesus Christ died for us upon the Cross before ascending to heaven; that He wanted to remain among us in the Host in the tabernacle; that He deigned to make Himself the food of our souls; that it is the priest who changes the bread and wine into the Body and Blood of Our Lord Jesus Christ when he pronounces the words of Consecration during Mass and that from this moment on the Host is no longer bread but it has become the living Body of Jesus Christ; that Jesus is hidden in this Host; that when one receives Holy Communion he receives God into his heart and that, therefore, he must before receiving cleanse his soul from all stain of sin."

Moreover, the *Instructions* further observe that in addition to the knowledge of the Eucharist as already described, the child ought to know and understand *to the best of his ability:*

That he has been created by God;

That this God, the Creator and Sovereign Master of all things is One only God;

That there are Three Persons in God: the Father, the Son, the Holy Spirit;

That the second Person became Man for us, suffered and died upon the Cross to save us;

That the person who with the grace of Jesus Christ does good by observing the law of God will be rewarded by God in heaven;

While the person who does evil by disobeying the law of God and who dies in the state of mortal sin will be deprived of the vision of God in heaven and will be punished eternally in hell.

It is important to note the stress laid upon the two phrases, *according to his capacity* and *to the best of his ability*.

The Church does not demand a profound knowledge; she requires only a knowledge proportionate to the age of the child. It is not necessary for him to know bookish formulas by heart; nor is it sufficient for him to learn by heart explanations which he recites like a parrot. The child should *understand—according to his capacity*, yes—but he should truly understand.

Eucharistic Education (2)

BESIDES the knowledge of the truths of faith which the child should have according to his age and intelligence, the Church requires of him the desire to approach God in the Eucharist before admitting him to his First Holy Communion. Diocesan statutes state:

"It is essential that, knowing the infinite love which brings our Divine Savior to him and the desire Our Lord has to give Himself and to unite Himself with him in Holy Communion, the child should on his part desire to approach Jesus and give evidence of his veneration and his love for Him."

This sufficient devotion supposes:

"The pious recitation of the prayers essential for the Christian: The *Our Father*, the *Hail Mary*, the *Apostles' Creed*, the *Acts* of *Faith, Hope, Charity* and of *Contrition* and dispositions of reverence toward the Holy Eucharist."

At what age can these conditions be realized?

Canon Law avoids setting a mathematical age. It states:

"All the faithful of either sex who have attained the age of discretion, that is to say, the age of reason, ought to receive the Sacrament of the Holy Eucharist at least once a year, during the Easter season, unless on the advice of his own confessor and for a reasonable cause he be justified in differing for the time being from the accomplishment of this precept." (Canon 859)

We can readily understand that because of differences in intelligence, receptivity of soul, educational environment, and the catechetical instruction obtainable the *age* required for First Holy Communion can vary. It is up to those charged with the spiritual care of the child to determine whether he has attained the *correct age*. Children attain it sooner than we might think in many cases.

If parents want to stimulate a desire for Holy Communion in their child, is it not evident that they themselves must have an ardent hunger for It? A mother who seldom receives Holy Communion will hardly be able to instil in her little ones a desire to receive Jesus. Should she none the less succeed in imparting to them a burning desire for Holy Communion, how will she then prevent their astonishment at her own lack of eagerness to communicate? What is good for the children is good for mamma, too, isn't it?

All things considered, is it not also true that what holds for the mother holds equally for the father?

Certainly there may at times be sufficiently justifiable reasons why papa and mamma cannot receive Holy Communion so often as their children and the reasons can be given to the children. However, it is well to remember that a child uses admirable logic. He will not accept as a precious treasure something which no one around him appears to appreciate.

Further there is nothing that so convinces and draws him as example.

Eucharistic Education (3)

It would be a mistake to limit the Eucharistic knowledge of the child to an understanding of the Real Presence and the nature of Holy Communion.

As soon as possible and in proportion to the unfolding of his understanding, the child should be initiated into the Mystery of the Eucharistic-Sacrifice, or in other words, he should be given an intelligent appreciation of the Mass. This naturally supposes that those instructing him have complete and correct information on this vital subject—unfortunately, this is not often the case.

It is easy to explain even to relatively young children—as was evidenced in the Children's Crusade—that Our Lord did not want to limit the offering of His immolation on the Cross to a single day, to Good Friday only.

Because sins were going to continue to swarm the earth, it was fitting—although certainly in itself not necessary, but assuredly fitting—for Our Lord to repeat His *elevation* between earth and heaven, to put Himself as a screen—the screen of His nail-pierced Hands and open Side—between the justice of God perpetually outraged and the sins of humanity.

Consequently, before dying, Our Lord gave to His Apostles and their successors the power to change bread and wine into His Body and Blood, the power to offer Him anew, the power in each Holy Mass to lift him up again between earth and heaven.

Since every day is marked by sin and the betrayal of Judas, by the crimes of men, by forgetfulness and ingratitude without name on the part of so many people, it is fitting, says Bossuet, *that every day be a Good Friday.*

Our Lord in every Mass has again in the hands of the priest the dispositions of complete sacrifice that were in His Heart at the moment of the First Eucharistic Offering and which He kept throughout His Passion and His agony on the Cross.

In this way will the Offering of His Sacrifice be perpetuated.

It is not a different immolation from the immolation of Holy Thursday at the Last Supper; it is the same. Nor is it a different immolation from the immolation on Calvary. There it was a bloody sacrifice; at the altar, in the Mass, it is an unbloody sacrifice. The form alone is different.

In order to stress the identity of the Mass and the Sacrifice of the Cross—for it is a dogma that they are one and the same sacrifice—the Church provides carefully that at every Holy Mass a great number of details recall the immolation of Jesus on Calvary.

The priest may not celebrate Mass unless there is a crucifix above the altar. The altar stone beneath the altar cloths is marked by five crosses which recall the five Wounds of Our Lord. All the objects the priest uses and the vestments he wears have reminders of the cross.

There should then not be too much difficulty for the child if he is alert to become well informed about the ineffable mystery of Christ's renewed or rather continued immolation. Then he will get the habit—and a very essential habit it is—of receiving Holy Communion not only *to receive* but also *to give;* not only *to benefit* by the Living Bread but to unite himself with Jesus in the very act of His perpetuated Sacrifice.

Eucharistic Education (4)

SHOULD children be led further in their Eucharistic education than the phases discussed so far? That is, should they at such an early age be introduced to the subject of grace, particularly the ineffable grace given to the world through the Sacrament of the altar?

It may be advisable to wait a bit before introducing them to the subject of grace but it should be kept constantly in mind. We ought not take it upon ourselves to dispense to these little Christians only a part of Christianity.

Before we can penetrate to the depths of the Eucharistic mystery, we must understand the great doctrine of our incorporation in Christ: Our Lord, in order to restore to us the divine life which we lost by original sin, was not satisfied to redeem us *from without* by paying our debts with the merits of His life and sacrifice; He wanted to make us *one* with Him which, as I have already understood in my meditations, is the culminating point of Christianity. Our Lord in order to redivinize us made us *one* with Himself.

Thanks to the bloody grafting Our Divine Lord was willing to endure for love of us on Calvary, we were made capable of being joined, set and established as branches of the Living Trunk. Baptism made this sublime incorporation effective for each of us.

Since Calvary, then, we are of the body of Christ—Christ's mystical body: Jesus plus us. *I am the Vine, you are the branches.*

A beautiful and strictly logical consequence follows: Just as the Divine Redeemer dying on the Cross offered Himself as Head of the whole human race, so in this pure oblation He offers not only Himself as Head of the Church to the Heavenly Father, but in Himself, His mystical members as well.

Since Calvary, Jesus is not separated from His members. A person passing through a door does not first put his head through and then fifty feet later bring through the other members of his body; he goes through as a unit at one time.

Is it so difficult to get our little Christians to understand that? Naturally, we will attempt to explain it to them only after we have made them conscious of what their baptism means to them and the splendor of their status in Christ.

We tell ourselves too easily that it is difficult and under this satisfying pretext we neglect to give the young the relish and the knowledge for their splendor which they are actually capable of enjoying.

I will teach my children as soon as possible to find in the Eucharist Christ's great plan for proving His love. "He has made us *one* with Him. In the act of sacrifice through the hands of the priest, whose word alone has brought Him to be present on the altar the Faithful themselves with one desire and one prayer offer to the Eternal Father the most acceptable victim of praise and propitiation for the Church's universal needs."

Eucharistic Education (5)

WE OUGHT to get the children into the habit of going to Holy Communion not only *to receive*, although that in itself is a tremendous privilege for *Unless you eat the Flesh of the Son of Man you shall not have life in you* but most of all *to give*. We have considered this point before, but it is worthy of much thought.

How can we expect to enter into a true union with One who is both the *Immolation* and the *Immolated* if we do not strive to nourish the spirit of sacrifice in the very depths of our being? To join together two beings one of whom is in the state of sacrifice and the other not, one who is imbued with the spirit of generosity and immolation and one who is not would be but a juxtaposition of two totally different beings. Is that union?

The spirit of sacrifice then is the prime disposition we should foster in ourselves if we wish to profit the most from the Eucharist. The priest at the Offertory puts a few drops of water into the chalice. We must pour our whole selves into the chalice to be offered.

The desire to give much more than the desire to receive should move us. To offer our generosity; to understand the call to sacrifice, to a united sacrifice, that is the Eucharistic spirit.

If only we could inspire all our religious practices and activities with this disposition which means so much to us when we are participating in the highest act of worship possible, the Holy Sacrifice of the Mass.

For how many is their whole life of prayer only their prayers of petition! They are in difficulty, they need something and they hold out their hand, "Lord, give me...." Such a prayer is not forbidden, but that is not all there is to prayer.

"Prayer," says the Catechism, "is the raising up of our minds and hearts to God...." Why? In order to adore Him, to thank Him, to beg His pardon and to implore His graces.

The petition for graces comes last in the order of prayers. First and foremost is the prayer of adoration, it is our homage ascending to God. It is toward Him and not toward ourselves that our souls are to be directed in prayer. "I praise You, O God, for Your great glory." That is the fundamental sentiment of the *Gloria in Excelsis*. *My soul doth magnify the Lord* is Mary's exultant prayer, the *Magnificat*.

In the prayer of *Thanksgiving*, there is some thought of ourselves but we are secondary. We pray because we have received a gift from God. We thank Him for His beneficence. This kind of prayer could be much more frequent! There are so many who are in the habit of receiving without ever so much as a "Thank You."

In the prayer for pardon, he who prays is surely present in his prayer; he has sinned; it is of himself he speaks. The prayer is excellent just the same, but it is only third in order of excellence.

How much prayer would there be left in the lives of most Christians if their prayers of petition were omitted from their worship of God?

How do I stand in this matter of prayer? Is it my principal effort to interest God in my affairs rather than to interest myself in Him?

I ought to broaden my concept of worship. I will teach my children to petition, to implore, to thank, but above all I will teach them to adore.

Training to Purity (1)

THE child is naturally innocent. Moreover, if baptized, it possesses with infused faith a special quality of innocence which comes to it from the presence of the Holy Spirit in its soul.

We must avoid any diminishing of this innocence. It is a great mistake to think that because the child is innocent, "it doesn't understand," and consequently to take no precautions; to be lacking in vigilance over the child's bathing and dressing; to let it run about without clothes, unsupervised before its brothers and sisters.

The adults of the family, too, should avoid any immodesty either in posture or dress before the little one; they should keep out of its way pictures of questionable decency. True, at the time, the harm may be slight or even negative, but the child has eyes and a memory; it registers everything, stores it all away.

Only when the child is still a baby should it be allowed to stay in bed after it is awake. Great care should be exercised for bodily cleanliness to prevent the formation of bad habits that might result from discomfort. It is best to separate the sexes for sleep and to give the children a bed that is not too soft.

As the children grow older, we must be vigilant over their choice of playmates. We should protect them from any pictures, statues, advertisements or entertainment that can disturb them. We are wise if we keep the children busy even to the point of fatigue, but a fatigue in keeping with their age and strength. Never should we praise children for their beauty, especially little girls. We ought also to inspire them to absolute confidence. In addition we must seize every opportunity to show them positively the grandeur of purity.

People sometimes attempt to rear children as if they were without sex. Children are either little boys or little girls. Long before the awakening of their sex instincts, in fact from their babyhood, their personality is distinctly individual and gives foreshadowings of fatherhood or of motherhood. Sex, although its characteristic functions do not become active until the onset of puberty, impregnates the whole physical and moral being from the beginning. Consequently, it is important to foresee long in advance the unfolding of that providential power which is still dormant yet capable of being influenced beneficially or detrimentally at this early stage according to the wisdom of the folly of its training.

It would be well, then, to heed the strong injunctions of a one-time educator: "We must never forget that certain organs of the child which still serve him only in the processes of elimination will become for him during adolescence the seat of the powerful passion of the flesh and that then certain acts, looks, attitudes which now may be only vulgar or immodest can easily be after the awakening of sexual urges impure and perverse. Further, such acts and attitudes can arouse unhealthy and troublesome sexual excitation prematurely and during the crisis of adolescence turn spontaneously into the development of a vice which seems to be rooted in the soul from its budding forth so truly is habit second nature; and habit is difficult to break even in early childhood."

We should not, however, be satisfied with a purely negative training to holy purity, a training made up for the most part of wise precautions. There is need, too, for positive training in this beautiful virtue. This positive training will in part consist of education in true facts, a discreet and chaste explanation of the functions of the generative organs according to God's plan; an explanation as complete as the age of the child permits or requires. The duty of giving this instruction falls largely upon the mother who only too often finds herself inadequately prepared.

Training to Purity (2)

It is a fact that even very young children become curious about the difference of the sexes as well as the mystery of generation and they express their curiosity with embarrassing candor and directness in blunt questions: "Where do babies come from?"

In general, no one is better qualified than the mother to give the initial instructions and information delicately, without wounding innocence or troubling and shocking the child's keenly susceptible soul by confronting it too brusquely with disturbing new concepts. It is better for the father to instruct the boys. Parents have the grace of state; furthermore, they know or they ought to know how to speak to their children and exactly what to say according to what the child already knows or does not know, according to its impressionability, its probable emotional reaction, its intelligence, its imagination.

The initial instruction must always be strictly individual, never group instruction.

Such instruction should be given early enough, in time, but never prematurely. Rarely should a mass of information be given at once, but nearly always imparted progressively. One must never give any false information, but neither is one obliged to tell all there is to be told at one blow. Only such knowledge should be given as is necessary to clarify the present difficulty, to satisfy the child's curiosity at the time. Later when occasion offers to complete the information, it can be completed.

The introduction of the child to the facts of life must be made with simplicity, without excessive preambles and beating about the bush, objectively without clumsiness; they must be presented as something quite natural but explained in an atmosphere of earnestness, dignity and respect. There must be nothing affected or borrowed in one's manner or tone, only calmness and a natural everyday voice uncolored by emotionalism. The child, however, must be made to realize that he has been given no new subject for chatter with his playmates and friends; if there is something he wishes to speak of later regarding his new information or if there is something he does not understand, he will always be able to ask mother or father about it; he should speak to them about it.

A very sensible mother concluded the instructions she gave her little one with these few words: "What I have just told you is a secret, *our* secret. Now that you know it, give me your hand and promise me that you will not question other people about it or ever speak to anyone else about it, but only to me."

A little child will be flattered by such a mark of confidence and being naturally pure will sense the reason for this recommendation as clearly as if it had been expressed.

In addition, if the child is used to living in an atmosphere of filial trust and abandonment, of respect for itself, of training in sacrifice, supernatural generosity, daily contact with the invisible world through prayer and love of God, its instruction will prove singularly easy.

We cannot overemphasize the fact that "training to purity must be set in the framework of a solid all-round training of the will, the conscience, the emotions, the imagination and the whole body." To enlighten the child regarding sex will serve for nothing and can even be harmful if it has not first been established in fidelity in the light of spirituality, and in energy of will.

In other words, formal training to purity must be preceded by training pure and simple. It will be possible to speak clearly to a child who lives in an environment that is deeply impregnated with Christianity. In his tranquil soul, innocent and disciplined as it is, useful initiations can take place with profit and without causing any trouble; his delicate conscience will understand; his refined and mortified emotions will yield readily to the requirements of modesty, and he will not be stimulated to an unhealthy curiosity.

Training to Purity (3)

SATISFYING the child's legitimate curiosity is not of itself a sufficient antidote against evil; the nascent passions aiding a precocious corruption in which the mind could effect a premature awakening of troubling instincts could very easily be the starting point of impure habits. It is essential that *with* or preferably *before* we enlighten the child's mind on sex, we inspire him with a love for moral beauty and develop in him a generous will.

When we have done this, how should we proceed in teaching the child the mystery of life?

There are two aspects to the lesson: to explain the role of the mother in generation which is relatively easy; to explain the role of the father which is more delicate and which should consequently be given much later.

For the explanation of the first phase of this lesson there is no better starting point than the *Hail Mary*, "*Blessed is the fruit of thy womb, Jesus.*"

"How beautiful it is," said little Guy de Fontgalland to his father one day, "how beautiful it is that little Jesus, wishing to come to earth like us, hid Himself for nine months within His mother, in His mother's womb! How beautiful it is! I learned that today when I said the Hail Mary; I understood it. How little Jesus must love us to do that for us!"

In *Formation de la chasteté* by Ernst, we read an example of how easily and simply a mother went about the instruction of her child. "Where do babies come from?" queried her seven-year-old son. She answered with a story:

"Your father and mother love each other very much. Therefore, they wanted a child with all their hearts. You know that little children come from God: He created the first man and gave all people life. But when He wanted to make another man, He made use of parents and He put love into their heart. He makes the little baby grow from a tiny little seed which he leaves hidden for almost a year in a dark little hiding place. You know flowers, plants and even big trees come also from little seeds. (It is good to call children's attention to that fact very early as it makes a good background.) Now each grain must first of all remain some time in the dark earth. The *seed of the child* has been placed by God's plan in the womb of the mother; that is its hiding place. That is where you, too, remained quite near my heart and God made your body and soul. How? No one really knows but God Himself. You grew until you were big enough to be taken in my arms.

"Even though the mother suffers great pain and may be in danger of losing her life when the baby comes into the world, she is glad to bear it all for love of her little one. Besides her joy is greater than her pain. Parents thank God for His gift and promise Him to take good care of the child and rear it well."

There will be no difficulty if these instructions are given before puberty when the opportunity arises.

The need to give the facts about the father's part in the marital act is much less pressing. Such details can be given when adolescent boys or girls ask specific questions on this point revealing that the problem is uppermost in their mind or when lack of knowledge if delayed would cause them troubles of mind or soul; even when the subject is not on their mind or causing them any difficulty, it may still seem advisable to instruct them by way of preparation for life, as for example, before they go away to school or enlist for military service, or take a vacation job or any similar occasion. How much better a revelation made with delicacy and love than a brutal shock to conscience through conversations, reading or impure pictures!

After giving the necessary details about the physiological aspect of marriage, parents should never fail to lead their child's mind as quickly as possible to a consideration of the glorious purpose of generation—a participation in the creative power of God.

Training to Purity (4)

EVEN though there may be cases where it seems advisable to give all the necessary explanations in a single sitting, in general it is better to spread the lessons over a well-spaced period of time and to grade them according to the development of the child, its suspected temptations, and its needs of soul.

Wise are parents and educators who *show concern* for the child, foresee its needs, guess its worries, answer prudently and discreetly its silent or expressed questioning. They need much self-sacrifice and intelligence; but it is their role in life—the most beautiful part of their role.

After impressing the child with the fact that everything in the mystery of the origin of life is sacred, divine—the union of the parents, the generation of the child, which gives another elect soul to God and another member to the Mystical Body—is there any need to call attention to the gravity of the desecrations that the perversity of men perpetrate against it?

Certainly such an idea should not be a starting point in our explanations; the child's first ideas about the origin of life must not be mingled with the concept of sin. The idea of magnificent grandeur should dominate. Later on, at an opportune time and as the need arises, we can explain how contrary to God's plan it is to interfere in any way with the generation of life whether through selfishness or fear of suffering; we can point out how God has surrounded the use of the reproductive organs with special protections; we ought to emphasize the safeguarding character of modesty and call attention to the tremendous thought of God's divine presence within us, making respect for our bodies imperative since they are living temples of the Holy Spirit. We will tell them, too, that God punishes severely the wicked use of the creative power He has entrusted to His creatures, spiritually by loss of grace and by hell and often corporally by disease.

What we must avoid above all is to give the children a sort of obsession in regard to these matters. It is much better to divert their attention from this subject than to concentrate it there. One writer aptly says, "The best sex education is the kind in which sex holds the least place possible." Another, "The sacred work of nature must be enveloped by the triple veil of modesty, silence, and obscurity."

We must say enough to enlighten the child, to silence his curiosity, but refrain from saying more than necessary which would excite further curiosity and trouble. We should approach the instruction from its noblest side so that the thought of the mystery of life will always be linked with the thought of divine splendor. We need to pray much so that the child by means of our efforts and despite dangers from within and without will remain faithful in purity always, faithful to the grace of his baptism; constant in living by the light of faith. That means we cannot limit ourselves to purely natural explanations but must steep our teaching in dogma—the divine life of the Christian, his incorporation in Christ.

From these religious principles we can show that it is not enough to have a beautiful ideal; we must live out this ideal, an ideal that is both human and Christian. The necessity of Confession, direction, and frequent Holy Communion, in achieving the ideal ought to be stressed.

It is primarily in this endeavor that the words of Our Lord have special significance: *Without Me you can do nothing.* And again, *The spirit is willing but the flesh is weak.* It is folly to expose oneself to temptation and wise to moderate one's love of comfort and pleasure, to learn how to conquer oneself. Better still is it to learn how to spend oneself in the service of others. Nothing is a better protection against failings in self than the gift of self to others. The first beneficiary of the apostolate is the apostle himself. We ought to encourage youth to join in one or other of the special Catholic Action groups of the Apostolate such as a C. Y. O. group, a Sodality, or Catholic scout work. It will help discipline the body while training the soul.

Reading

LAMARTINE's mother wrote in her diary on June 19, 1801: "I was thinking again today about the danger of light reading. I believe that I would do well to refrain altogether from it; it would be a sacrifice at first, a sacrifice that would certainly please God since such reading is one of the most dangerous pleasures in the world. Besides, when I am taken up with this distracting kind of reading, serious and useful reading wearies and bores me; yet, I certainly need it to become capable of instructing my children. For their sakes I have finally decided to deprive myself of the pleasures of frivolous reading."

Parents should exercise care in their own reading. They, too, must avoid all that could sully their souls and rob them of virtue. They can go even further and like Lamartine's mother give up reading that consumes the precious time which could be spent in useful reading. One needs to know so many things to rear children! Making due allowance for needful and useful distractions, one ought always to choose reading matter that will enrich the mind and foster the qualities needed for the delicate ministry of parenthood.

What good fortune to be helped in advance by one's children: "For their sakes, I am finally decided to deprive myself of the pleasure of frivolous reading."

But the parents' reading is not the only problem. There is another, the children's reading. What great imprudence is evident in many families where all sorts of reviews, magazines, newspapers, and books definitely unfit for children are left lying about in their way; where unwise freedom of the library is granted and children can ferret out books that are often harmful to their morals and Christian convictions.

Jean Jacques Rousseau's story is well known. Born a Calvinist of parents who could scarcely be called commendable, he met with nothing but disturbing examples in his early childhood; however, he manifested a singular purity in resisting all interior and exterior temptations to corruption. He became a Catholic later and felt himself drawn to the priesthood. But his superiors decided at the end of a few weeks that he definitely did not have the makings of a good priest in him.

Some time after he left the seminary he was perverted morally by his benefactor, Madame de Warrens, who by most culpable relations shamefully debased the youth she called "Little one" despite her claim of wanting to act as "Mother" to him.

Awakening to a realization of his condition, Rousseau wrote in 1738: "O my God, pardon the sins I have committed up to this day, all the evils into which I have fallen.... Accept my repentance, O God,... I will remember that You are the witness of all my actions.... I will be indulgent toward others, severe toward myself; I will resist temptations; I will live purely.... O my sovereign Master, I will spend my life in serving You."

But unfortunately a library was opened to him and he "perused books with a sort of frenzy," with no direction, no discernment. He fell under the influence of Diderot, and became a recruit for the Encyclopedists.

We know the rest. His story should incite us to serious thought. On what does the orientation of a life depend? An unlocked door, momentary forgetfulness, negligence—and a soul is perverted forever!

The conclusion is evident: Never to have bad books in the house. What good comes of them?

If for purposes of study or other reasons, books which might prove dangerous for the rest of the family are absolutely essential, they must always be kept in a locked place. Children are curious, so too are the help. Harm is quickly done!

Training of the Emotions

MANY parents are too soft in the training of their children.

In order not to pain their offspring, they give in to their every whim. If the little one wants to be kissed, it is kissed; more often than not its desire for the kiss is anticipated by the parents to satisfy a desire of their own and to shower upon the little one proofs of an exaggerated tenderness. Should the child want a piece of candy, an object to examine, the parents rush to give it; they give him everything he wants or they think he wants.

What is the result? A child incapable of self denial; a child who seeks only one thing, the satisfaction of his little cravings. What a great danger for later life!

Father Viollet, director of the *Association of Catholic Mothers*, speaking at its convention in 1929 said:

"Consider a mother who has obeyed all the corporal whims of her child; she has in so doing prepared for all the child's future falls. The little one lives as it were only by the senses of taste and touch. If a mother satisfies every sensual desire of the child in the delight of the palate and bodily comforts, she unconsciously makes it a slave of its desires; are we not correct then in saying that she herself has paved the way for the child's powerlessness later to control its sexual life?

"When sex urges appear, it is only a matter of a change of place for the sense cravings: The desires that in the child were but the hankerings of its palate will spread at the age of puberty to the other parts of the body. If the child has not been accustomed from little on to control his sense of taste and touch, how do we suppose he can escape becoming the slave of sexual sensuality? This is a point that cannot be overlooked."

Some parents are too demonstrative toward their children. Of course, there is no question of forbidding all marks of affection so natural on the part of the parents for their children and the children for their parents; that too would be an extreme. It is simply a matter of moderating tender caresses, of keeping them in their proper measure, well-ordered.

Just as it is essential for children to be reared in an atmosphere of joyous confidence, loving simplicity, harmonious companionship penetrated through and through with mutual love, so too it is essential to avoid excess in demonstrations of affection, endearing expressions, caresses and fondling. Excess in this just as excess in any other respect is a defect. It is easy to fall into such excess. Canon Dermine, a very understanding man, made this comment:

"Parents, older brothers and sisters, maids, governesses, friends of the family are inclined by the attraction of their own feelings to shower babies with hugs and kisses. These immoderate manifestations, although they have nothing indecent about them, are not without danger, for they nourish in the child a need for tenderness and a sort of sensuality which can easily become a predisposition for the awakening of the passions. Here moderation should be the rule."

The training of the children begins in the training of the parents. They ought to moderate their own feelings if they do not want their children to give evidence later of some dangerously exacting needs. There is one kind of glutton who stuffs himself with food and sweets; there is another who is consumed by a need for caresses.

Let us be moderate ourselves on these points so that we can teach the children to be moderate. Training is built on wise and intelligent moderation.

The Child and Laziness

It has been said that a great difficulty in child-training is to know when to caress and when to whip.

While it is true that many of the child's faults arise from his physical condition, we should not exaggerate that fact; however, until we have proved that the fault is not the result of a physical state, an embrace is of more value than a whipping.

But here is a child whose faults are moral not physical, nor is there a psychological difficulty involved; he is sensual, he lies and he steals. There is nothing for it but to use restraints and punishments, without, however, neglecting wholesome encouragement at any manifestation of good will.

This is all very simple in theory, but the practical application of it is not always easy especially when the fault in question happens to be laziness. When a normally intelligent child dawdles at his work; when in spite of all efforts to stimulate him with high motives of courage, hope of reward and similar attractions, he persists in his inertia, chances are that he has something physically wrong with him or he is suffering from poor hygienic conditions. There was, for example, the little boy who appeared to be disgustingly lazy. One day, however, an attack of appendicitis made an operation imperative for him. Six months later, the child was at the head of his class.

Another child was in a classroom that was overcrowded and the atmosphere was so vitiated that he had difficulty breathing. He was sent to the country and immediately his work habits improved.

Whipping in either of these two cases would have been no help in curing the laziness of the children; all that was necessary was to make conditions favorable for work.

But there are truly lazy children; theirs is a moral laziness: They won't work at all because they don't have the least bit of energy. The Catechism defines laziness as "an excessive love of rest which makes one avoid every painful duty." That is exactly what it is.

Now people who work do so either through a taste for it, through self-respect or because of duty. The problem, then, with the really lazy child is to try to stimulate in him a liking for work or awaken in him a legitimate self-respect or develop in him a sense of duty.

Stimulate a liking for work: Sometimes children dislike school work especially because their beginning lessons in a subject were poorly taught. The child was repulsed by initial difficulties. That is often the case in mathematics.

"My son is getting along all right," a mother explained, "but he is a little weak in Greek." The fact was that the elements of that language had been badly explained to him. A clever professor took him in hand, showed him that Greek was easier than Latin once the first difficulties of the alphabet, the declensions, and the conjugations had been conquered. The boy won a *first* in Greek.

Awaken a legitimate self-respect: Some children prefer rest and comfort to all else. The last place bothers them very little. They seem to have no ambition; they are utterly indifferent to success. We need not fear to humiliate them but we must be vigilant not to discourage them. The dunce cap worn too often frequently produces a real dunce. We must be ingenious to find a way to make that pupil succeed in something at least once. This could be a good starting point; then, if nothing comes of it, punishment should follow. We are, it must be remembered, considering the case of a child who does not succeed, not because he lacks the means, but because he does not work.

Develop a sense of duty: "You ought to work because

papa and mamma wish it and God asks it." Bring into play a filial spirit and love of God.

Parents must know correct child psychology. They are the ones who have given him his physiological being. It is up to them to examine whether anything in his physical condition explains his inertia at work; they are in a better position than anyone else to determine this. If the deficiency is psychological, they have the responsibility for seeking into its cause and supplying the appropriate remedy. It is up to them, without substituting their own activity for the child's to teach him how to will by stimulating his will.

Lazy Children

CHILDREN who do not work or who work badly are of several types.

There are sickly children: Here the remedy is up to the doctor.

There are poorly endowed children: They are not exactly ill; people can be in splendid health without being very intelligent. Some children have little talent. Rare are the parents who have the courage to recognize it; they are ashamed, and wrongly so, of the weak instrument their offspring has received. They ought to pity the child whose mind is less keen as they pity the child who is crippled or in weak health. Besides with patience they can sometimes achieve excellent results.

Then there are children who are badly trained by their parents or poorly taught by their teachers. They have been allowed to acquire habits of disorder and caprice or they have been roughly treated, overwhelmed with tasks beyond their ability to the point of being crushed by their work; they have been taught neither discipline nor a good method of work. In their case poor pedagogy is to blame.

Finally, there are the actually lazy children: They are sufficiently endowed, sufficiently healthy to do normal work, but they refuse to apply themselves, go at their work grudgingly and seek to do the least possible amount of work.

Such evil is frequently traceable to an early childhood marked by too soft a training, an inadequate training in effort and endurance. The child did not start early enough to use profitably the opportunities to exercise liberty, to assume responsibility and to attack work. The parents acted for him instead of trying to form him. They lacked skill in transforming play into work and work into play. They gave him toys which offered him no chance to use his intelligence, his constructive bent, his imagination and creative powers. And whenever they held out the prospect of school life to him they led him to regard it as a task or punishment: "If you are not good at home we will send you to school soon," instead of "If you are good, we shall be able to send you to school and you will have the joy of beginning to work."

The child who is poorly trained will get accustomed to cutting his life up into two parts: the principal part belongs to pleasure with the other part thrown in from time to time—those boring moments assigned to work. He should have been impressed with the idea that work is the law of our whole life; it is the unfolding and the extension of our powers and if it brings with it a certain amount of labor, it also brings with it a greater amount of joy which results from overcoming difficulties, acquiring new knowledge and opening up additional possibilities for advancing farther into the field of truth. Recreations, games are but opportunities to relax and to stretch out into the open as it were to grasp new strength for further work.

Work should be presented not as a drudgery but as a conquest. Very early in life the child should be led to envision his future career or mission: "If you want to become an engineer, a sailor, then...." Or "You will be a mother maybe and you will have to keep house." They should see that papa and mamma find pleasure in work and better still that work pleases God. We must all of us sanctify ourselves in the duty of our state at each moment whether we like it or not. If we like it, so much the better. If we do not like it, then we ought to put greater generosity into it and offer our suffering for a worthy cause, such as the missions, the sanctification of priests and religious, one's family and many similar good intentions.

Care should be taken not to overdo the reward idea, especially rewards promised as a prize for work requested; that develops calculating hearts. Ask for work for the reasons previously indicated and wait for an opportunity to give an appropriate recompense on some other occasion; it will be so much more a prize since it will be unexpected.

Training in Sincerity (1)

THE CHILD is exposed to two sorts of lies: the lie of which he himself is the victim; the lie of which he makes others the victim.

The child has an imagination that never ceases its activity. His first contacts with the world have been with dream powers; he knows nothing yet of reality being much too little to grasp it; he makes a world for himself, a world in which he is king and lord. Even later when he does begin to get in touch with reality, he will use it only as a springboard to project himself into the stars. Dream and reality overlap in his little head without harming each other; they merely embellish each other and he will not be able to recognize the line of separation. That accounts for so much fantasy in his conversation and the astonishing liberty he takes with what we adults hold as true.

Weighed by our standards, it is clearly evident that the child's stories sound to us like downright inventions. He himself will be taken in by his own game. He will distort with delight, improvise the strangest scenes without shame. Will he always be able to distinguish whether he is the dupe of his imagination or not? Whether he is sincere or not? He is a wonderful builder of castles in the air and he will often endeavor to persuade those about him with the solidity of his edifices. Shall we call him a liar?

—Certainly not, rather an actor, an artist, a poet.

Parents and educators know well how advantageously they can utilize this power of recall and creation that children have. Consequently, they know no better way to amuse them and keep them quiet than to tell them stories —stories that are entirely fictitious, tales of magic, picturesque legends in which ghosts, fairies or devils play enchanting roles.

Let us not carry water too generously to the fountain. Yes, certainly, we can tell the little ones charming stories but with moderation. Make the children want them; however, avoid killing their effect by telling too many in close sequence. Children must be able to think over the stories, mediate on them, and through them discover life as it is. If the stories resemble each other or follow in too close succession, the child's imagination will jumble everything; the profit is considerably lessened.

One precaution is vital: The stories, which will surely always be very appealing and not without some suggestion of complication and mystery, must definitely present virtue in a beautiful light; otherwise, the child will be occupied, entertained and kept interested but he will not be educated or inspired. Since he is possessed of uncompromising logic he will be quick to draw dangerous conclusions if he sees vice rewarded; and the unpleasant results may not be slight. From this standpoint some puppet shows are not so innocent as they appear. We must not be pharisaical but we must know how to foresee danger. With children everything is important.

Even one or the other of La Fontaine's fables have questionable merit for children. Fortunately, with these fables, the children are much more interested in the activities of the characters than in the moral demonstrated. As one child put it: "Fables are entertaining; it is a pity though that there must always be a tiresome closing at the end." He was referring to the final two or three lines, the author's moral tag, which pointed out the lesson to be taught.

Let us not forget that the most beautiful stories are not *made-up* stories, but stories that really happened. "Did that really happen, mamma?" What a joy to be able to answer *yes* to that question. Why not take the bulk of our stories, if not exclusively at least mostly, from the lives of the saints, from the Gospel stories? Where can anything more wonderful, more truly wonderful, and at the same time more authentic, be found?

Training in Sincerity (2)

THERE is another kind of lie possible for the child, one that has moral significance, and that is the lie told with the actual intention of deceiving.

He may categorically deny his guilt when accused of a fault he has actually committed, or he may invent falsehoods through vanity. In the first instance he is seeking to exonerate himself; in the second, to make himself more important.

Often the reason the child tells the first kind of lie is that the punishment he gets for his little pranks and misdemeanors is out of all proportion to his offense. So many parents punish under the influence of anger that cruel words, exaggerated expressions and sometimes mean acts escape them. The child unable to resist by strength seeks to escape by deceit.

Sometimes the child lies for the sole satisfaction of excusing himself; not to mention the case, which is not at all fantastic, where the child lies for the sake of lying through an unhealthy tendency which is fortunately rare. In cases of this kind, the little offender must be shown how ugly such a fault is, how unworthy of him and how saddening for his parents.

Wise indeed was the mother who used the following technique on her four-year-old daughter the first time she tried to deceive her.

"My little girl has lied to me. This is the first time that anyone has lied in this house; therefore my little one may not have any dessert today because she deserves to be punished and mamma will not eat either because she will not be able to; she feels too sad."

Even when children are older such a method is good. A certain colonel had entrusted his sixteen-year-old son with the honor of keeping the flag of his regiment in his room; he took the privilege away from him as a punishment for a small lie.

The following counsel ought to be adopted as principles of conduct by those who want to inculcate an appreciation of sincerity in their children:

1. To create and to maintain an atmosphere of loyalty, of uprightness and of utter truth in the home. To instil a horror of sham, of pretense, of playing-up through policy. To encourage simplicity in everything; to take it for

granted that no one will seek to pass for what he is not; that if one has done wrong he will admit it. To refrain from upbraiding and to tolerate no tattling. To praise another for his truthfulness particularly if it cost him something.

2. Never to set an example of lying or give any encouragement to lying. No bluff: "When the teacher asks you if you did your homework all alone say *yes*." None of that!

3. Never to give a child the impression that we believe him to be a liar, but rather to manifest confidence in him. That will encourage him to be truthful and develop his self-respect.

4. Never to demand any immediate avowal of faults in the presence of others.

5. Never to laugh at any clever little lie told by the child to get out of facing up to a mistake or fault.

6. Never to lose an opportunity of praising for honesty and reproving for duplicity.

The last and most important of all advice is to inculcate in the child the sense of the Divine Presence. Help him to realize that God is everywhere, as the proverb puts it, "God sees a black ant on the blackest marble in the blackest night." Above all help him to understand that God dwells in the depths of his baptized soul. "You are a living ciborium. You can deceive your parents, your playmates, your friends. God accompanies you everywhere: Be firm out of respect for the divine Guest who does not leave you."

Training in Sincerity (3)

THE best way to encourage a child to be truthful at all times is to use strong positive appeals.

1. *Appeal to personal dignity and pride:* General de

Lamoricière used to say, "I shall die without ever having told a lie." And little Guy de Fontgalland, "I have never lied; I have too great a horror of untruth."

Beneath the doorway of the Church of *Santa Maria in Cosmedin*, at Rome there is an immense slab of antique marble on which is drawn a face with a wide open mouth—*The Mouth of Truth, La bocca della verita*. Legend has it that it closes mercilessly on the fingers of liars. The biographer of the Empress Zita relates that when she was a little girl she used to plunge her fingers into the *bocca* positive of withdrawing them intact because as she explained, "I have never lied." Is not the reproach, "you are a liar" one of the most devastating?

2. *Appeal to Courage:* The story of George Washington and the cherry tree is a classic. We all know it. The father appreciated his son's courage and praised him with the words: "Your honesty is worth more than the most beautiful cherry tree."

According to Corneille, to be honest is to be a gentleman:

> He who calls himself a gentleman and lies as you do
> Lies when he says it, and will never be one.
> Is there vice more vile, is there stain more black
> More unworthy of a man...

3. *Appeal to Love for Peace:* Corneille wrote his play *The Liar* to show that he who deceives others is not happy. Once he has entangled himself in the web of deceit and dissimulation, he needs a good memory for all the tales he has invented. What if he were to give himself away, reveal his deceit? That must be a constant worry.

How truly psychological was the answer of the individual who responded to the question, "Are you really telling the truth" with the statement, "I never lie; I am too busy; lying would befuddle me too much, get me too involved."

Truthfulness is further a guarantee of success. Sincerity is the best policy; we mistrust one who is known as a sly fellow, a dissembler, without integrity. We are not wary of an upright person. To be honest is the best way to be clever.

In general, a frank admission of guilt disarms. Madame Acarie, an outstanding Christian of the seventeenth century often said to her children, "Even if you would turn the whole house topsy-turvy and destroy it, but admit it when questioned, I should pardon you; however, I will never pardon you the smallest lie. Even if you were as tall as the ceiling I would get some women to help me hold you rather than allow a lie to slip by without punishment; nor would the whole world together succeed in getting me to pardon you."

The conclusion is evident. I will strive to give my children the Gospel principle, *Let your words be yea, yea; nay, nay*.

The example of that upright soldier General de Maudhuy could well be an inspiration for me; he composed the following soldier-prayer for his boys, "My lord, Saint Louis, Sir Bertrand du Guselin et Sir Bayard obtain for me the grace to be brave like you and never to lie either to myself or to others."

Honesty and Tact

To TEACH children to be honest and at the same time to develop in them a feeling for the requirements of tact so that they learn to keep to themselves opinions which might wound or embarrass others is a delicate undertaking.

While a child may occasionally be given to lying, he is, unless perverted, much more inclined to speak the truth. He will blurt it out regardless of place or circumstances.

Has he not often won for himself the epithet *terrible* for no other reason than his disconcerting honesty?

—"Godfather, are you going to stay a long time this evening?"
—"Oh, just about the usual time. Why?"
—"Because, Mamma says there's just no way of getting you to leave."

It is necessary but not easy to make the child appreciate where sincerity ends and indiscretion begins; to teach him, without dulling the lustre of his honesty, that it is not always good to say everything just because it is true and that politeness and even charity require us to practice self-restraint and not give free rein to the expression of all feelings.

In his play *The Misanthrope*, Molière gave us the character of Alceste who on the plea of honesty flung the unpleasant truth about others into their very face. He succeeded not in converting them but in bringing shame upon himself and wounding seriously the self-respect of those he insulted with his intemperate frankness.

Always to mean what one says is not the same as saying all one thinks or all one knows.

Human beings are called to live together in society and there can be cases where social life requires that words, those external symbols of thought and feeling, be used outside of strict material meaning or even contrary to it. We should not call such statements lies or we will create a disturbing confusion in the mind of the child who must be thoroughly convinced that a lie is never justifiable.

Much of the difficulty will be cleared away if we make the child understand that the purpose of speech is not only to express the truth but also to foster life in common. We must insist that lying is absolutely forbidden but likewise explain that to defend one's secrets against the curious, one's purse against thieves is a legitimate act which need not involve a lie.

Catholic morality is the morality of truth and honesty; but being human and social, it is also the morality of prudence, of justice and of charity.

Is Self-Accusation Obligatory?

WE HAVE seen the difficulty and the necessity of giving the child a correct notion of the consideration due to politeness and charity in the true spirit of sincerity.

There is yet another difficulty: Many do not sufficiently distinguish the exact limits of sincerity or rather the degree of obligation to speak the entire truth.

"There is no obligation to speak the entire truth to one who has no right to know it. We can use words in their usually accepted meanings: we can allow circumstances to modify the meanings of words: we can allow the hearer to deceive himself:"

St. Thomas à Becket, Archbishop of Canterbury, had to flee from the anger of Henry II, the King of England. He was pursued by the king's emissaries. As he rode along on a horse with neither bridle nor saddle he was stopped by armed men. "Are you possibly the Archbishop of Canterbury?"

—"Well, my friends," he answered, "look and judge for yourselves whether or not this is the equipage of an Archbishop."

"Deceit and sharp practice!" some will protest. Not at all. Simply a clear knowledge of the exact extent of the duty of truthfulness.

Take a case more directly concerned with education. Here let us presume that those who question have a right to the truth, the parents for example. There is even in this case a principle intervening which does not allow them to push their right to know the truth by demanding an avowal of guilt.

And this principle which all moral theologians recognize and which is founded on great wisdom is that *no one is obliged to accuse himself*. It is up to the accusers to prove the guilt and to punish accordingly if the guilt is proved. If the culprit does admit guilt it should be a reason for lessening the punishment. But to make self-denunciation a necessity is excessive.

Consider the case of a little child suspected of a fault. "Did you do that?" he is asked. According to correct morality, he cannot be *forced* to accuse himself. If the child says the whole truth, perfect! He is not obliged to. When he does, he is generous, doing more than he must; he has a right then to marked leniency. "A fault confessed is half pardonned." But one oversteps his power by commanding him to hide nothing, by telling him that he sins if he does not accuse himself. He does the better thing in accusing himself but commits no fault in not accusing himself; he is guilty of an imperfection but no sin.

Certainly it is better to accustom the child to admit the truth at all times, but to make it a formal duty in every case is to urge the law beyond reason and to confound a generous attitude with an obligatory attitude. One of the most essential points in the formation of the child's conscience is to teach him to discern what is commanded from what is simply though earnestly counseled.

Training to Confidence

CONFIDENCE is necessary. Nothing is so sad as those chasms which divide parents and children, causing them to lead lives practically isolated from each other, with no contact of soul, no intimacy between them.

Difficult moments will come, temptations will arise, decisions will have to be made and action determined. If children have no confidence in their parents, to what dangers they will be exposed!

But this confidence is difficult to get.

One important reason for the difficulty arises from the physical or moral temperament of the parents and of the children. The parents must know how to vanquish their little ones' fears, consent to their advances and not be afraid to give in.

Sometimes this confidence is blocked by other reasons which parents only too often overlook. There are for example parents, who because they are not sufficiently supernatural, openly show more affection for one child than another or give fewer marks of affection to one child. The child who believes himself slighted may turn inward and become sullen and jealous.

Again there are parents who are unbalanced in their punishments or fail to be just. There are others who are woefully ignorant of psychology and as a consequence seriously wound the self-respect of a child. He retaliates by closing up his heart.

A mother once laughed at a candid confidence her little boy revealed to her. He was hurt.

—"Papa," he said, "I don't love mamma anymore."

—"What's that! Is it possible? Why not?"

—"Why?... Well, that's just how it is. I don't want to tell her anything anymore... never anymore."

The father tried in vain to reason with him but he remained obstinate.

—"No, that's the end. I don't love mamma anymore!"

It may have been mere caprice and doubtless it was; time would probably clear it up. Yet, who knows?

Like all fragile things, the child's heart is easily scarred. And as with all things that have been marred it is not easy to restore the lustre, to efface all the blemishes.

Parents who want their children's confidence must know how to listen, to listen untiringly. They must be able to show interest in their triumphant little stories as well as in their grievances. They may never ridicule them, never rebuff them through irritation or nervousness and never deceive them.

They must know how to read their children without trying in any way to force an entry into their hearts or consciences; rather, they must be clever at inviting a confidence, dispelling a cloud, evoking a smile, creating a diversion in case of a mishap or tempest. They must show understanding always and make the children feel that they can tell them everything. Not that they approve of everything, but they take everything into consideration; if then adjustments are called for they make them; if rewards are merited, they bestow them. And when they must punish they do so with only the good of the child in mind so that, if the age of the child warrants it, they will explain the reason for their actions.

If in spite of all this, a child still persists in being withdrawn and uncommunicative, reserved as a hermit, there is nothing else to do but pray. Parents should not grow discouraged. Of course they should try to discover whether this reticence is the result of temperament or conscience worries. It might even be necessary for them to turn to someone else for help, someone who will be more successful because more competent. In many cases this could be a priest. It is a great mistake for parents to want to be the only recipients of their children's confidence. The child, the adolescent must be able to confide in someone. If we are not the one, and someone else is, let us accept the fact humbly. Such renunciation is very meritorious especially for the mother.

"All My Trust"

"I GET all my trust from my mother," Joan of Arc used to say.

Pauline Jaricot, the foundress of the Society for the Propagation of the Faith, could say the same. Every evening her mother used to gaze into her eyes to read the story of the day's fidelities to God's law which she had explained to the little girl with much unction.

Something similar took place in the training of the boy Augustine in Malègue's *The Master is Here*: Never did his mother reprimand him for his failings without reminding him that he had grieved Little Jesus. "It makes Little Jesus sad when you stamp your foot because you want to go home; when you refuse to leave the table so that it can be set just because you are busy doing a water color in your Christmas drawing book."

Each day he was expected to learn two Catechism questions:

"Every morning after breakfast in Big Catherine's kitchen, mamma heard the recitation of the two Catechism questions she had explained the evening before. Tiny sister Christine balancing herself on her yet unsteady legs used to pull at mamma's dress. That would be just the time when the baby would set up a howl in his cradle.

"Mingled with this morning hubbub were the words of Theology. They were difficult and impressive words. They were like the words grown-ups use when they don't want little children to understand what they are saying. It is true that mamma put other words in their place to explain them."

Happy the man to whom God gives a saintly mother!

This verse of Lamartine will always be profoundly true!

Who can tell the mother's great power to make the Faith take root in the mind of the child and to plant seeds of the most beautiful virtues in his heart. And will we not have to give primary credit to these first lessons of childhood for whatever remains of trust in the mind that has reached maturity and for whatever generosity exists in the souls that have been buffeted by life? The forces of mature age owe much to the lights and inspirations of early age.

Monsignor d'Hulst in one of his famous conferences at Notre Dame in Paris referred to this idea: He said that when a man wants to justify his moral principles he will search his past to find their origin; he will discover that they seem to trace back farther than the beginnings of his conscious thought; they will seem to him as submerged in that distant past when his life was still bound closely to that of his mother and he was as yet unable to sustain himself without the tenderness of her supporting arms.

Should it happen that a child loses his mother at an early age, her memory will remain and protect him. But if she lives what a help she is above all if she has a great soul, a soul that knows how to watch and to pray; to watch without being too obvious about it; for she will not want to awaken haughty resistance; to pray more silently still without however neglecting her duty of good example in prayerfulness.

Ozanam writing to a friend stated that he seemed to benefit almost every moment by the nearly constant presence of his mother.

Let me as a mother examine my conscience. By bringing children into the world I have accepted a sublime mission.

To give birth to children is in itself something wonderful. But to rear children, how much more difficult! How close to God I must be to lead all my little ones or my big ones as the case may be to the heights of the divine and to help them live on this high plane.

I must grow. I must educate myself. I must acquire what I lack.

Formation of Character (1)

CHILDREN are naturally upright. They are weak and easily become afraid like the rest of us but they are upright.

They know what they ought to do and what they must not do. They discover that very quickly since they are not only aided by the restraints and prohibitions of their family but also enlightened by the interior verdict of their conscience.

They have no difficulty surmising that if they do not do what is good they will grieve Mamma and Papa and likewise God; furthermore they realize that they will incur a punishment in proportion to their wrong—the principle of the proportion between the sin and the punishment familiar to the Doctors is already implicitly in the heads of these little theologians.

To be sure, it is in no abstract fashion that they acquire such knowledge; they achieve it in situations that are part of their everyday life, to the accompaniment of emotional experiences which are often quite impressive. They feel an inward approval, peace and joy when they have been good and, on the contrary, disquiet, unease, and interior reproach if they have not fulfilled a command. They do not have precise ideas on the subject but an intense feeling; they would not be able to explain the words *responsibility*, *law* or *liberty;* however, a real and profound experience discovers moral reality to them. They were supposed to behave well and they have acted badly, they are in the wrong and deserve to be punished. They feel it, they know it, and they suffer from it. Their childish language, their very silence and embarrassment bear witness to it. The day they learn the correct vocabulary for all of this they will be capable of putting these realities under their proper classification. Before they have ever learned the words for these realities they have *lived* the realities.

What a precious advantage for the child to be brought in this way into the region of the invisible!

The great philosopher Ollé-Laprune stresses this point:

The child "who it seems is entirely controlled by sense impressions, he whom visible nature seems to dominate by its charms and the thousand causes for fright it spreads about him, stops respectful and troubled before an invisible law. Invisible also is the Master, invisible too the Judge whose presence this law makes the child feel. God—the august and Sacred Name that he used to pronounce with docility but without comprehension—now becomes for him a mysterious reality whose invisible smile or secret threats are for him the most precious cause for hope or the greatest reason for fear. God—whom he does not see but who sees him, God—whom he knows so little yet by whom he is perfectly known. God—of whom he thinks only at intervals but who is constantly mindful of him. God—all powerful, wise, good completely good, better than a father, better than a mother, perfectly good and just and holy; what care he must take not to displease such a God! what misfortune to offend Him. How good he ought to be himself, how he ought to be truthful, to be just to all, to do good to others because those are the things God loves; those are the things He commands; those are the things God Himself does in His own sublime fashion, and he must resemble God.

"Invisible grandeurs, invisible beauties: the child who

enters into life with all his senses open and avid for stimulation of every sort can nevertheless fall in love with these realities that are inaccessible to the senses; he can aspire to know them better some day, somewhere and finally to look forward to the joy of possessing them then as the best reward for good will and the pain of being deprived of them as the worst punishment for an evil will. This is the way the moral and religious life of the child gets its start."

Formation of Conscience (2)

THERE is a story that at a certain Honor's Day a prize was offered to a lazy little fellow by way of consolation; since he did not come in for any victories in achievement, he was given a prize for the best health. He must have had a flair for rhyme for according to the legend this was his response:

> I don't care for the prize I did not really earn;
> Why, to get my good health, I did not make a turn.

To be rewarded for something which had caused him no effort, which represented no attainment on his part seemed odious to him. Lazy though he was, he did not lack intelligence or a sense of disinterestedness.

Most children are quicker to understand the notion of punishment as a just consequence for a wrong done.

They are well aware that to be able materially to accomplish an act is not one and the same thing as being permitted to do it. Children very quickly grasp the idea that Monsignor d'Hulst explained in one of his masterful talks at Notre Dame in Paris:

"We can compare physical necessity to a rigid iron or wooden barrier: As long as it holds out it is impossible to break through; if one does succeed in breaking through it is only because the barrier was knocked down or broken.

Duty, moral obligation, is also a barrier, but a spiritual barrier; we can cut through it as we would through a ray of sunshine. Its bright line marks out very clearly the limits beyond which we must not pass; if we happen to violate it, it lets us pass but closes behind us to continue forming a frontier of light between good and evil."

Whoever does break through this bar of light merits punishment.

How easy it is to profit by the awakenings of morality in the child to help him see clearly into his conscience. We teach him his prayers, the Act of Contrition for example: "O my God, I am very sorry..."; he has no trouble understanding; he knows he has acted badly, that he should not have pulled his sister's hair, disobeyed papa, wanted his own way. He has broken through the bar of light. Even if mother did not see him, someone did and that was God; a kind of inward voice tells him very quietly that he is guilty, that he must make up for it by being sorry, by asking forgiveness, by accepting the little pain that will come to compensate for the pleasure that he had no right to take.

Perhaps it will be necessary to reverse the order of the words, proceeding from the natural to the supernatural. Nothing is simpler: *"Regret, sorrow, penance, offense against God, a God infinitely good...."* How many difficult words; yet their meaning will unfold bit by bit.

Then when the time for confession comes, when he must say "I confess to Almighy God" only the word *confess* will seem strange, but only the word not the act; the child will have no difficulty making his accusation. Get him into the habit of making his little examination of conscience; he will tell you his "sins" out loud. I "confess" that is I "admit"; he will understand that he ought to admit and admit to God who is so good all the wrong that he has done.

"Through my fault," I should not have done it. But

when I have confessed it, it will disappear, it will be wiped out. And then, of course, I must not do it over again; I must not break through the bar of light again. "Therefore I beseech You..." Another difficult word he must learn, but a reality which he does not yet see... to be good he must have God's help. By himself everything would be too difficult! How children do stumble over that "by means of Your holy grace" in their Act of Contrition and sometimes we don't blame them! Yet beyond the vocabulary so poorly adapted to them lies a reality which is quite within their power to grasp!

Formation of Character (3)

SOME children, perhaps the majority of them, readily admit their peccadillos.

There are others though who are very proud, very jealous of that little interior kingdom where an intimate voice, God's voice, is heard, where they can judge their conduct in the light of what that voice demands; into this domain they want no other person to penetrate.

We must respect a child's interior life and not seek to enter there without being invited, not try to learn what he does not wish us to know of that interior life, nor try to find out what he hides with a sort of naïve but respectable modesty. Neither should we remind him of painful scenes, now past and forgiven, in which he was clearly off his good behavior; there is danger of humiliating him, of causing him to close up. Discretion always!

This virtue will be an absolute necessity later; it will be no easy virtue to practice either. How painful for the father and the mother not to know what happens in the intimate life of their child! True there are indications that everything is all right or that something is wrong: Eyes that can no longer meet one's gaze, the tilt of the head, the sudden blush of shame, the general appearance that has become less vibrant and more embarrassed may tell much. But there are some young people, boys and girls, who excel in putting on an act and who never reveal their true depths; they remain closed temples.

It is ideal if parents do know everything about their child. They must however be willing to know only a little and in some cases nothing at all.

One very important lesson we must teach a child is not only to observe the *number* of his peccadillos but the *kind*. He should learn to distinguish between important matter, a slight infraction, and simple imperfections. It is a sin when one resists a command of God, an imperfection only when one resists a simple desire of God. When there is question of a command of God, he must know too if the command is concerned with something serious, for then the infraction of that command is a mortal sin provided of course that there was full knowledge and real consent.

Most scruples are caused by inadequate and ill-adapted Catechism instruction at the age when the first conscience problems arise.

It is vitally important that we take great care not to cause the child to live in a perpetual fear of sin. Let him learn to be motivated by love. It is easier by far; the child quickly advances beyond attrition or imperfect contrition and finds love and perfect contrition much more understandable.

Souls that have been warped in childhood by exaggerated fears are in danger of living for the rest of their lives with nervous consciences, without freedom of spirit or joy.

We are to form children of God and not future prisoners of an iron-collar religion. The Gospel is not for a convict squad; we are at ease in our Father's house.

Many defections of later life are due to inadequacies of

education. A false conscience is easily made; a soul is easily warped.

Education in Reverse

It has been said that education is the art of developing in a child all the faults he has received from nature and adding all those nature failed to give him.

In this same vein a rather facetious author dared the comment, "Providence gave us parents to show us how we ought not act toward our children."

Someone else even more caustic drew up an infallible recipe for rearing children badly. All he had to do to determine the ingredients was to observe the behavior of certain parents. Could we not put definite names behind a few of the points ourselves. All we must do is observe; examples unfortunately abound: Here is the infallible recipe:

1. Begin from babyhood to give the child everything he asks for.
2. Discuss his wonderful qualities in his presence.
3. Observe in his presence that it is impossible to correct him.
4. Be sure to have father and mother wrangling in his presence and in disagreement about him.
5. Let him get the idea that his father is only a tyrant and good for nothing but to chastise him.
6. Let the father show little respect for the mother in his presence.
7. Pay no attention to his choice of playmates.
8. Let him read anything he wants.
9. Try to earn much money for him without giving him good principles to live by and let him have money freely.
10. Let him have no supervision during recreation.

11. Punish him for a mere awkwardness and laugh at his real faults.
12. Take his part against teachers at school or in college when they try to make him come to task.

As far as punishment goes for wrongdoing, how many parents prove cowardly and unwise. Consider the mother's statement, "The only way I can keep my authority is by not exercising it." What a confession of failure!

Some parents let their children do anything and everything. Others intervene but in what a clumsy fashion:

—Perhaps they are profuse in threats. "If you do that, this will happen." The child does the wrong and "*this*" does not happen; the punishment threatened remains hanging in the air. The child knowing what to expect is no longer impressed. We must never make a threat we do not intend to carry out when the infraction has been committed!

—Then again they may take to bargaining: "If you do that, I will give you this present." Or they may stoop to argument to force compliance:

"Louis, take your coat."

"But, Mamma it's not worth while."

"Yes it is; take it because it looks threatening. I looked at the barometer and it's low."

"But, Mamma, I tell you it won't rain..."

"Thursday, you didn't have your coat and you were soaked to the skin."

"Yes, but Sunday you made me wear it and it didn't rain..."

And so it goes on and on...

Then parents sometimes permit coaxing to lead them into multiple concessions: A child may be convalescing and wants something to eat which would harm him.

"No, you many not have it."

"Oh, yes Mamma, give it to me."

"You know very well the doctor said you should not have it."

"Only this once, I won't ask again."

"Well, just this once since you want it and because you are sick but it will be your own fault if you get worse."

Who is to be pitied in all these instances? The child whose every whim is satisfied? Or the parents whose inexperience or weakness lead the child to the greatest dangers?

Lack of character in children is often the outgrowth of lack of character in the parents. One can give only what one has.

Important *Nevers*

Never make a promise you don't intend to keep. It brings discredit on you and teaches your child to lie.

Never shout. To rear a child you must control him. Now we are controlled only by qualities we do not have ourselves, a talent beyond our reach. If there is one quality a child does not possesses, it is calm, which is the direct opposite of the extreme mobility of his nature, his impulsive impressionability. Calmness controls him, not shouting.

Never deceive: "Give me your whistle; you will see what fine music I can make." The child with no defence gives you his whistle and you put it in your pocket: "Now with the whistle there, you can't annoy us anymore."

Or if you want the child to take some disagreeable medicine, you may say "Oh but this is good! Drink it, you will see." The child sips it and pushes away the deceiving cup. You have failed him in your words. A few scenes of this kind and the child will lose all confidence in those who speak to him. If we wish to be believed, we must not abuse belief.

Never do yourself what the child with a little time and ingenuity can do himself otherwise he will never learn to take the initiative. On the contrary, confront him as soon as possible and as often as possible with tasks that are beyond him but which are capable of challenging him a bit so that he learns to gauge his strength, to remain humble because of non-success and eager for struggle because he wants to conquer the obstacle.

Never tolerate backtalk to a command, or grumbling, or any argument about it. Never take back a prohibition especially if the child tries to work its recall by tears and coy manoeuvering.

Never present a task to the child as beyond his capabilities as "Could you do that? Don't you think you would be afraid to do that?"—so that he gets the idea of a possible sidetracking of the issue or a sliding out of it altogether. No, tell him squarely what to do as if it were just an ordinary simple matter. "Do this. Go there please." In this way the child will not question his ability to do what is asked. If he says he can't do it or shows that he can't do it, there will be time enough to chide him for his cowardice or lack of nerve.

Never seem to attach importance to little scratches, bumps, and bruises he gets (naturally proper attention should be paid to real needs). The child often cries when he hurts himself just to get attention, being pitied makes him a more interesting individual. If you do not appear excited, he will understand that it is useless to make a tragedy of the affair. Care for the hurts that need care, and far from magnifying the case, explain that it isn't anything much: "You will have many others! Try to have more nerve about it!" The child grows calm.

Never inflict a humiliating punishment in the presence of others, except in the rare case that might need it to punish an ineradicable pride. Aside from such a case, however, you would be degrading a child beyond reason: "Look how ugly he is!" "How clumsy you are! etc.... Or what is worse—"Look at your brother, see how good he is!" Such comparisons are odious and only excite jealousy.

Never flatter either: "Isn't he darling!" The child knows it only too well. Encourage him but don't praise him. To praise him is to admire him for an advantage he has without merit on his part; to encourage him is to congratulate him on meritorious effort. Never tolerate the adulations of people who visit you either.

Training the Adolescent

To TRAIN little ones is difficult enough. When these little ones grow up the difficulty of educating them grows with them.

There is a particular age—between thirteen and seventeen—when the rise of new energies generally produces a crisis. The child is no longer a child; neither is he a grown-up. He is in a period of transition which we must not fear but which we must consider sympathetically; it is a time when we should be ever ready to come to his help at opportune moments.

It is also a time when restraints weigh upon him. Until now the child did not distinguish his individual identity much from those about him. What they thought and felt he was satisfied to feel and think in perfect harmony. But now his personality is emerging. Before this it was indistinct. Oh yes, at times traits of it would shine out and predict the future character but it was only a faint sketch. Now the design takes form and definite lines.

It is thrilling to see the dawn of manhood and womanhood in the young as they rise up to meet life. It is depressing to think of possible deformations! A design can so easily change into a caricature!

There is no question now of a dead image on inert paper! We are concerned with an animated potentiality, with an intense dynamism—a soul seeking itself. It is like a person lost in the night groping about here and there to find the right road. We can speak to the adolescent, guide him, but nothing takes the place of personal experience and it means much to allow the young the liberty to try their luck.

Even as a baby, as soon as he takes his first steps, the child uses all its baby strength to pull away from its mother. The mother had until then held him in her arms. But one day she put him down so that he could learn to stand and to put one foot before the other. As soon as he learnt this new game the little one is ready for his first expedition. And what mother, even though she rejoices at the prowess of the young explorer, does not suffer when she realizes that her arms and her heart can no longer hold back this little conqueror already setting out to meet life?

As the adolescent boy or girl grows older the span of their investigation widens. There is the immense field of their own individuality. How many realities, how many mysteries they encounter at every step! Fortunate that youth who, avid until now to ask questions, remains willing to ask some still! He wants to learn certainly, even more than ever before, only he wants to learn by himself so he withdraws into himself to solve his problems. Who could ever know as he does his little domain; he is jealous of it; he closes his arms about his riches; he yields to no one the right to violate his treasure.

We should not be astonished at this but stimulate their research unobtrusively, provide them, without appearing to do so, with the means to solve their problems; we should not pry into their confidence but rather cleverly inspire and provoke it. Let them realize that mother and father themselves formerly discovered this whole world that challenges their discovery; that mother and father can therefore serve as prudent but well-informed advisers to the young novices of life.

Then there is the whole world outside of themselves—the frame of their life, their surroundings, and other people; that is quite a universe. What is the significance of such a smile, such a silence, such an action? They thought everyone was good—that was a mistake! They thought that life was conquered without difficulty—they have to struggle hard: How much work to learn the least thing!

And then the whole domain of religion. It was all so simple formerly. Now there are problems on every side. And love? This whole transformation that they sense within themselves? Those impulses of feeling? Those sensations never before experienced, organic phenomena whose nature and reason they do not know?

We need great sympathy before their laborious and often worried seeking and also much vigilance mingled with a gentle firmness, high moral principles, and exceptional psychological insight almost bordering on prophecy. Above all we need much prayer.

Girls versus Boys (1)

THE training of adolescence ought to make much allowance for the difference between the sexes and for the difference of individual temperaments within each sex.

The boy as he grows older becomes more and more individualistic. Everything exists for him. His little person makes itself conspicuous without fear. He loves to make noise not only because of his love for activity but also to assert his presence. In games he likes to direct and if he envisions the future he always sees himself in the role of a leader....

He must be taught that other people exist and what is more, that he has the duty not only to refrain from harming them but to help them. Every opportunity for him to render service should be used to advantage—to take care of his little sisters gallantly and willingly, to run on errands for father or mother or someone else in the household. The boy and later the man is a great egoist. It is wise to counteract very early this tendency of his to make himself the center of interest, to turn his attention to careers of devoted self-sacrifice, to impress him with the repercussions his actions have upon others and to enlighten him on his duty to give much since he has received much and to penetrate him with the realization that he has a responsibility toward his own.

The little girl as she advances toward womanhood—and this begins quite early—very quickly becomes conscious of herself as part of a relationship. She feels herself physically weaker than her brothers and her powers of feeling orientate her even at that early age whether she is aware of it or not, toward love—in the beginning toward the *couple* "mamma and baby" but later toward the *couple* "husband and wife."

Much less individualistic than the boy—although she can be so in her own way and sometimes fiercely so—she is above all family-minded. She loves to rock the baby, to help her mother. If she prefers one study more than another, history, literature or mathematics, it is more often because of the teacher who teaches it than the subject itself. Early in the little girl's life are verified the words of George Sand concerning woman, "Behind the *things* that she loves there is always *someone*."

Because of the complexities of feeling, the education of the adolescent girl is more delicate and more difficult than the education of the adolescent boy. The boy is more heavy, more blunt, more matter of fact, less given to fine distinctions; the phenomena of puberty are more tardy in him and are generally not at all or scarcely ever accompanied by any fits of feeling but rather a mere hunger for sensations: he is still the individualist.

Because of her periods, a phenomenon which often troubles the adolescent girl even after its mysterious significance has been chastely and adequately explained to her, she becomes more curious and uneasy about all that bears on the problem of life and is much more susceptible to emotional unbalance and the fascination of abandoning herself to daydreams than a boy of her age. If the adolescent boy is healthy, he doesn't indulge in dreaming; he makes noise or pulls all kinds of pranks. The girl, even when she loves study, loves still other things and she is much attracted by the perspective of an eventual giving of herself.

Beautiful is the task of giving her a clear idea of her essential vocation; to guard her from false notions; to get her to be diligent in the tasks of the moment, her house duties and school assignments; to direct her need for unreserved giving so that what is but a vague instinct within her becomes translated into terms of clear duty; to impress her with the immense responsibility of having been chosen to give life unles God chooses her to renounce this power, for love of Him, in virginity.

Girls versus Boys (2)

EVERYDAY experiences give many examples of the distinctive differences between the two sexes especially during their adolescence: the egocentric interests of the boy, the self-radiating tendencies of the girl. The boy thinks about his future exploits; the girl dreams of possible children. In the one, love of glory; in the other love of love itself.

The following bit of conversation between two sisters is in itself an amusing commentary on feminine adolescent psychology.

—"What are you thinking of," the twelve year old asked her fifteen year old sister, "of your future husband?"

—"A husband," protested the elder, "I am too young. I have a lot of time before I begin thinking of a husband!"

—"Well then what are you thinking about?"

—"I was planning what kind of trimmings I would have on my wedding dress."

Even when we take into account the differences created by nature between boys and girls, we still must make allowances for different temperaments within the sexes. Each child lives in a world of his own, in a world that is strangely different from the world of those about him. With one individual maternal influence will have greater force; with another, paternal influence. One child may have vigorous health, whereas another is delicate. In the one a melancholy temperament may predominate; in another, the exact opposite, the sanguinic with extrovert tendencies conspicuous. One child may be calm and poised; another, a little bundle of nerves ... Consequently, if the educator has but one method of dealing with all, a single and only method, he can expect to meet with disappointments.

However in providing for these individual differences a real problem must be faced: It is not sufficient to correct the one child and refrain from correcting the other; to congratulate the one and ignore the success of the other and so on through all the possible variations that might be in order. All this must be done while preserving the impression of treating all alike. If children perceive, as they sometimes do with reason, that there is partiality shown to one or other of the family, authority is broken down, jealousy enters and soon constant wrangling results.

The ideal is to maintain poise, serenity, evenness of temper, and a steadiness of behavior that nothing can upset.

Superiors of religious orders are advised to make use of a practice which is beneficial for all—an honest examination periodically of their faithful fulfilment of the trust confided to them. Have I given evidence of any partiality or any unjustifiable toleration of wrong? Have I seen to it that the rules have been observed, the ways of customs of the order and its holy traditions held in honor?

In what way are things not going as they should? One can pass quickly over what is as it should be, thanking God humbly for it but direct attention by choice to what is defective and faulty to determine to make the necessary corrections either in one's person or one's work. Mussolini's comment has a point here: "It is useless to tell me about what is going along well. Speak to me immediately of what is going badly."

If only parents would make it a habit to practice this counsel suggested to monks: Stop a moment to observe the train pass; look to see if the lighting functions, if the wheels are well oiled, if there is any need to fear for the connections. People do that from time to time in regard to their personal life and we call it a *Retreat*. It is strongly advisable to make a retreat to examine oneself on the conduct and management of the home, of one's profession; such a retreat should be sufficiently frequent to prevent painful surprises.

Our Lord said that when one wishes to build a tower, he sits down to calculate the cost and requirements for a solid structure. What a tower is the Christian home! That is something to construct! How necessary are foundations that will not crumble, materials that will hold solidly! How essential an able contractor, attention to every detail, care to check every stone, exactitude in the measurements for every story...!

Perhaps I have forgotten to sit down... to calculate... to get on my knees. There is still time!

A Father's Letter

RACINE the great classic dramatist wrote a letter to his son urging him to complete fidelity in his religious duties and to love for the interior life.

You beg me to pray for you. If my prayers were good for anything you would soon be a perfect Christian, who hoped for nothing with more ardor than for his eternal salvation. But remember, my Son, that the father and mother pray in vain for their children if the children do not remember the training their parents gave them. Remember, my Son, that you are a Christian, and think of all that character makes of obligation for you, all the passions it requires you to renounce. For what would it benefit you to acquire the esteem of men if you would jeopardize your soul? It will be the height of my joy to see you working out your salvation. I hope for it by the grace of Our Lord.

When Racine was thirty-eight and at the height of his power, his religious directors through the misguided zeal of their jansenistic spirit commanded him to give up writing for the theatre which he did with untold pain. Consequently, when he spoke to his son of the practice of renunciation, he could speak with authority.

Especially sensitive to physical suffering, he accepted sickness humbly and generously: "I have never had the strength to do penance; what an advantage then for me that God has had the mercy to send me this."

It is a great grace for children to have a father who

teaches the divine law with firmness, and who moreover lives this divine life, joining personal example to precept.

Am I sufficiently attentive to give my children the supernatural equipment they need? Am I sufficiently careful about that still more important duty of giving them a good example always and in everything.

If there was too much severity in Racine's manner it was due to his own training at Port-Royal, the Jansenist center. When his brother Lionval was only five years old he insisted that he would never go to the theatre for fear of being damned. Madelon, at ten years had to observe Lent to the very end even though she felt ill because of it. The mother kept them in step. Did she not command young Louis Racine who had indulged in writing about twelve stanzas of poetry on the death of a dog to betake himself to Boileau for a good scolding?

There must be no exaggeration in the exercise of authority; it would no longer be Christian in character but an erroneous way of understanding the morality and perfection of the Gospel. It is essential to retain a zealous will on the part of the children and a courageous practice of generosity. We must however always remember that they are children and not impose upon them too heavy a yoke thereby running the danger of giving them an incorrect idea of religion or of disgusting them even with its most balanced practice.

We must be mindful too that some day they will be confronted with fearful difficulties. They will need a training that is not *harsh* but *strong* otherwise we can fear shipwreck or at least ineffective returns.

If my profession or my health prevent me from fasting, am I careful to get a dispensation, to substitute another mortification for it, to manifest an exemplary moderation on all occasions, in general, a real detachment from food and body comforts; to deny myself amusements that might prove dangerous?

Misunderstood Children

ANDRÉ BERGE in his book on "Bewildered Youth" gives us the story of a young man who had been left completely to himself by his parents. Taken up with their own affairs, business and pleasure, these parents let their son grow up with no concern at all for his soul, his ambitions, his difficulties, his temptations, his failings.

At first, the youth relished this liberty which he interpreted as reserve on the part of his parents. But soon he came to realize that it was nothing more than cowardice, abandonment of duty and flagrant desertion of obligation on their part; he was living in the home but was not of the home—a mere boarder in a hotel. As soon as he was out of his childhood, they showed no more care for him; he found himself confronting life alone, confused, cut off. He should have been able to expect counsel, affection, protection, light. Nothing of the sort did he receive. Instead he met with selfishness; faced by loneliness, life began to pall upon him; he had no one to untangle his problems, no one to point out definite steps to follow on the bewildering way.

Unable to bear living any longer in this way with no vital ties binding him to those who should have been nearest to him, he decided to break all connections, to go away. Material separation from his own would but serve to accentuate the separation of their souls.

He left this note as an explanation of his conduct and a reproach for theirs:

To my parents,
Why do you desert me? You do not understand that I am stifled between these walls and that my heart is bursting.

Do you not understand that I am growing up and that life is calling me, that I am alone all day with its voice? You who could have so lovingly directed me in life, why do you abandon me?

Well, so much the worse, I will meet life alone. I am so far from you already through your fault.

How heavy the obligations of parents! Let us not consider now the case of grossly selfish parents as described in the preceding story. We shall consider parents who are concerned about accomplishing their mission.

Are they not in danger of two extremes in the fulfilment of their duty: either to exaggerate their control or to exaggerate their reserve.

If they try to exercise too much control over the young adventurers in freedom who are making ready for their first flights will they not incur the blame of tyranny, excessive watchfulness and supervision?

If, on the other hand, they try to avoid this reproach, are they not going to lack firmness? By trying to win confidence through a gentleness that gives free rein are they not going to see all the restraints which they deem good broken down and the advice they judge opportune utterly ignored?

How have I succeeded in this problem of training? Do I steer my bark with proper mastery? The reefs are many; a solid craft is needed, a steady hand at the helm. Am I acquainted with the route, the true merits of my crew?

My God grant me the grace to know how to rear my little world as you want me to; to know how to form each of my children according to Your plans; to know how to attain balance in sharpness, firmness and restraint. Grant that the youth formed in my home may never be confused, lost before life but rather know always where to find counsel, support, the warmth of love and guidance, an understanding and patient heart that can give help with enlightened insight.

A Defaulting Father

A RELIGIOUS was trying to extricate a young man of twenty-two from a distressing and almost insurmountable difficulty; the young man wrote him the following explanation for falling so low:

"... I was endowed as any normal person and would have been able to succeed in my studies as any one else but for some wretched habits—and I say these words, trembling with a powerless rage—wretched habits which came to poison the work of God. A cousin and a friend bear with me the responsibility for the first steps toward those devastating sensations that enkindled the odious flame which in turn upset my mental and physical health. No more willpower or rather no more strength despite good will; no more memory; all these results followed in succession. I blame my parents especially my father who had given up all religious practices. He never spoke to me with a view to understanding me; never did we have the least conversation which could indicate any common bond of ideas or feeling; he fed my body, that is all...."

What a terrible indictment are these words! How they prove the necessity of watching the associations of the children, their work, the reasons for their laziness; the importance of keeping their confidence, of knowing how to win that confidence; of showing them understanding and a willingness to help; of giving them an assurance of victory.

"I was endowed as any normal person and would have been able to succeed." Nothing more readily weakens the resilience of the powers of the mind and the heart than lust. What the young man said is exactly true; he had abandoned himself to impurity, he lost the keenness of his intelligence, the retentiveness of his memory and a relish for effort. Even grave physical injuries sometimes result. "Devastating sensations" and "the odious flame" quickly depleted and consumed vital energies.

"A cousin and a friend." How absolutely necessary is vigilance over the friendships that circumstances and relationships often provide, and sometimes alas that certain corrupted individuals seek to establish to give vent to their secret taste for perversion.

If the child had confided in someone at the onset of the first serious difficulties! But nothing in the attitude of the parents invited confidence, a request for enlightenment, a humble avowal of imprudence or faults already committed. How many children, how many youths yearn to speak! Someone, their father or mother or a director must take the first step. Nothing happens. Nobody imagines that they want help; nobody deigns to interest themselves in them. The mother is absorbed in her worldliness or completely oblivious of their needs; the father is wrapped up in his business; the spiritual director if they have one at all does not find the time or the means to help...

And the child, the young boy or the young girl carries the weight of inward suffering and is stifled by it.

"I blame my parents... never did my father speak to me with a view to understanding me; never did we have the least conversation which could indicate any common bond of ideas or feeling; he fed my body, that is all."

Did this father realize that even while he was nourishing the body of his son, he was contributing to the death of his soul by a double sin of omission! He did not help his son in his moral life when he needed it; he gave him a very bad example by openly abandoning the Christian law.

Such sins are paid for and paid for painfully. How prevent lack of training and mistakes of training from producing their disastrous effects?

To develop the body is fine, commendable, and a duty.

Even more important is it to develop the soul, to protect it, to strengthen it, to uplift it.

A Mother to Her Son

WHEN Léon Bloy was about twenty years old, he fell into one of those crises not uncommon in youth, particularly in youth whose environment brings contact with unbelievers and persons of loose morals, and he drifted from his religion. He was wretchedly unhappy besides, unhappy because of the very direction he was taking; but an involuntary confusion and probably a certain amount of wilful pride prevented him from breaking with doubt to return to the path of light.

The mother read her son's soul clearly. She did not reproach him, nor did she speak to him exclusively nor immediately of his religious problem; she attributed his interior troubles to different causes of an inferior order which more than likely played a part in his wretchedness. She wrote to him:

How is it my dear child that you do not write to us. I feel heavy hearted because of it for I am sure that you do not realize what is taking place in your poor soul; all kinds of things are conflicting within it—it is ardent and lacks the nourishment proper to it; you turn from one side to the other and you cannot tell what really bothers you. Ah! poor child, be calm, reflect. It is not that you feel your future lost or compromised; at your age one cannot have established his future or despaired of it; it is not for most persons your age still uncertain. No, it is not that, Your work, your studies do not show sufficient progress? Why? Perhaps because you want to do too many things at once; you are too impatient. No, not that either? Your mind is willing enough but your heart and your soul are suffering; they have so many yearnings that you are scarcely aware of, and their unease and their suffering react upon your mind sapping from it necessary strength and attention.

You are suffering, you are unhappy. I feel all that you experience and yet I am powerless to console you, to encourage you much as I should love to do so. Ah! that we might have the same convictions! Why have you rejected the faith of your childhood without a profound examination of your reason for and against it? The statements of those whom faith irritates or who have no religion for lack of instruction have made an impression on your young imagination; but just the same your heart needs a center that it will never find on earth. It is God, it is the infinite you need and all your yearnings are driving you there. You belong to that select number of elect to whom God communicates Himself and in whose regard He is prodigal of his love when once they have consented to humble themselves by submitting to the obscurities of faith.

What a frightening duty mothers have! To bring forth the bodies of their children is a beautiful ministry; to rear their souls is an even greater ministry.

What anguish for a mother when a grown child, a son in early manhood or a daughter in early womanhood cuts loose from faith, and considers God lightly! If ever she feels that she has lost her hold over her son or daughter, that they are escaping her, it is when she sees them follow the paths of doubt or fall under the spell of the intoxicating enchantments of flirtation.

A mother must continue to bring forth her children all her life. In this sense they are always her little ones. Not that she makes them feel their bonds of dependence any longer but that she watches over them. And she prays! Except for a brief reminder from time to time, the clear statement of her hopes joined to the definite but loving message of the father, an occasional letter in which true principles are recalled, the chief role of a mother whose adult child has strayed is prayer, patient waiting and sacrifice—the persevering effort to become a saint.

What if she were to die before she sees the return of the Prodigal? What if the Child were to die before she has seen him "return"?

She should not be discouraged. Can we know the mystery of souls? Can we know what takes place in the last moments? Can we know what goes on within when the exterior reveals nothing? Can we know the value of a mother's tears? Monica will continue to the end of time to convert Augustine; but Monica must be a saint.

Tick Tock

THE mother of Cardinal Vaughan had fourteen children—eight boys and six girls. Remarkable educator that she was, she believed that she owed the best part of her time to her little world.

The children's special room looked like the nave of a Church for each little boy and girl had his statue to care for and they never failed to put flowers before it on special occasions.

With what art this mother settled a quarrelsome boy or a vain or untruthful little girl! With the littlest ones she was not afraid to become a little one and like them to sit on the ground. Thus, placed *on their level*, as the biography of her Jesuit son expresses it, she used to put her watch to their ears and explain to them that some day God would stop the *tick tock* of their lives and that He would call to Himself in heaven His children whom He had lent to earth.

In the course of the day, Mrs. Vaughan loved to pick out one or other of her band, preferably two, chosen on the basis of their earnest efforts or some particular need for improvement, and make a visit to Church. Yes, they should pray at home too; they had God in their hearts; but in each village or in each section of town, there is a special house generally of stone where Our Lord lives as He once lived at Nazareth except that now He remains hidden under the appearances of a little Host. She explained to them that prayer consists not in reciting set words but in conversing with Jesus. And if they had been very very good she would let them kiss the altar cloth and sometimes the altar itself, a favor the children regarded as most precious. When they had beautiful flowers in their green house they brought them to Church; happy and proud were the ones who were entrusted with delivering the bouquets or the vases of flowers!

Besides the visits made to *"Jesus, the Head"* there were also visits to the "members of Jesus," *What you do to the least of My brethren you do to me.* And Mrs. Vaughan explained to each child according to its capacity to understand the great duty of charity and the reason for this duty. She did not hesitate to take them into sordid homes. Sometimes people were horrified to see her take the children to see the sick who suffered from a contagious disease. Wasn't she afraid her children would contract it? But kind, firm Mrs. Vaughan did not allow herself to be the least disturbed by such comments. "Sickness? Well if one of them contracted a sickness while visiting the poor, that would still not be too high a price to pay for Christian charity. Besides God will protect my children much better than mother-love can."

Here was true formation in piety, true formation in charity. Here too was encouragement to follow a high ideal.

Herbert, the eldest of the boys, was once quite concerned over a hunting trip that the weather threatened to spoil. "Pray mamma," he said, "that we have good weather!"

And Mrs. Vaughan more concerned to lift her son's soul than to secure him a pleasurable time answered smilingly, "I shall pray that you will be a priest!" How the boy took such an answer at the moment is not recorded. We do know this: Herbert was . . . the future Cardinal!

Mrs. Vaughan also gave her children an appreciation of the fine arts. She herself played the harp delightfully. From time to time she gathered her household about her for a gala time playing, singing, and a bit of mimicry; she always used the occasion to remind the children that there are other melodies and other joys more beautiful than those of earth.

Training in Generosity

THE child is instinctively selfish, but he easily learns generosity.

His training should be directed toward it.

Little Rose of Lima's childhood was marked by a series of accidents, maladies, and sufferings which the crude treatment of that time often aggravated rather than relieved. When only three months old she crushed her thumb under a trunk lid and the nail had to be removed. She also had to undergo an ear operation which was followed by a skin disease that began on her head; her mother treated it with a salve which burnt her so severely that the surgeon had to treat her for weeks, removing proud flesh so that the healthy skin could heal.

Thanks to her mother's exhortations, this little girl of four years bore the cruel pain with an astonishing calmness and in perfect silence. Are not the staggering mortifications we see her imposing on herself later due to her early training?

Like all little girls, she was vain and took considerable care of her hair which was very beautiful. Her brother used to throw mud at it and get it all dirty just to tease her. Rose became very angry, but the brother, recalling perhaps some sermon he had heard, assumed a preaching tone on one of these occasions and said to her solemnly, "Take care, vanity will be your ruin; the curled hair of girls are cords from hell which bind the hearts of men and drag them into the eternal flames."

Rose did not answer, but bit by bit began to understand ... and she detached herself. That detachment prepared her for greater sacrifices and soon we see her offering her virginity to God.

Jacqueline was another little girl, a little girl of our own day, who learned the lesson of sacrifice. She was sick and suffering much. "Oh, I believe nobody has ever had pain like mine!"

—"Where does it hurt?" she was asked.
—"In my stomach, in my head, everywhere!"
—"Think of St. Francis who had a red hot iron applied to his eyes as a treatment..."

This time her attention was caught. She forgot her own misery to sympathize with her dear saint whom people had hurt.

—"Did they cure him after all that?"

Guy de Fontgalland had to have many strychnine injections in his leg.

—"Offer it to Jesus, my darling," suggested his mother. "He was crowned with thorns for love of you."

—"Oh yes, that is true and He kept the thorns in His head while they quickly removed the needle from my leg."

A mother had three children; the oldest was four, the second, three, and the baby, twenty months. It was Good Friday. Why not encourage them to offer Jesus on the Cross some little sacrifice which would cost them a little?

—"My children, I will not deprive you of your chocolate candy at lunch today; but little girls who love Jesus will know themselves how to sacrifice their chocolate."

She made no further reference to it. None of the children answered. That evening the mother was very much moved to see the three chocolate bars at the foot of the Crucifix. Our Lord must have smiled at the childish offering; one of the candy bars bore the teeth marks of the baby who had hesitated before the offering and begun to nibble on her chocolate.

These stories of successful lessons in generosity are encouraging. What others have achieved, can I not achieve too?

Mothers and Vocations

WHEN Motta was elected to the Swiss Federal Council his first act was to send this telegram to his mother: "To my venerated mother, who remaining a widow while I was still a child, engraved in my heart the concept of duty by teaching me that duty dominates all interests, all selfishness, all other concerns."

To be sure God remains the Master of vocations. Motta was not entering upon Holy Orders. His providential position was to be quite different and very fruitful besides.

What is certain is that never—or shall we say rarely, very rarely—is a vocation born into a family unless the mother has inculcated in her children a sense of duty and a habit of sacrifice. Of course, all children who receive a strong supernatural training do not enter the priesthood or religious life, but no child enters upon any career calling for great self-sacrifice, prescinding some unusual influence which is rare, if he does not acquire early in life a solid spirit of renunciation and generosity in the accomplishment of duty.

On the other hand, where mothers know how to go about

teaching and above all practicing complete fidelity to duty and total renunciation, where they always put the supernatural love of God before material love for their children, Our Lord finds it easy to choose His privileged souls.

Monsignor d'Hulst said many a time to Abbé Leprince, "It takes a truly Christian mother to make a good priest. The seminary polishes him off but does not give him the substance, the *sacerdotal spirit*."

All things considered, that holds true for novitiates and religious life. Nothing replaces family training, above all the influence of the mother. But that training and that influence must be wholly supernatural.

Madame Acarie, foundress of a French Carmelite Convent where she was known as Sister Marie of the Incarnation, strove earnestly to rear her six children for God. She explained to them: "I would not hesitate to love a strange child more than you if his love for God were greater than yours."

However, individual free will always remains and God is Always Master of His gifts. That thought ought to calm the fear—unjustifiable as it is but humanly understandable—of certain mothers who think, "If I conduct my home along lines too thoroughly Christian, if I instill into my children too strong a habit of the virtues which lead to total renunciation, to an all embracing zeal, I shall see my sons and daughters renouncing marriage one by one and setting off for the priesthood or the convent."

If that were to happen, where would be the harm? But that rarely happens in practice. Furthermore, is marriage a state of life that does not require a sense of duty or abnegation?

Let there be no anxiety on this score but perfect peace. The important thing now is not that God might choose so-and-so but that the home give Our Lord maximum glory;

that each child whatever its destiny serve an apprenticeship in generosity and the true spirit of the Gospel. Everything else as far as the future is concerned should be left to God.

Priests in the Family

THE supreme honor for Christian families is to give priests to God. The father can do much to inspire a priestly vocation but the mother who is often closer to the children can do more. For this she needs a priestly soul, a gift that is not so rare in mothers as one might believe. "There are," said René Bazin, "mothers who have a priestly soul and they give it to their children."

The lack of priests is a terrible sickness of the world today, a sickness that is growing worse. The war has depleted their number and the absence of priestly influence in many parishes before and during the war has damaged more than one vocation.

It is necessary that Christian families desire to give priests to the Church; that they beg God for the grace to prepare to the best of their ability for the eventual flowering of the priesthood.

Christian families should desire to give priests: Such a desire presupposes a profound esteem for the priesthood on the part of the parents. What a pity it is when a child who broaches the subject of becoming a priest meets with his father's unreasonable anger, "If you mention vocation to me again, I'm going to strangle your confessor for it!" Can there be any greater blessing than a priest in a family?

Christian families should pray: A priestly vocation is a supernatural favor; prayer is essential to obtain it. God's gifts are free, that is true, but we know that He makes some of His choice graces depend upon the prayers of His friends.

Christian families should prepare for vocations: Parents should know how to detect the germs of a vocation. "I hear the grain growing," said an old peasant as he walked about in his field. No one can better read the soul of a child than the mother. "I know him through and through as if I had made him." This rather common but profound statement expresses very well the sort of intuition mothers have for all that concerns their child. Although the boy himself may not have discovered the divine germ, the mother, if she is keen and close to God, has been able to discern it.

How then help this germ to bud?

Help it *gently*, for there must be no pressure brought to bear upon the child. Suggest, yes; force, no.

Inspire great esteem for the priesthood. Consider a priest's visit to the home as a privilege and a festive occasion. "From the age of seven," declared Father Olier, the founder of the Sulpicians, "I had such an esteem for a priest that in my simple childish mind I believed them no longer human." When asked the source of his great esteem, he said, "From my father and my mother."

"Dear child, since you love to go to church so much and since you are so good in public speaking, you ought to become a priest," suggested the father to his son, the future martyr, Blessed Perboyre.

Often the mother has quicker insight and longer-ranged vision. The father sometimes resists the vocation of his child. Such was the case with Saint Francis de Sales and Saint Alphonsus Ligouri. The father of Saint Alphonsus refused to speak to him for a whole year.

Sometimes though the father is the one who inspires the love for the priesthood. At the time of the confiscation of Church property in 1905 in France, a father perched his son on his shoulders to watch the pillage of the churches to incite in him a desire to become a defender of the Church later and if possible a priest.

Madame de Quélen did not hesitate to bring her son to the prison of the Carmelite priests to visit the priests interned there. The bishop later chose the Church of this Carmelite prison for his See.

If a child seems drawn to the priesthood show him the high motives that can lead him to embrace such a calling—the desire to imitate Our Lord and the desire to save souls.

What a reward the parents reap at their son's ordination or on the day of their death. That repays them for all the sacrifices they willingly made; repays them with interest.

The Mother of a Saint

MADAME DE BOISY, the mother of Saint Francis de Sales, brought many precious virtues with her to the chateau of Thorens in Savoy where her husband lived. Unassuming and kind, she considered the village households around her estate almost as part of her family; she showed concern for their poverty and sufferings, settled their differences and exercised a control over them that was highly successful for the simple reason that she was careful not to make a show of it. Watchful to see that her servants were truly a part of the family, she encouraged them, without constraining them, to practice their faith and offered to read spiritual books to them herself after the evening meal; she invited all of them to attend the family prayer.

Unfortunately her marriage promised to be sterile. At Annecy in a church dedicated to Our Lady of Liesse, she begged God to give her a son, promising to "exercise all her care to make him worthy of heaven." On August 1567, Francis de Sales was born. He was so frail a child that all feared for his life.

As he grew older, the child had no greater delight than to show kindness to the unfortunate and to distribute among the poor the delicacies his mother gave him for this purpose. It is said of him that by way of thanking his mother he promised her, "When I am my own master, I will give you a beautiful red silk dress every year."

At the same time she was training her little boy to almsgiving, Madame de Sales was also educating him to love of God and to sacrifice.

Soon the hour of separation struck. The child had to leave for the school of La Roche and later for the College at Annecy. He was beloved by all, excused the faults of his comrades and one day even took a whipping in place of his cousin Gaspard de Sales. Shortly after his First Holy Communion he told his mother that he wanted to receive the tonsure some day and that therefore she ought to have his beautiful blond curls cut now.

Francis had two brothers. To characterize them and himself, he developed a comparison between the trio and the seasoning of a salad: "Jean-Francis with his violent temper furnishes the vinegar; Louis with his wisdom the salt; and I, the good-natured chubby Francis, put in the oil because I love mildness."

Francis possessed a secret of which his mother was the confidant: He wanted to be a priest at any cost. Madame de Sales shared his dream and upheld her son in it. After six years at Jesuit schools and colleges accompanied by outstanding success he entered the University of Padua. Here he astonished his professors with the brilliant way he defended his thesis although he was scarcely twenty-four at the time.

The father already envisioned his son as a great lawyer, then a senator, and the founder of a fine family, but Francis, enlightened by a providential experience he had one day while riding through a forest, decided not to delay his consecration to God any longer.

His father objected. The mother intervened: "Can we dispute with God over a soul He wants for His service?" Secretly she had clerical clothes made for Francis. The post of provost of the Cathedral Chapter became vacant. The father finally gave in and on June 8, 1593, Francis was ordained to the diaconate. In the opinion of his father, who missed the joy of seeing him a bishop, Francis preached too much and didn't put in enough Greek and Latin when he did preach. But Francis knew how to talk to souls as his famous missions at Chablais strikingly demonstrated. Rich and poor besieged his confessional.

On December 8, 1602, Francis, who was then thirty-five gave his first episcopal blessing to his mother, who soon put herself under his spiritual direction. One of the last joys of this noble mother was to read her son's *Introduction to a Devout Life*, a book which met with spectacular success.

A stroke brought the saint's mother to the point of death. The holy bishop of Annecy came hurriedly to her bedside. She recognized him, took his hand and kissed it, then putting up her arms to draw his head closer to her to kiss him, she said, "You are my father and my son!"

Francis closed her eyes at death. Broken by sorrow, he wrote to Madame de Chantel, "It has pleased God to take from this world our very good and very dear mother in order to have her, as I strongly hope, at His right hand, since she was one of the sweetest and most innocent souls that could be found."

Sons are worth what their mothers are worth.

Parents of Saints

SAINT FRANCIS DE SALES was the first child of Madame de Boisy. Saint Paul of the Cross was the first of sixteen children. The saint in the family is not always the oldest. Saint Bernard was the third of seven. Saint Thomas Aquinas was the sixth child in the family. Saint Therese of the Child Jesus was the last of nine children. Saint Ignatius of Loyola the last of thirteen.

What glory would have been lost to the Church if the parents of these children had consulted their *selfishness* rather than their duty of parenthood and had left buried in the realms of nothingness these little beings destined to become saints! It brings to mind the conversation between two women, the one voluntarily sterile, the other surrounded by fine children. The first woman explained to the second that she just couldn't be tied down. The second responded with the classic argument: "And suppose that your father and mother had reasoned like that, where would you be?"

The saints are rarely *only children* for two reasons: The first, that there cannot be any sanctity without a habit of renunciation and this habit is much more readily acquired in a large family where each one must forget self to think of others; where the rubbing of character against character whittles down selfishness; where the parents do not have time to overwhelm their offspring with a foolish indulgence that spoils them. The second, that God gives the grace of a holy call, by preference, where there is an integral practice of virtue, where virtue is held in honor, where the parents do not fear difficulty but trust in Divine Providence.

Saint Vincent de Paul was one of five children and Saint Vincent Ferrer, one of eight, Saint Aloysius Gonzaga, Blessed Perboyre, Saint Bernadette were each, one of eight children. In the family of the Curé of Ars there were six children; in that of Saint Margaret Mary Alacoque, seven; in that of Saint Benedict Joseph Labre, fifteen. In the family of Saint Catherine of Siena, there were twenty-two children of the same marriage. And how many more examples we could still find!

There is a charming Breton legend that carries an equally charming lesson. One day Amel, the fisherman, and his wife Penhov, who used to bring fresh fish to the monks, had left with their child to bring in the nets. They were overtaken by the tide. The water rose higher and higher and higher. "Wife, this is our last hour; put your two feet on my shoulders; in this way you will hold out longer.... and love my memory." Penhov obeyed. Amel sunk into the sand like a post driven in with a hammer. Penhov seized the child and lifting it above her said, "Put your two feet on my shoulders; in this way you will hold out longer. And love deeply the memory of your father and mother." The mother too sank beneath the water and soon only the golden hair of the child floated on the water. An angel of God passed by. He seized the child's hair and pulled. "My, how heavy you are!" Another blond head appeared, that of Penhov who had not let go of her boy's feet. "How heavy you both are!" Then Amel appeared for he had not let go of his wife's feet.... By the child the father and mother had been saved!

Who knows whether or not some parents will enter Paradise because an angel has seized their child by the hair! What a beautiful letter of introduction for Heaven is a child and above all a canonized child!

Training in Charity

JEANNE-ANCELOT-HUSTACHE gives us a picture of her little daughter Jacqueline in the book entitled *The Book of Jacqueline*.

She is a well-endowed child; she is made much of, in fact, too much petted by her grandmother, by her father, by her sister who is extremely proud of her and by all the guests of the home. She is in danger of becoming a charming little self-centered individual as so many children are.

Happily, attentive care watches over her and strives to give the child the spirit of charity, love for the poor, for children, for the weak and the suffering. Little by little, Jacqueline opens her heart to this love, toward the suffering of the world.

She finds exquisite words, unexpected delicacy in greeting people, in thanking them, and in easing every wound that she guesses with a subtle and tender intuition. She is embarrassed rather than triumphant because of the special advantages she has over companions who are less gifted, poorer and less endowed. She pities the poor beggar on the boulevard; she brightens the lives of the aged sick in the hospice of Ligny with her refreshing graciousness. At seven years this is how she prays to the Blessed Virgin for an unfortunate servant:

"O my Mother, my Mother, please deliver Yvonne. The poor little one. Nobody wants her. Her father doesn't want her, her mother is now far from her. She stole, she is in prison, she is sad and never will any one take her from it, never until her death; I alone on earth love her, I love her because she seems to say to me, 'If they would let me alone with you, I would never do anything bad.'"

"I alone on earth, I love her." That is the answer of Jacqueline to the secret appeal of the merciful Christ: She will give herself entirely to those who have no one to love them; she will be their *Sister of Charity*, their *Little Sister of the Poor*, their *Sister of Mercy*.

The hour of God for this privileged child was to come in an unexpected way. She was to die while still very young and she was to go to the Christ of the extended Arms, the Christ who loves little children who are charitable and pure.

What an advantage for the child's later life, if the parents have succeeded in making it alert to the refinements of charity, to a concern for the needs of the world.

They do not lack opportunities. Perhaps mother and child are taking a walk. Here comes a poor grandmother, gathering dead branches, leading along an emaciated, sickly child. "Suppose we go to their aid?" suggests the mother to her little one.

Christmas comes. In many families some good little children will have nothing, not the smallest present. Their papa is too poor; he earns just enough to provide bread to his household. Playthings? By no means; playthings cost too much. "Suppose we bring them that doll you don't play with anymore. Mother will dress it again so that it will look fine." Or, "Suppose you look for that mechanical horse you relegated to the attic. Papa will repair it so that it will seem like new."

Then there are the Missions. A terrible flood in some land has been reported. How many people are suffering! Let us fix up a bank into which each one can put his little alms! When we have a nice sum, we can send it over there. Or perhaps there is an occasion to ransom a little pagan baby so that it can be reared as a Christian. The opportunity to explain that spiritual alms are superior to material alms should not be passed by.

Once a child's eyes have been opened, how well it will know how to be good!

Training in Social Responsibility (1)

To AWAKEN the child to solicitude for the poor and the wretched is a splendid thing. However parents do not fulfil their whole duty, if they fail to give it a sense of responsibility for the common good and a true concept of co-operation.

Instinctively the child refers everything to its own small personal interest. If it is not taught very early to concern itself for others, it will be in danger of becoming narrow and selfish, of being forever oblivious to the general welfare, in other words, of never achieving a *social sense*.

While the child is very young this training will not consist in formal instructions but rather in a constant directing of attention on a thousand different occasions to the fact of having to be concerned about others. It will be taught to go upstairs without making a noise because mamma is resting; not to slam the doors because little brother or little sister is asleep; not to play noisily near papa's study. The child will learn very early in this way the social consequences of its actions.

The child may be with the whole family to meet someone at the station; the parents will have a fine opportunity to show it how selfish it is to stand directly in door ways and passages as it loves to do, since that obstructs the entrances and exits for people coming in from trains or those who merely wish to leave that way.

If a little girl accompanies her mother on a shopping trip, she can be taught not to ask the clerk to display more goods than necessary because it will all have to be refolded and replaced after she leaves.

At basketball or football, it is not so important to be a star player oneself as to bring the team to victory. It is true sportsmanship and true nobility to renounce a personal triumph by passing the ball to a fellow player who will assure the victory because he is in a better position or better qualified.

"Point out to us the lessons of the football game," a young sportsman asked his older friend. And he gave the one that extols the virtue of renunciation: "I will pass my chance to him"—the sacrifice of selfish or vain calculating with a view to the result for the whole.

The child can be shown that when there is question of committing an infraction of discipline in school, he ought to avoid it not so much because of the effect on the teacher—"He who budges will have to deal with me"—but rather the disturbance it causes for his comrades whose attention is distracted and progress retarded. Discipline was not invented for the comfort of the teacher but for the good of the pupils.

In this way, theoretical teaching is preceded by the practical background of the child in an atmosphere of cooperation, of social interchange of help. Every occasion for practice of this type should be accompanied by an explanation that later they must always act with like consideration in the office, the factory, the army or in whatever community they may be.

Once the children are old enough to understand more theory, every opportunity to instill doctrine should be seized: An international problem arises: Selfishness or mutual help? What does the Church say on this point? What does the Gospel say? Or perhaps it is a problem of relations between employer and workers, a strike in the father's factory or in the city. Here too, what does the Church say? What does the Gospel command. Selfishness or reciprocal understanding?

Trained in this fashion the young will be ready and quick to understand the social or international doctrine of the

Church when they are old enough to be taught it academically. They will not oppose correct principles, as they only too often do with a wall of prejudices or pseudo-traditions, when their religion or philosophy teachers explain them.

Training in Social Responsibility (2)

WE HAVE accomplished a good deal if we have accustomed the child to put itself as much as possible "in the place of others." "If I were in such and such a situation, what would I do, what would I think?" We are all wrapped up in ourselves as in a cocoon, the child more than anyone else; particularly if it has been coddled, if it has been born into a family that is comfortably fixed, if it gets accustomed or others make it accustomed to being waited on.

The child must be encouraged to wait on itself and to give service. If for any reason the mother needs to hire help, that is no reason for the child to monopolize such help to its own comfort; it should never be permitted to give direct orders to domestic help.

As much as possible, especially in the case of little girls, the child should be given the opportunity to do many little tasks that make family life run more smoothly: to set the table, to dust up a room, to arrange a bouquet, to take care of the baby. Such assignments should not be presented to them as burdensome tasks but as an aid toward the common good, a lightening of mamma's work so that they are joyful about it even if it demands an effort, upsets their well-laid plans or requires a sacrifice. Often the child will be delighted, proud of its importance. However care must be taken to appeal not to vanity but to responsibility.

A delicate point to consider is the question of friendships. Should the child be permitted to associate with children who are not as we say *of their class?* They will meet in school. If these possible friends are morally good and well-mannered, why not? It will offer a fine opportunity to show that money is not everything, that the only true worth is virtue and human dignity. The child may be too much inclined to pair off only with those who belong to the same social circle or environment; that flatters its vanity. The parents should react to this tendency by teaching the little one that it ought to share with a comrade who is less privileged and while avoiding indiscriminate associations with anybody and everybody, seek out as friends not the best dressed but those who are the best students, the most truly pious, the strongest personalities for good, in a word, those that deserve most esteem.

Should the family circumstances require sacrifices, show the child that there are people who are poorer; silence all jealousy. When the time comes for a choice of profession direct the boy or girl to choose judiciously not according to possible profit or financial returns but according to the possibilities for best serving society, the common good.

Generous parents will not hesitate, if the child's qualifications are adequate and the opportune moment presents itself, to speak of vocations of complete consecration, the priesthood, religious life. There are so many needs in the world. *The harvest indeed is great, but the laborers are few.* They enlist their children's interest. A priest? Why not he? A religious? Why not she?

That supposes a spirit of detachment in the parents, an informed appreciation for the needs of the Church, love of the general good of Christianity, the sacrifice of little hopes for building up a new family. Yes, it means that.

Such parents will often call attention to the distress of the world; to the struggle of nations among themselves. They will explain to their children that union alone is fruitful; furthermore that union alone is truly Christian.

What an inspiring example do those children have whose father has always been a man of broad sympathies and a generous heart, highly social-minded; if in his profession he has always tried *to serve* rather than merely to earn money; if a lawyer, he has always been concerned for justice; if an industrialist, he has applied himself to bettering the human aspects of production; if a merchant, he has been attentive to injure no one; if a doctor, he has sacrificed himself to do the most possible good; if an employee, he has given his time loyally and honestly to his work—a worker eager for work well done and the social defense of his profession.

The boy and girl learn from this to consider their chosen professions or careers as future *social service*. They get out of their narrow selfish views which formerly warped their characters—they emerge with souls truly formed.

Training in Social Responsibility (3)

If we are alert to seize the occasions, everything can serve to teach children to guess or at least to understand the needs and requirements of others.

A little girl who could no longer be called a baby had not as yet any brother or sister. One day she noticed her mother busy with the details of a layette: "Is all that for Liette, mamma?" She was Liette. "No dear, not for Liette, but for a little brother or sister who is going to come."

Liette was utterly stupefied. What was this? Mother was not working only for her then!

The first school for social consciousness is the *family*. What a handicap if mother has never worked for anyone but Liette, if Liette remained an only child! We can readily guess what selfishness she would have been capable of displaying.

The family is together: "It's so stuffy here, I'm going to open the window."

"No, grandmother has a cold."

The child understands it is not alone; others count.

The family lives in an apartment. The children are making an uproar. "Gently, children; we must not disturb the people downstairs. Not so much noise." Others count.

The little girl is learning how to keep house. She shakes her dustcloth out of the window. "Did you look to see if someone was passing by?"

To know that other people exist and to understand that we must restrain ourselves for them is the root of social consciousness. A person would think that we all would have it and to spare.

Unfortunately experience proves otherwise.

Mother and child go to a neighboring park for play. How tempting to make little sand piles all along the bench beside mamma! "You will see, I will not get you dirty mamma."

"No, my little one, but you are not thinking of the people who may come in a little while to sit on this bench."

The street as well as a public garden can offer opportunities for such lessons. "Step aside dear. Don't you see that mother who is pushing her baby buggy; let her pass."

On the *streetcar:* "Give your place to the lady."

In a *train.* "Take turns sitting by the window." "Let's not speak so loud; it will disturb other people's conversation or their reading."

On a *visit.* "The steps have just been scrubbed; clean your shoes on the mat and walk along the edge so as not to track them up for the lady."

All this is rounded out in Catechism lessons. "Then in heaven I will be with some poor little child, won't I?"

Children of poor families should be taught the dignity of poverty and labor, the duty of contributing one's best efforts to lift the living conditions and social status of their group.

Children of wealthy families should be taught their responsibility toward the working classes; they should be taught how far material, moral, and spiritual destitution can go and what they ought to do to learn how to remedy it.

Training in Social Responsibility (4)

WE HAVE not done everything when we have given children the idea and the desire of going to the aid of the poor. There is something better to be done. That is to teach them gradually to try to prevent misery from invading the poor world. We shall never succeed completely in checking it, but what a beautiful work it is to try to spread more happiness among men!

As children grow and reach an age of keener perception and of deeper reflection show them that the problem involves:

—The relations of social classes with one another;
—The relations of nations toward one another.

Within a single country, there are those who have what they need, those who have more than they need, those who have not even the essentials.

Is it not fundamental to establish a condition in the world in which the fewest people possible lack the necessities of life or better in which the most people possible can attain a sufficient possession of the goods of the earth, the culture of the mind and the knowledge of supernatural riches?

To the degree in which we are impregnated with the spirit of the Gospel, we will desire that our *brothers* about us are not only cured of their wounds but preserved as far as they can be from possible wounds and established in a state of adequate human development, and of adequate divine development.

To dress a wound that has been infected is a good deed; to prevent a wound from being inflicted is a better deed. To prearrange indemnity for those who fall into unemployment is good; to strive for a status of work in which unemployment is prevented is better.

Now the conditions of modern living, the economic equipment of society, have thrown a whole section of society into a situation in which life has become very hard, in which "earning one's living" has become a terrible problem.

Young boys and girls must be taught to realize these facts as they grow up. They must open their minds to an understanding of the social problems in their most agonizing aspects; they must prepare themselves to work to the best of their ability to counteract these evils.

When the social questions are concerned with relations between peoples of different nations, then how many problems crop up! Wars, even after treaties have been signed, leave hearts embittered. New difficulties arise. A very correct idea of patriotism is of capital importance!

Is periodic war between nations justifiable? Ought we not do everything in our power to constitute a state of peace in the world by an honest agreement between nations?

What procedures should we follow that these desirable understandings be effective?

What virtues must be developed in order to reconcile at one and the same time concern for national dignity, love of peace, brotherhood according to God.

How can we get different peoples to live together side by side without the grave interests of any group suffering even though each nationality remains deeply concerned for its own greatness?

A whole education on these points must be given.

The Family and the School

To CHOOSE a school and then to help the school are two great duties of the family.

1. *To choose a school.* It is quite clear that a Catholic family ought to choose a Catholic school. On every level of education when there is a choice between a Catholic school and a public school, Christian parents have the serious duty to prefer the one which speaks of God and Christ rather than the one which sins by omission.

It is a duty and a serious duty for many reasons:

First of all when Catholics practically bleed themselves to death financially to maintain their schools, not to profit by their sacrifice is to do them grave injustice.

Then, and this is serious, even when there need be no fear of the danger of immorality, the very fact of the mixed religions necessarily involved is a danger for the child's faith since because of this variety, the education offered is severed from all allusion to things eternal. It is by a regrettable amputation that educators pretend to isolate in the human being, the merely human vocation and the supernatural vocation. We have not been created to be human beings pure and simple but divinized human beings. Educators can work in vain, secularization will accomplish nothing in changing this truth. It is just that way. The same holds for the education the parents give to supplement that of the school; it is immeasurably harmful for the moral life of young minds and young hearts never to hear mentioned that which alone counts for life. That is, however, how so many generations have become accustomed to put life on one side and religion on the other as if they were separate water-tight compartments.

To count on the school alone, especially when it is *neutral*, to equip children adequately for life is a grave delusion.

Spencer, that English realist, once wrote:

"The one who would want to teach geometry by giving Latin lessons or who believed he could teach pupils to play the piano by drawing would be considered crazy. He would be just as reasonable as those who pretend to improve the moral sense by teaching grammar, chemistry or physics."

An education, even a solid education that is purely secular is insufficient for the full development of the moral sense and the adequate formation of character.

2. *To help the school.* After the school has been carefully chosen, the family still has the duty to help the teachers in their task. Therefore, parents, older brothers and sisters should:

—show new interest in the children's studies not as they often do through vanity but through real interest in the children.

—should never contradict the disciplinary measures that teachers thought necessary; if a punishment has been inflicted at school or a schedule decided upon, the pupil's family ought to support it and express themselves as being in accord with it.

—should, if necessity has obligated them to put a child in a secular school, supplement the regrettable deficiencies of the school by competent religious instructions; they must also exercise vigilance over the friendships and associations the children form.

They should exercise vigilance in this regard even when the school is of the highest moral standard; particularly careful must they be of the influences of doubtful companions the children might become acquainted with on their way to and from school. Along with the school and the home we must take account of the influence of the streets.

The Secularism of Christians

WE ARE not concerned here with refuting the doctrines of secularism. Every Christian ought to know the mind of the Church on this subject; we need not go back to ancient documents either to discover it. It is enough to recall the Encyclical *Summi Pontificatus* issued by Pius XII in 1939 at the beginning of the Second World War.

Denouncing the aggressive encroachment into the field of religion by some present-day particular doctrines, he traced even farther back the source of the evil which has poisoned the whole life of Europe; he pointed to the doctrines which tried to build up the present and the future of humanity by getting rid of God and getting rid of Christ.

The problem now is to determine which of the unfortunate species of secularism has invaded me, my home, my habits, and which now may dominate me.

Of course there is no question of a denial of God or of Christ. But what place do they hold in my family life? In my daily life, in my profession, in my participation in civic affairs?

Has it not often happened that in choosing schools or colleges for their children so-called Christian parents often evidence a utilitarian materialistic spirit; they give lame reasons for choosing the secular colleges instead of a Catholic college—the teachers are better, the chances for success after graduation are more certain. Are they so sure? And if by chance it were true? Do the souls of their children mean less than a diploma?

Has it not often happened that the influence of such Christian parents in their social and civic life was practically nothing as far as bringing the doctrines of the Gospel and the teaching of the Church to bear on those domains?

And even though they neglected nothing of the essential practices of their religion, was it not primarily mere formality rather than solid convictions; conformity or fashion rather than true worship? There was a great disparity between their external actions, their attitudes and real prayer, the living knowledge of the gift of God?

Is not following the doctrines and the morality of Christ nothing more than letting them be evident in my life and my family?

The world must be made over. In the light of an Apocalypse, terrible ruins have been effected. The edifice that was the European world appeared solid; the foundation stone was deficient. Are we going to build the new world on an equally fragile base? If we are, then, the causes remaining the same, the results must inevitably be the same. And we shall continue indefinitely to see renewed destructions. If God has no place in the foundations of the City with all that His inclusion implies, then how can the City remain standing? That is a thought expressed in an ancient psalm; there is no exception—the truth of this fact remains. The stability of nations and of society is bound up with eternal principles.

Am I sufficiently convinced of this? Do I not have much more confidence in human formulas than in the rule of complete truth? Do I not unconsciously try to establish human life only upon the human? Am I not still and always, in spite of the lesson in world events, the victim of a deficient ideal, of inadequate principles?

I must Christianize *my* Christianity. I must make it evident in every department of my life—in my relations with my family and with society; in the opinions I hold regarding national and international issues. In all that depends on me there shall be one hundred percent Christianity.

Family Affections

THE family spirit, that traditional ensemble of convictions, ideals, and domestic practices which constitute the sacred patrimony of people united by the same blood, can exist without a very strong affection among the members. The family spirit is in itself something precious; but when it is merely a sort of collective egotism, it has been blemished; it is a beautiful fruit injured by a worm.

What an inspiring and noble reality family affection is! One author refers to it poetically:

"... Beautiful families that travel as a group and as a choir on the road to heaven after the pattern of stars that are united in constellations in the firmament..."

How we ought to pity those husbands or wives and often young boys and girls who find the hours spent at home long; those husbands and wives who are bored with each other; those brothers and sisters who find one another's company monotonous and whose glance is ever on the door, the gate or the garage!

Mutual Love of Parents and Children: Joseph and Mary did not grow bored with Jesus; Jesus did not tire of the company of Mary and Joseph. It is said that love does not go backward. We do not find too many examples of parents who do not love their offspring but how many children neglect their father and mother with painful disregard! They explain it by saying that young people like to be together. But there is a time for everything. There are some who do not make enough of the part of the home in their lives. How strange it is that children can be so loving when they are little, so demonstrative, and when they grow up so adept at saddening their parents?

Brotherly and Sisterly Love: Where will we find love if not between brothers and sisters? "Who then will love you," Bishop Baunard asks, "if you do not love your brother. It is like loving yourself. I believe the etymology of the word *frater, brother,* is made up of these two words *fere alter,* that is nearly another self."

The Count de Mun wrote in his *Memoirs,* "It is sweet to me to have to speak in the plural when recalling the first years of my existence. I have a twin brother who has never been so much as a step away from me in my career. My life is his life, my joys have been his, and his successes mine. It is not Anatole and Armand, he and I, it is *we*."

Marshal Lyautey had a brother who was a colonel during the war of 1914; this brother manifested to all who spoke to him not only his admiration for Lyautey, the Governor of Morocco, but his deep affection.

One only had to hear Father Foch, a fine type of Jesuit, mention his brother Marshal Foch to sense his love; though he showed a complete reserve it was more eloquent than any discourse; his was a warmth of heart which a few restrained but touching words sufficed to express.

There should be place in the home for the affection that grandparents, uncles and aunts deserve.

On the children's birthdays, why not invite the godparents; they would enter better into their office. "Men and women who have held children at the baptismal font, I remind you that you will have to render an account of them before God." For their part, the children will get a better realization of this beautiful institution of Christian sponsorship.

If all the members of the family are to understand one another and love one another, each one must have a great virtue. The same training and the same blood are not sufficient; self-conquest is necessary. Bossuet expressed it well: "Natures are always sufficiently opposite in character to create frequent friction in a habitual society. Each one has his particular disposition, his prejudices, his habits. One sees himself at such close range and one sees oneself from so many angles, with so many faults in the most trifling occurrences! One grows weary, imperfection repels, human weakness makes itself felt more and more, so that it is necessary to conquer oneself at every hour."

The Hierarchy of Duties

APOSTOLIC work if carried on inopportunely or immoderately can take a woman away from her home too much.

Beyond a doubt, there are immense needs: help for the sick, catechetical instructions, guild meetings for the Sisters, spiritual conferences, and in all of these, great charity can be exercised. It is much better for a woman to spend her time in such things than in lounging, or in numerous and useless visits, in exploring for the hundredth time some enticing department store. Nevertheless, the duties of the home remain her principal work: To plan, to arrange, to mend, to clean, to sew, to beautify, to care for the children. Insignificant duties? But what would that matter if they represented the Will of God? Are we not too often tempted to want a change? Impetuous zeal, poorly directed service, caprice under the guise of generosity seek to substitute for daily duty which perhaps has not much glamor about it but which is just the same wanted by God.

Would not the greatest charity in such a case be not to engage in works of charity but to remain faithfully at home and devote oneself to works which no one will speak of and which will win no one's congratulations? Later when the children have grown up and settled, there may be leisure; then a large share in the apostolate will be open according to one's strength and time. Until then, my nearest neighbor, without being the least bit exclusive about it but merely judging with a well instructed understanding, will be this little world that has established itself in my home. . . .

Another danger besides excessive apostolic works that might ensnare some wives and mothers of families would be to give exaggerated place to exercises of piety. Did not one of the characters in a novel by George Duhamel lament this tendency: "I have heard priests say that some women have spoiled their married life by excessive attendance at religious ceremonies and they sighed, 'Why did they get married if they had a religious vocation.' "

There are unfortunately some husbands so superficially Christian that they see exaggeration in the most elementary and normal practice of piety on the part of the wife and mother. That is only too sadly true! Their judgment is worth nothing.

We are referring only to an actual excess which would really be considered such by a competent judge.

There is no doubt that a married woman, if she is a good manager and is not encumbered by some job outside the home, can find time for normal religious exercises and can even provide for meditation, spiritual reading and a relatively frequent assistance at Mass and reception of Holy Communion; time, after all, is something that varies in its possibility for adaptations and compressibility and woman excels in the heart of putting many things into a small place. . . .

If she suspects that her husband finds certain exterior acts of piety exaggerated, attendance at weekday Mass for instance, let her increase her private devotions somewhat, a little more meditation or spiritual reading when he is not around; whether he is right or not, it is better not to irritate him if grave consequences might result. That is how Elizabeth Leseur managed; never did she betray the least annoyance when disturbed in her devotions; she always answered her husband's call or his outbursts of irritation with a pleasant face.

Never neglect a duty but observe the order of their importance.